ADVANCE PRAISE FOR

# Unyielding Resolve

"Only in the 2020s, with Russia's brutal invasion of Ukraine and its determined imperial justification by Vladimir Putin, has the liberal democratic West begun to understand the nature of Russian imperialism and its persistence through the centuries.

"US ambassador and professor Lev Dobriansky was one of the few scholars in the West to write about the fate of the non-Russian captive nations throughout the Cold War. He continued making his case in the 'Kumbaya-la-la' years after 1991, when Western governments seriously believed that with the collapse of Soviet Communism, Russia and its subjugated peoples would live in free-market democracies.

"Today as Russia, with its heinous and brutal war, tries again to make Ukraine, Georgia, and others its captive, Dobriansky's analysis and his concept of the captive nations of Russia is striking in its predictive value for understanding Russia and the threats to peace and to the West today."

—Toomas Hendrik Ilves, former president of Estonia (2006–16)

"At a time when almost no one in politics, diplomacy, academia, or media looked at the Soviet Union as a continuation of the Russian colonial empire, Dr. Lev Dobriansky dedicated his life to advocating freedom and the right of national self-determination for nations held captive by Russian imperialism. Dobriansky understood that the USSR was a prison of nations struggling to break free and did everything he could for decades to help bring independence to those nations. His views were vindicated when the Soviet Union collapsed in 1991 and now, when Putin has brutally invaded Ukraine and proved Russia's intent to re-establish its repressive, colonial empire. What some considered his unconventional thinking has become accepted wisdom today. I am honored that Dr. Dobriansky was my professor, mentor, boss, and friend, and am deeply grateful for his indefatigable efforts to define and fight Russian imperialism and colonialism. His legacy is immeasurable."

—Kateryna Yushchenko, First Lady of Ukraine (2005–10)
and director, National Captive Nations Committee (1982–84)

"Lev Dobriansky and I worked together for decades to defeat Communism and honor its countless victims. He was the leading exponent of the idea that Soviet Communism was really a new form of Russian imperialism. The dissolution of the Soviet Union and the continuing aggression of Vladimir Putin has proved Professor Dobriansky right. This book recounts, in fascinating detail, how he developed his theory of Russian imperialism while engaging in vigorous public policy advocacy. His historic achievement is the Captive Nations Week Resolution (Public Law 86-90), which has been proclaimed by every US president from Eisenhower to the present."

—**Lee Edwards**, cofounder,
Victims of Communism Memorial Foundation

"Professor Lev Dobriansky has been an unsung freedom hero of the Cold War for more than a generation. *Unyielding Resolve* is his account of the intellectual, political, and public battles he mobilized to inform— and influence—America's leadership and the American public around the plight of the people of the captive nations under Moscow's control. It is a tale of remarkable resolve and of the impact one person can have on the history of the world, and it is a wonderful read."

—**Edwin J. Feulner**, PhD, founder and retired president,
The Heritage Foundation, and chairman emeritus,
Victims of Communism Memorial Foundation

"Lev Dobriansky's *Unyielding Resolve* illuminates the importance of traditional Russian nationalism—in particular its authoritarian character and imperial ambitions—to understanding the sources of Soviet conduct and, avant la lettre, of Russia's conduct under Putin. In an era in which experts are addicted to popular ideologies and fancy theorizing, Dobriansky's trenchant analysis also demonstrates that mastery of nations' languages, histories, cultures, politics, and religions remains indispensable to grasping the logic of geopolitics."

—**Peter Berkowitz**, Tad and Dianne Taube Senior Fellow,
Hoover Institution

"This is a timely and immensely useful book during a tumultuous time of woke cultural and political confusion. Dobriansky provides a clear warning to the free world: be vigilant lest we lose our freedoms at home. At the same time, the book calls on us to advocate for the remaining captive nations, such as China and Cuba. Anyone interested in freedom must read this book."

—**Bob Fu,** founder and president of ChinaAid
and Tiananmen Square student leader

"Lev Dobriansky devoted his life to addressing one question: Taking the hardest case that the whole history of the twentieth century gives us, the case of the captive nations, how can we do what is right and decent? How can we help them grasp and maintain their liberty? This is the work of a brilliant, passionate, and very good man."

—**Peter Robinson,** Murdoch Distinguished Policy Fellow,
Hoover Institution, and former speechwriter to
President Ronald Reagan

"As a Uyghur woman witnessing the ongoing persecution of my people in China, Lev Dobriansky's *Unyielding Resolve* resonates deeply with me. This book serves as a powerful reminder that the struggle against oppressive regimes is far from over. Dobriansky's insights into the forces of legitimate nationalism and the unyielding human spirit provide time-less lessons for those of us fighting for freedom today. This book is not just a recounting of history, it's a call to action for all who stand against tyranny."

—**Muetter Iliqud,** China Programs,
Victims of Communism Memorial Foundation,
and Uyghur activist

# Unyielding Resolve

# Unyielding Resolve

*Captive Nations and
the Path to Freedom*

By Lev E. Dobriansky
*Edited by* Paula J. Dobriansky
*and* Pratik Chougule

HOOVER INSTITUTION PRESS

Stanford University | Stanford, California

*hoover.org*

**Hoover Institution Press Publication No. 739**

Hoover Institution at Leland Stanford Junior University,
Stanford, California 94305-6003

First printing 2025
31  30  29  28  27  26  25      7  6  5  4  3  2  1

Manufactured in the United States of America
Printed on acid-free, archival-quality paper

**Library of Congress Cataloging-in-Publication Data**
Names: Dobriansky, Lev E., author. | Dobriansky, Paula, editor. | Chougule, Pratik, editor.
Title: Unyielding resolve : captive nations and the path to freedom / by
   Lev E. Dobriansky; edited by Paula J. Dobriansky and Pratik Chougule.
Other titles: Hoover Institution Press publication ; 739.
Description: Stanford, California : Hoover Institution Press, Stanford University, 2025. |
   Series: Hoover Institution Press publication ; no. 739 | Includes bibliographical
   references and index. | Summary: "This memoir documents the role of nationalism in
   the Cold War resistance to Moscow's domination over non-Russian peoples and details
   efforts to pass a US law designating Captive Nations Week"—Provided by publisher.
Identifiers: LCCN 2024038903 (print) | LCCN 2024038904 (ebook) |
   ISBN 9780817926557 (paperback) | ISBN 9780817926564 (epub) |
   ISBN 9780817926588 (pdf)
Subjects: LCSH: Dobriansky, Lev E. | Anti-communist movements—United States—
   History—20th century. | Anti-communist movements—Europe, Eastern—History—
   20th century. | Nationalism—Europe, Eastern—History—20th century. |
   Nationalism—Soviet Union—History. | Captive Nations Week—History |
   Cold War—Personal narratives, American.
Classification: LCC E743.5 .D558 2025 (print) | LCC E743.5 (ebook) |
   DDC 973.9—dc23/eng/20240920
LC record available at https://lccn.loc.gov/2024038903
LC ebook record available at https://lccn.loc.gov/2024038904

# Contents

*Photo section follows after page 140*

# Foreword

I t is my honor and privilege to write the foreword to Dr. Lev Dobriansky's book. I was fortunate to have met him, become his teaching
assistant, and eventually graduate to being his friend.

I first met Lev in 1976 when I arrived in Washington, DC, as a young
refugee from the Soviet Union. I came by myself, had lots of time on my
hands, and was keenly interested in anything that dealt with what to me
were the key existential questions: what made the Soviet Union the evil
regime that it was and what was its future. Being deeply fascinated by
these issues, I found myself drawn to Lev's unique scholarship.

I brought with me a plethora of personal observations and beliefs,
drawn from my experience growing up in the Soviet Union. Having
begun to study Western scholars, who sought to provide explanations
for the "sources of the Soviet conduct," I was not impressed. I did not
buy into the "convergence theory" that held that Soviet behavior,
externally and internally, would eventually ameliorate. I also did not
agree with the assignment of the paramount role to communist ideology; in the world where I was growing up, precious few Soviet citizens,
including government officials, took communist ideology seriously.

Lev's unique perspective ascribed pivotal importance to the dominant imperialist strain in Russian history and statecraft, regarding it as
the most compelling driver of Soviet domestic repression and external

aggression. As we continued to discuss these issues, I was impressed by Lev's combination of rigorous scholarship and vigorous political activism.

There are many scholars and many policy players. Lev was both— and then some. He taught at both Georgetown University and the National War College, traveled around the world lecturing in dozens of countries, debated with his peers one-on-one and in academic conferences, and served as an ambassador. He also was one of the most influential Ukrainian Americans, chairing for decades the Ukrainian Congress Committee of America (UCCA) and relentlessly lobbying both Congress and the executive branch.

Over the course of many discussions with Lev Dobriansky (and having read several of his scholarly books), I began to appreciate that he did not just reject the most common explanations of the sources of Soviet conduct; he had developed a unique comprehensive explanation of his own—the captive nations concept. For centuries, Russia has expanded by taking over adjacent lands, in both Europe and Asia, and incorporating them into Moscow's imperial framework.

Since forceful annexation of neighboring countries was both resisted by other powers and resented by the people, who were annexed against their will, Moscow's foreign policy was consistently aggressive while its domestic policies were consistently repressive. To be sure, the degree of aggression and repression has varied, but the strategic trends have remained the same.

Lev and I also focused on two major, related issues that animated Russian imperialism: its ideological justification and Moscow's assessment of its place in the world. As far as the first issue is concerned, empires have always sought to justify their behavior by invoking an ideological framework. In the pre-Soviet period, Moscow's ideological construct was that it was the Third Rome, the guardian of Orthodox Christianity, whose perpetual mission was to restore something loosely resembling the Second Rome, the Byzantine empire.

Not surprisingly, this Third Rome building was accompanied by the oft-proclaimed belief that, without empire building, persecution and woes would afflict Orthodox Slavs. Hence, the Russian style of empire building was allegedly a necessary self-preservation strategy.

During the Soviet period, the Third Rome ethos was replaced by the Marxist ideology that building a global communist state was the key goal of Moscow's statecraft. The view that the Soviet Union was surrounded by implacable foes who sought to destroy it remained unchanged, with the explanation for this hostility being partly a dislike of all things Russian and partly an intense dislike of Marxist-Leninist ideology.

As far as the second issue is concerned, we debated at length whether Russia was a European or an Asian power. Our discussion was rooted in the vigorous debate among Russian and Western historians who have sparred about this for centuries. Interestingly enough, Lev's view was that Moscow was always perfectly prepared to reassess its place in the world. I was not convinced.

As a tribute to his scholarship, subsequent events have proved Lev's point. The new self-assessment, reflected in the report by a commission of Russian historians convened by Russian leader Vladimir Putin, is that Russia was, is, and will be an Asian power. The related new interpretation of Russian history is that the period of Mongol domination of Russia, which has been long decried as a national tragedy, was actually a blessing: Mongol domination lessened the pernicious impact of Western civilization on Russia.

My yearslong conversations with Lev Dobriansky were heavy on intellectual and analytical discourse, but they also involved discussions of more pragmatic political considerations. This is because Lev was more than an academic; he was a skilled community organizer, adroit lobbyist, and superb policymaker. Thus, having developed the captive nations concept, he worked tirelessly on having it embraced first by the Ukrainian American community, second by the American people at large, and, eventually, by American politicians.

The Captive Nations Resolution (PL 86-90) was enacted with a bipartisan vote. A proclamation to celebrate it has been issued by every president since Dwight Eisenhower. Its enduring legacy and its viability, despite the ebb and flow of US-Soviet relations, are un-matched by any other congressional legislation.

It's worth emphasizing that the presidential proclamation wasn't mere rhetoric; its annual issuance provided an invaluable context for preserving America's commitment to self-determination for the captive nations that had been forcibly incorporated into the Russian empire and, later, the Soviet empire. It played a particularly important role during the Reagan presidency and was an integral part of Reagan's challenge to the legitimacy of the "evil empire."

The George H. W. Bush administration that harnessed the results of Reagan's policies toward Moscow offered another opportunity for the captive nations concept to play a major role. It contributed to the resolution of administration debates about Ukrainian independence and eventual embrace of it.

The evolution of Russian policy toward the former captive nations, particularly Ukraine, further underscores the intellectual vitality of Lev's analysis. Putin's description of the imperial nature of Russian foreign policy, his passionate embrace of the notion that Ukraine must be a part of Moscow's empire, and his justification for Russian conduct are all perfectly captured by Lev's captive nations paradigm.

In Lev's obituary, which I had the honor to draft, I stated that there are very few people in this world who develop a big idea, spend their lives working on making it a reality, and see it profoundly vindicated. I can now add to this that, years after Lev's death, the key developments in Europe—Moscow's empire rebuilding—further dramatize Dr. Dobriansky's analytical prescience and intellectual brilliance.

He was a remarkable man, and reading this book will provide invaluable insights to both ordinary readers and US decision makers. I admire Lev greatly and am honored to have been his friend and an intellectual sparring partner.

David B. Rivkin
Washington, DC

# Preface

In our conversations toward the end of his life, my father was particularly concerned about the imperial, authoritarian ambitions of Russia. He expected that Ukraine would be a primary focus of the Putin regime's strategy to restore Russia's empire and posited that "Russia minus Ukraine equals zero." My father feared that an inadequate defense of Ukraine could invite Moscow's aggression. Both the brutality of Russia's 2022 invasion as well as the national will that Ukrainians have marshaled to defend their freedoms were consistent with his analysis.

My father wrote this book to document the history of captive nations and the passage of PL 86-90, the law designating Captive Nations Week, in order to describe the meaning of the concept itself and to detail those key developments that "vindicate a trail of thought and conviction extending back to the 1950s."

Dr. Lev Dobriansky worked on this manuscript for several years until his death, in January 2008, leaving it unfinished. I was fortunate to enlist Pratik Chougule, a talented writer in the field of political affairs whom I came to know at the State Department, to assist me with finishing the manuscript. This required making certain refinements for publication that my father did not have the opportunity to complete. These include adding clarifying details; reorganizing the chapters for better chronology; and adding material to the front and back of the book that contextualizes my father's work within the current geopolitical landscape. As we were completing this manuscript after the death of the author, we were unable to locate or verify the sources of all of his materials. Endnotes that he left in his manuscript have been retained but may lack particular identifying details; some additions and updates have also been inserted.

This memoir reflects my father's strong opinions on the matters discussed and contributes a potent first-person perspective on anti-communist activities in the United States in the twentieth century. Significantly, it provides a unique account of the "captive nations" concept, which heretofore has not been methodically documented. Scholars have the opportunity to study the original manuscript, along with Lev Dobriansky's other papers, in the Hoover Institution Library & Archives.

Ambassador Paula J. Dobriansky
Washington, DC

# Acknowledgments

At the time of his writing this book, Dr. Lev E. Dobriansky wrote, "In the rightful order of acknowledgment, words alone cannot adequately express my heartfelt gratitude and thanks to all who assisted me in researching, preparing, and advising on the material selected for the work. For their encouragement and valuable services, I am indebted to Colonel John P. Glasgow, Dean of Students and Executive Officer, National War College; and to Mrs. Sarah Mikel, librarian, National Defense University, and her staff members: Tim Renick, Rosemary Marlowe-Dzuik, Barbara Neal, Ann Sullivan, Sandor Clarke, and Vivian Fisher."

Before my father died in January 2008, he shared with me each chapter of this book and wanted me to read and review it. It was a real task because my father handwrote all the chapters on legal size paper. When he passed away, I had an electronic manuscript created and am indebted to Helen Ellis, who did yeoman's work turning the handwritten manuscript into a typed manuscript.

Upon conclusion of my tenure as under secretary of state for global affairs, a former State Department colleague, Pratik Chougule, reached out to me to discuss my father's work—in particular, the "captive nations" concept. Pratik took on the most challenging task of editing my father's manuscript, researching quotations and references, and proofing the entire book. His longstanding and unwavering commitment to seeing the book to completion is nonpareil. I highly valued Pratik's superb editorial skills and am indebted to him not only for sticking long term with the book project but for providing thoughtful, insightful comments at every stage.

Heartfelt thanks go to David B. Rivkin, a dear friend of my father and someone whom he thoroughly enjoyed having a good debate with about his ideas. David was a key sounding board to me about the manuscript. His intellect, analytical prowess, and profound understanding of my father's views were of great benefit.

I am also grateful to The Fund for American Studies, which provided institutional support to prepare the book for publication. In particular, I thank the Fund's president, Roger Ream, and Chairman of the Board Randal Teague for their ongoing support. My dear friend Ambassador Barbara Barrett, twenty-fifth secretary of the Air Force, also rendered enthusiastic support for the book right at the outset. Dr. Lee Edwards, Heritage Foundation fellow and my father's close friend and professional colleague, gave crucial advice contributing to the book's publication.

The Hoover Institution at Stanford University proved to be an ideal partner in terms of both publishing the book and archiving many of my father's related papers. Eric Wakin, research fellow and deputy director of the Hoover Institution and the Everett and Jane Hauck Director of the Hoover Institution Library & Archives, arranged for my father's papers to be housed in Hoover's Ukraine collections. Eric also reviewed early drafts of the book and provided guidance that ultimately led the Hoover Institution Press to accept the book for publication. Thanks also go to Anatol Shmelev, Hoover Institution research fellow and Robert Conquest Curator for the Russia, Ukraine, and Eurasia Collections at the Hoover Institution Library & Archives; Peter Robinson, Murdoch Distinguished Policy Fellow at Hoover; and Peter Berkowitz, Hoover's Tad and Dianne Taube Senior Fellow, all of whom provided valuable ongoing and thoughtful advice. At Hoover Institution Press, executive editor Barbara Arellano, editorial manager Danica Michels

Hodge, book production manager Alison Law, and editor Barbara Egbert ably guided the book from development through the publication process.

Several librarians and archivists helped us locate images and sources, including: Julia Dudley, access services supervisor at the Syracuse University Special Collections Research Center; Christopher Kaergard, communications manager and associate historian at the Dirksen Congressional Center; and John Zarrillo, head of archival processing at Georgetown University library. Michael Sawkiw, vice president of the Ukrainian Congress Committee of America, also assisted in finding historical photos of captive nations–related meetings and events.

Ambassador Paula J. Dobriansky
Washington, DC

# Unyielding Resolve

# Introduction

The demise of the Union of Soviet Socialist Republics caught most analysts and commentators in the world off base. Surprise and amazement punctuated the massive reaction. However, many institutions and circles of thought were notable exceptions. Those dedicated to anticommunist endeavors had, at the very least, their firm beliefs and faith confirmed. The range of these decades-long endeavors was widespread, involving labor unions, religious groups, ethnic organizations, liberals, conservatives, socialists, and others, as well as numerous civic bodies, pockets in our political parties, and individuals in government, the media, and academia.

On the downfall of the Soviet Russian empire, the question is not one of precise prediction as to exact time and place. However, a structure of thought readily and easily accommodated the historic changes in this decade of the 1990s. Just as a minor example: in one of my books, written over twenty years ago, a chapter caption reads "USSR – Ukraine = 0." With different motivations, the formula, which stretches back to Lenin and many others, predicted in its form the "what" but not the specific "when," the latter necessarily awaiting a confluence of major developments and catalytic events such as occurred in 1991.[1] Actually, the story is far more involved and revealing than this mere citation of "prediction."

The clinching reason why so many observers were jolted by what transpired in Central and Eastern Europe and Central Asia lies in their faulty overviews and stubborn misconceptions. The stupendous outcome constitutes the full and complete vindication—at least so far—of an evolutionary structure of thought embodied in the captive nations rationale and encapsulated in the now traditional Captive Nations Week resolution (PL 86-90). For those who comprehended the rationale and the law, the demise of the USSR was no cause for surprise. Without exaggeration, current realities strongly vindicate a trail of thought and conviction extending back to the 1950s.

Anticommunism, in its fervent spirit, motivation, and multiple directions, was not a sufficient cause for vindication. The fundamental problems of the anticommunist movement, both in the United States and abroad, centered on an inability to focus on the formidable forces at work in that empire (significant parts of which still remain), a failure to grasp the predominant idea of empire itself. Too many people wasted much time and resources in divining the doctrinal vagaries of a misplaced Marxism, the incidentals of totalitarian personalities, and relevant but essentially nondeterminative shifts in communist-controlled policies and administrations. Instead, they should have concentrated on the real historical forces of legitimate nationalism, well-established drives for independence from imperial systems, cultural preservations and resistance, religion, politico-economic self-determination and warfare, and similar fundamental realities.

It has always been mystifying in the course of the Cold War struggle how the consummate ends and ultimate values of American culture were "pragmatically" dimmed and even foreclosed in our dealings with communist party regimes. This was—and in the current historical context is—particularly true with reference to the inner sphere of Moscow's unprecedented empire, namely the Soviet Union. Human rights, national self-determination, democracy, and a free market economy were no less applicable in the 1950s, 1960s, and 1970s than they are now.

The negativism of anticommunism shared in these temporizing omissions and value understatements; so did the specialized governmental and private studies during the period. Explanations for this condition are numerous, ranging from the fear of nuclear war to plain ignorance. Our secretary of state enjoyed a laugh or two with a Russian ambassador over a supposedly nonexistent Idel-Ural (Tatarstan, et al.), not realizing that the last laugh was on him.

It has been my good fortune to be associated with Georgetown University and the National War College, both conveniently located in our nation's capital. Under the Jesuits, the former, philosophically and practically, facilitated this kind of academic experience, combining ideas and deeds; the latter, one of the highest governmental and educational institutions in our land, provided the summit environment for the exchange and clash of ideas and knowledge that proved to be an intellectual catalyst for me in authoring a law—PL 86-90, the Captive Nations Week law—that has persisted to the present date and contains much applicability and promise for the future.

As one should expect, where there is a conflict of ideas, there is invariably a contest of concepts. This was well punctuated at both institutions and far beyond in discussions and debates on the real nature of "communism," the fabric of the Soviet Union, the essence of a captive nation, the major anticommunist and anti-imperial forces, and so forth in a long series of related subjects. As a matter of fact, despite the objective significance of the historic changes, conceptual differences of determinative importance have continued into the 1990s. For example, is Russia the Russian Federation, as most writers presume, and has their oft-quoted "Soviet empire," which in name has vanished, still remaining? The case of Chechnya is only an initial eye-opener.

Needless to point out, poor and jaded concepts in whatever endeavor lead to misguided policies and substandard performances. The paper trail delineated here overflows with basic concepts that were and are distinctive and have stood in sharp contrast to those in other trails of thought, literally from the beginning of the Cold War between Moscow and us, even into the present. You will sense this as you follow this paper trail in unbending contest with those paved by others, and in the end you will make your own assessment. I would venture to say that a most productive and revealing study would be a comparison of these literary trains extending back to the early 1950s.

You will frequently come across the phrase "paper trail" in reference to the innumerable, apparent paths leading up to the empirically validated captive nations rationale. As we traverse the paper trail, we'll have abundant opportunities to witness the thinking and reactions of numerous political leaders, policymakers, media members, academic specialists, and other personages in what was rightly considered a most serious and even a mortal Cold War. It was a privilege for me to meet with extremely interesting and prominent personalities and engage in various undertakings. My memories are rich and indelibly imprinted. To mention only a few here who will appear on the trail are all of our presidents since Eisenhower.

CHAPTER 1

# Captive Nations, Then and Now

The paper trail of the captive nations rationale is marked by three phases of development: pre-1959, post-1959, and 1990 into the next century.

The pre-1959 stage was essentially a formative one. As we shall see later, developing ideas in the rationale were literally applied in piecemeal fashion along a broad front of subjects and issues that dominated our nation's concerns. Examples include the Voice of America, the Genocide Convention, forced labor, the pioneering and unique work of Congress's House Select Committee to Investigate Communist Aggression and the Forced Incorporation of the Baltic States into the USSR, NATO, early soundings on East-West trade, Radio Liberty, the UN Charter, the overall liberation policy, and diplomatic relations with Ukraine and Byelorussia. A little reflection later on these issues will establish their relevance to more recent events, such as the mission of NATO, the necessity for Voice of America and Radio Liberty (concerning the once-again independent nations and still communist-dominated countries), the Genocide Convention (not ratified by us until the 1980s but grimly pertinent to present-day "ethnic cleansing"), forced labor in mainland China, the nature of our diplomatic relations today with Ukraine and Belarus, and even some general components of the past, but gravely misunderstood, liberation policy.

The frenzied course of Cold War engagement generated additional issues in the post-1959 phase, right up to the 1990s. Both 1959 and 1990 represent decisive dividers in the trail. In this second phase, a whole array of issues and points of contention emerged, including the United States Information Agency (USIA), Vice President Nixon's reaction to Congress's Captive Nations Week resolution, a hard-fought endeavor to establish a House Select Committee on the Captive Nations and the strikingly indicative Dean Rusk letters, the unprecedented Captive Nations plank in the 1964 Republican National Convention platform, a House Judiciary Committee study on the USSR's population, the Shevchenko statue affair, the Vietnam War, resumed East-West trade, the Vienna Convention on Consular Relations, the USSR détente, human rights, the Goldwater resolution on religion in the USSR, and the final incorporation of the captive nations rationale during President Reagan's tenure.

Here, too, several positions and observations, held then, enjoy a range of applicability now in the third, post-1990 phase. Examples include the captive nations thesis in relation to the remaining communist party–dominated countries; perspectives on the manipulation of Russian population statistics, as overtly demonstrated in Chechnya; the "near captives" in the so-called Russian Federation; and the dangers confronting the "near abroad" (once-again independent countries of the former USSR) and indubitably facing those in Central Europe from a resurgence of Russian imperialism, without, perhaps, the mask of ideologic communism. In the short run, decisions on the distribution of Western aid and assistance, trade and investment, and diverse public policy undertakings will all be effectual and productive in their dependence on the right foreign policy decisions made on the dominant forces at work in the larger picture of geopolitical engagement.

This current phase of the trail's progression has not been without additional highlights. President George H. W. Bush's deviation from the captive nations' bent of his predecessor (marked especially by his now infamous "Chicken Kiev" address); the calculated Russian drive, begun at the Vancouver summit between presidents Clinton and Yeltsin, to eradicate the Captive Nations Week law; the West's disgraceful handling of the natural breakup of the Yugoslavia mini-empire; the blundering imbalance of our policy toward the liberated parts of the Soviet Russian empire; and the pressing need for a balancing Eurocentric policy in themselves suggest the reality of the trail. All of these issues and more find their respective place in the broad scope of the captive nations analysis, which presaged the imperial dissolution.

It should be evident from this brief portrayal of the trail that it embraces other features. Centered on the course of our foreign policy, which has always been crucial to our domestic well-being, the trail manifests a definite non-elitist characteristic. In or out of government, anyone who has had the experience of exchanges and arguments with officials influencing policy determinations will appreciate this characteristic. The condition alluded to is solely one of attitude, spiced by a measure of intellectual arrogance and a predisposition to insulate the policy of foreign policymaking from influence beyond the pale of a self-appointed few.

Constitutionally, of course, it is the president who has the final say. But it is naïve to think, as some elitists did in the early 1950s and later, that Congress, motivated institutions, the media, academics, and others do not play a role in the process. From its beginning, and with much contention and contest, the trail was paved by innumerable institutional and individual supporters. What's more, despite the elitist impress, a number of key figures in the White House, Department of State, Congress, state and local governments, labor unions, and other entities left their indelible marks on its development.

Judging by its effects and repercussions, Congress's resolution to establish Captive Nations Week undoubtedly represented one of the peaks in the unfolding trail. Every president since Eisenhower proclaimed the week and governors and mayors have followed suit. Over the years, the levels of congruity between the proclamations and the content of the resolution also make for a fascinating and revealing study in itself—in measured effect, what in policies was pursued and what should have been.

The second peak was the courageous Reagan elevation of the resolution in proclamations and consistent observances of the White House and also at the Ukrainian Catholic National Shrine of the Holy Family in Washington, DC—a veritable omen of things to come. In 1991, the third, towering peak of the trail was the full vindication of PL 86-90, at least up to now, of the principles and substance embodied by it. In terms of guiding perspectives on the trail, its conceptual framework continues to apply accurately in the present and for the future.

Concretely described in subsequent chapters, I give just a few examples of this vindication here. The liberation of the captive nations in Central and Eastern Europe and in Central Asia is the striking and foremost example. Contrary to the beliefs of most analysts who clung to the quarter-truth that the only captive nations were in Central Europe (Poland, Hungary, etc.), the liberation of those nations in the Soviet Union and the collapse of that state-empire provided the stunning vindication of the congressional resolution. Without exaggeration, most of them, given to errant theories and fantasies such as "convergence," "spheres of influence," "détente," and "pragmatic appeasement," missed the target entirely. By the end of the 1970s, such warnings and pleas, like "malaise" and "the will to fight," circulated from the presidential pulpit and the media to the popular domain. Meanwhile, the contents of the 1959 resolution targeted the core areas.

For the anticommunist movement, and the vast majority without, the struggle was generally and in declining proportion viewed as (1) against Marxism, socialism, and simply communism; (2) tinged with the preceding, also the freedom of the captive nations in Central Europe, including or not the Baltic nations; (3) in similar mode, but sparsely, the liberation of the non-Russian nations, and as a result the freedom of the Russian people itself; and (4) with even fewer analysts and observers, but also necessarily embracing most of the foregoing, the proliferation of captive nations on other continents. On the trail, the pungency of this classification of general views will be quite apparent.

A second example in this empirical validation is the resolution's balanced emphasis on the brute reality of Soviet Russian imperialism and the essentially political warfare tool called communism. The plain and open fact is that this perspective produced an explosion in the Kremlin, a significantly unrelenting attack by Warsaw against the law down to 1993 (also a ripe subject for historical study), and, of course, much contention and some eventual concourse in the spheres of our society.

The downfall of the USSR in 1991 has been popularly blamed on "the failure of communism." More accurately, this downfall began in 1921 when Lenin tactically opted for a "New Economic Policy," the pause necessary for the build-up of repressive totalitarianism throughout the re-created empire and mimicked by the Blackshirts in fascist Italy and the Brownshirts in Nazi Germany. The socioeconomic paucity and hollowness of theoretical communism was amply revealed in the early 1920s and perceived by objective Russian and non-Russian observers alike. And, increasingly fanning Western fears, the cumulating evidence since 1991 of what are depicted as "resurgent Russian imperialism," "Russian ultra-nationalism," and various campaigns for the recovery of the USSR also confirm the traditionality factor in the resolution's thesis.

Consider this basic question, which will be adequately answered later: Is the foundation of the heralded ending of the "Soviet empire" also now nonexistent? The indisputable fact is that the present Russian Federation is the consistent successor of Lenin's Russian Soviet Federative Socialist Republic (RSFSR), the primary imperial layer leading to the Union of Soviet Socialist Republics.

To cite one more example in the vindication of our PL 86-90, the crucial weapon of skilled propaganda as manipulated by the Russian Communists was not lost sight of in the formulation of the congressional resolution and its necessary exegeses. The unprecedented power and numerous successes of Moscow's huge propaganda machine, with its incessant themes of socioeconomic millenarianism, abolition of classes, liberation of subjugated nations, world peace, and boundless admixtures of myths and partial facts colored by Marxist trappings, were forcefully and remarkably demonstrated in all critical areas. The attraction of countless intellectuals and literati in the noncommunist world to its "cause," the hoodwinking of Western and other officials and politicians in interminable visitations staged in the traditional but modernized Potemkin village style, and the monumental deception of millions within the empire and beyond are sufficient for one to appreciate the efficacy of this weapon in Moscow's political warfare arsenal.

From the 1950s on, a number of very successful and highly principled businessmen, who were disturbed about our conspicuous lag on the propaganda front, asked me, "How could this possibly be—with us being tops in the world in advertising and publicity techniques?" During my ambassadorial tour in the 1980s in the Bahamas, one even virtually lectured our secretary of state on this. Briefly, apart from the factor of totalitarian control, the very range and multiplicity of subjects and issues manipulated by Moscow's heavily invested machine (in varying periods, thousands in percentage to ours) served to lure, confuse, and compromise untold numbers of souls around the world. The playing field was far more complex—culturally and technically—than that for specific, commercial products in competition. Ironically, while during the entire Cold War period, the indoctrination of communism within the empire degenerated into rote Babbittry, outside it, Moscow's seizure of issues, skewed information, disinformation, and crass fabrication nevertheless held sway.

Doubtless, you're asking yourself, "Given our underinvestment, how did we cope with this formidable machine and its propaganda labyrinth?" The simple and real answer was—in different contexts today, still is—by telling the truth, with credible facts and sound editorial interpretation, with diplomatic finesse zeroing in on basics. Fitting questions about resources, subordinate policies, and bureaucratic management belong in a different and more complex order.

But as to the additional and relevant question on how Congress's resolution and its implementation entered into all of this, it is also on two counts a simple one. First, separating the propaganda wheat from the chaff, the resolution zeroed in on the two most vulnerable and basic realities of the USSR, namely Russian Communist imperialism and empire-building via communist party dictatorships. As indicated, Moscow reacted sharply to this and, significantly, has been concerned about PL 86-90 to date. Second, in terms of the resolution's content, public policy surveillance and intervention were exerted with regard to policy and programming of the Voice of America and Radio Liberty. Shown later, such action prevented a flawed USIA plan that would have spelled disaster for the aspirations of the non-Russian nations in the USSR. Overall, as every reliable post-1991 survey has disclosed, Voice of America and Radio Liberty, in addition to Radio Free Europe—all three covering Captive Nations Week observances—played a fundamental role in sustaining the hopes and resistance of millions.

The myths, illusions, and half-truths of Russian Communist ideology were not the only objects of attention for those who sponsored the dramatic resolution and sought its every measure of constructive implementation. On this front, a direct attack on the propaganda spawned by Moscow and its communist satraps was relatively easy, and this showed in their vitriolic reactions. Far more disturbing and time-consuming was the other object of concern, representing a sort of second front from within. This was the whole array of equivalent myths and unbalanced analyses that saturated noncommunist studies on communism and the Soviet Union, not only in the United States and Canada but also in Western Europe, Asia, and Latin America.

Apart from deep differences on the myth of communism and the reality of Soviet Russian imperialism, brisk contention and disagreement marked discussions over orientations, concepts, and the meanings of terms. The causal reasons for this orientational and conceptual divide are numerous. They involve backgrounds in history, patient logical analysis, sheer habit, semantic slovenliness, intellectual bias, and so forth. These reasons are also ripe for another study and are of no relevance here. However, the ruling misconceptions displayed the limits of our understanding of the playing field and, by the same token, indicated to the enemy our handicaps in the global competition for the hearts and minds of peoples.

Persistent criticisms of such misconceptions and misguiding half-truths as "the Soviet nation," "the Soviet people," "Great Russians, Little Russians, Georgian Russians," "national minorities," "USSR equals Russia," and so forth were consistently brushed aside on this second front as "mere semantics." Such contorted views could have dire consequences in our everyday lives. On the plane of lethal, global political warfare, consequences could be incalculable. The stubborn fact is that words do have meaning: they reflect ideas and concepts that measure capabilities and steer us into courses of action leading to alternative performances and results. Both before and after the congressional resolution, the endeavor to rectify our deficient condition was ceaseless.

The proof of this sound, critical endeavor was the collapse of the Soviet Union and the emergence of an informational pattern in striking congruity with the counter-concepts long advocated. In this post-1991 period, the essentials of the resolution bear poignant application to the Russian Federation, which most observers now misidentify as Russia and in which exist "near captives" that form a neat parallel to Moscow's favorite usage of "the near abroad." Explained fully later, the currency and analytic applicability of the resolution extend also to the former Yugoslavia, mainland China, and others under communist party dictatorship. As in the case of the USSR, the valuable concept of empire applies to mainland China.

On the vital idea of empire, it can scarcely be denied that President Reagan's skillful and courageous use of the "evil empire" theme psychologically rocked the Soviet Russian political warriors far more than his drive for the Strategic Defense Initiative (aka Star Wars). The latter was more a material calculation of spent and future cost resources for the Kremlin, the former pierced the very heart of its global strategy. For over twenty years, Moscow railed against the resolution and its basic empire concept, bamboozling many of our leaders in the process. But with Reagan it reached the presidential level. As indicated, he nourished the theme throughout his administration, an action that all preceding administrations timorously avoided.

What is not generally known is the fact that this empire concept has been rooted in PL 86-90 and is still quite applicable to the Russian Federation and Red China. Reagan was the first to elevate the congressional resolution to the presidential pulpit. Going as far back as President Wilson's time, Reagan was the only president who officially, with this concept, recognized the fundamental imperialist substance in Russian Communism. President Truman, who thoroughly and instructively sensed it, but did not officially utilize it, was a near exception. His secretary of state, Dean Acheson, did—with beautiful succinctness and truth.

Others, conditioned by post–World War II history, sometimes referred in their presidential declarations to the "empire of the Soviet Union," but this was never the same thing as properly identifying the USSR itself as an empire. In most instances, the underlying assumption was that the only captive nations were in Central Europe; in others, with Moscow leaping over the so-called containment line, some unstructured awareness of Moscow's reach into other continents gained momentum. Similarly conditioned, most analysts failed to comprehend the Soviet Union as Moscow's basic empire—the inner empire with two layers—and thus followed the same fallacious line. For both officialdom and media, the fate of the Baltic nations in 1940 (vowed by the Russian Bolsheviks after World War I) should have been a clue for them as to the real nature of the USSR, but it made no impression.

As a matter of fact—on the basis of my faithful participation in the annual independence day observances at both the Lithuanian and Latvian legations in Washington—I learned that in the mid-1960s intense fear was expressed by their representatives of an impending de-recognition of their status by our government, following suit of others in Latin America and elsewhere.

Now for several more aspects to savor one's interest in tracking
the vindicated trail: just as, some thirty years earlier, Khrushchev had
well understood the incisive implications of Congress's resolution,
so did Gorbachev bristle over Reagan's repeated designation of the
USSR per se as an empire. Because of his deeper experience and more
intimate relations with the non-Russian nations in the inner empire,
Khrushchev was unquestionably more sensitive to the resolution's meaning and significance than was Gorbachev. Khrushchev displayed this
for five years, commencing with his outbursts to Vice President Nixon
and his *Foreign Affairs* article in 1959.[1] Gorbachev grew rapidly in
his understanding of the Reagan theme and seized every opportunity
to inveigh against it, highlighted by his book *Perestroika*.[2] His
political opponent, the Siberian Boris Yeltsin, doubtlessly aware of a
century-long Siberyak drive for independence, seized the non-Russian
card and astutely played it to oust the indecisive leader.

The underlying truth of this continuity, as portrayed later, is that
Reagan's theme rhetorically and pointedly encapsulated the contents
of the 1959 law. When enacted, the law not only emphasized the
empire concept but also, with a few necessary exceptions at the time,
enumerated captive nations from the very beginning of Lenin's Soviet
Russian aggressions and imperialist exploitation. Since that enactment, down to the end of the 1970s, the Captive Nations List, as envisioned and accommodated in the resolution, grew steadily. Riveted
by time-honored principles of civilized existence, the resolution focused realistically on an expanding imperial system, not on a bogus
ideology. Moscow's failure rested in the disintegration of its imperial
system, not in the erosion of a tool that still possessed a potency of
deception in other parts of the world.

In this post-1991 period, literary and oral expressions abound
about the end of the Cold War. Looking ahead, however, and intelligently guided by lessons of the recent past, we cannot but soberly
recognize the many lingering questions that remain and for which
answers must be found if the cherished hope is not to become objectively a grand illusion. Emphatically, the Cold War meant political

warfare between Soviet Russia and its subservient nations within the several spheres of its empire, on the one hand, and primarily the United States and its allies in the noncommunist world on the other.

Were there to be an unfortunate resumption of the Cold War, now between Russia within the Russian Federation and the democracies, would the latter regain the will to see it through to victory again? Yeltsin in 1994 already gave expression to a "cold peace." This and similar questions bear on the threat of Russian imperialist recidivism, the possible collapse of the Russian core economy, and its certain impact on the "unity" of the Russian Federation. The role of our traditional, basic principles and ends pertaining to human rights, national self-determination, democracy, and free market economy are either dormant or overlooked to suit domestic political expediencies—until a real and preventable emergency arises.

In short, all of these questions and more fall as possible winding paths on the proven trail of captive nations rationale and analysis. The trail has embraced an organon of thought with a historically founded overview to determine and assess policies conducive to the realization of our proclaimed ends, both in short- and long-term frameworks. It has encompassed historical, political, diplomatic, military, cultural, and other considerations as they have affected the course of our overall foreign policy. Firmly rooted in the past-present-future continuum, it has produced questions and answers to a notable series of debated subjects and issues that have dominated our collective endeavors during the entire Cold War period, and even now and into the future.

Philosophically, although it can be plausibly argued that the "ifs" of history constitute reality as do the actual "whats" and "whens," it is not my intention to speculate afar on what might have happened and when had our policies been more attuned and adjusted to the trail's blazers in the three decades preceding President Reagan's turn of events—again, both conceptually and strategically. It can't be objectively proven—as was the belated Reagan strategy itself—but one can be reasonably inclined to believe that our enormous Cold War costs would have been substantially lower than what was incurred. Estimates of the total cost fall in the $3 trillion to $7 trillion range.

At the minimum or maximum, that is a lot of money, much of which could have been saved and spent in alternative investments had a couple grave, myopic mistakes not been committed decades prior to the emergence of our Cold War. But, given the Cold War and its necessary military outlays, a far more sophisticated politico-economic warfare strategy and tactics could have reduced the cost considerably. A greater and less costly emphasis on creative diplomacy, propaganda as truth propagation, support of citizen anti-communist forces worldwide, focused intelligence, and numerous other conduits in the strategy might well have shortened the period of the Cold War itself. Despite our involvement in the Korean and Vietnam wars and in social crises at home, our state of politico-economic health and strength was constantly far superior to that of Moscow's empire—this, contrary to Moscow's fabricated propaganda, as well as our own academic and governmental outputs. The muddling-through nature of the empire's politicized economy indicated its basic instabilities and sector paralyses long before its so-called Brezhnev stagnation in the 1970s.

This work aims to contribute to this value, for the future more so than the past. In following the trail, one will also be given to ponder the question, "Is the Cold War *really* won, when no substantive peace has been achieved?" This is no purely academic question. Lest we forget, in the last century we gloriously won two major world wars, only to lose a real peace. Essentially, a real peace means the absence of any war precipitated by foreign aggression—even with an evolving pattern in the short run in seemingly remote regions by standards of common knowledge (like Vietnam, Bosnia, and Chechnya)—threatening our national interests and those of our allies. Conceptually, it denotes a steady and evolving development in world affairs that is progressively characterized by expansive economic exchange in trade and investment, effusive cultural contacts and knowledge, an unmistakable and monitored international bent on the part of sovereign states toward the lessening of tensions and conflicts, whatever their character, under accepted rules of international law and conduct, and the marked erosion of politico-economic empire building.

Unless America forsakes its world leadership—for which it is both spiritually and materially best endowed—the inescapable challenge, the politico-moral responsibility, and the historic opportunity to carve a long-run, real peace rest on us as heavily and intensely as they had in our winning the Cold War. Short-term myopia, pragmatism unaligned with principle, and avoidable mistakes and omissions breed only nightmares and tragedy ahead. Congress's input in 1959 provided both a structure of thought and a vision that not only proved to be a political clincher that was eminently vindicated by what ensued, but fundamentally applies today and in the future.

Down the alternate paths of the twenty-first century, unquestionably, the trail of captive nations rationale and analysis will continue to wind its envisioned course of development. Logically, whatever the path of official policy pursued by us and our allies, the nature and context of the proven analysis will realistically accommodate the politico-economic variables at play, furnish its critical assessments, and submit in public advocacy its respective positions, as has been consistently done in the past.

Indubitably, there are general and supporting policies—at times conflicting—within the permanent spectrum of reconciling means to ends, short-term objectives to long-term goals. The trail has been studded with these primary considerations, including simple balance-of-power equations, and undoubtedly will continue to be. However, its differentiating factor and quality have been a controlling overview lodged in a structural context that enables a ready discernment of discrepancies and deviations in policies, between ends and means, between principles and dubious pragmatics.

There's nothing purely idealistic in all of this. It's just reflective of a philosophical bent best depicted as principled pragmatism. Firmly imbedded in the congressional resolution, the historically founded context alone projects the trail well into the future. The still existing captive nations under communist party dictatorships in mainland China, North Korea, Vietnam, Laos, and Cuba—far exceeding in population that of the former captive nations—guarantee the relevancy and applicability of the analysis in years ahead. Also, the entire area of the former Soviet Union is certainly not beyond the purview of this analysis.

The imperial foundation of the evil empire in its first layer still exists in the form of the Russian Federation, the successor of Lenin's contrived RSFSR. "Near captives" in it, like North Caucasia (Chechnya an example of attempted liberation), Idel-Ural (Tatarstan, etc.), and others cannot be overlooked or taken lightly. Neighboring, once-again independent states like Latvia, Ukraine, etc.—which Moscow dubs "the near abroad"—certainly can't. And, justifiably, those in Central Europe share in the same underlying fear of another recovery and reconstitution of the Russian Empire without the utility of a communist mask. All the necessary levers for such recovery exist. In brief, as a short-term real possibility, the liberation section of the proven Captive Nations List (CNL) could contract in such a severe reversal. It happened before, and with the direst of historical consequences.

On the global scale, the powerfully troublesome and critical areas are the Russian Federation and mainland China. Developments within these imperial realms and the foreign policies adopted by their strongarm governments will determine the latitude for the liberation of the remaining captive nations, "the near captives," and the longitude of world progress toward a real peace. Relatively small-scale phenomena, such as Iran, Iraq, Palestine, Bosnia, and others, are, of course, not unrelated to this larger sphere, bearing as they do far-reaching escalatory potency and significance.

Now, let's pick up the trail, with a constant bent toward the past-present-future continuum. In the next chapters, we examine the genesis, development, adoption, and effects of Public Law 86-90, the Captive Nations Week Resolution.

# CHAPTER 2

# The First Plateau

## *Public Law 86-90—Stemming the Tide*

The first plateau was the congressional passage of the Captive Nations Week Resolution in 1959, which President Eisenhower signed into Public Law 86-90. The second plateau, as I will examine in chapter 4, did not materialize until the Reagan administration.

The congressional resolution—the core of the central trail—contained a captive nations concept that has been flexibly synthetic in character and has effectively served as an overall framework for accurate analysis and interpretation to the present date, as well as being singularly and fully vindicated by the historic changes of the late 1980s and 1990s. Contemporaneously, and looking forward with our abiding sense of the historical continuum, it should be stressed that PL 86-90 has remained on our legislative books despite determined efforts by a few high-level opponents in our government to rescind it.

Since Eisenhower, every president has issued an annual proclamation commemorating the week, and year after year governors and mayors have followed suit—during the Cold War period and after. As we'll see, the liberation of the captive nations in Central Europe and most of them in the inner empire didn't signal the end of communist party dictatorship and imperial domination over the captive nations. The largest of them, mainland China, has continued as one, with an imperial hold over the captive peoples of Tibet, Inner Mongolia, East

Turkestan, and even Manchuria. Of special note, a prevailing myth in contemporary debates on US-China relations—similar to the past myth of USSR-Russia—is that the People's Republic of China equals mainland China.

Understanding the contents of PL 86-90 goes a long way to show why most analysts and observers in government and beyond were "surprised" and "puzzled" by the breakup of the Soviet Union. Instead of steeping themselves in the past and current histories of all the crucial nations in the law's framework, these analysts and policymakers in officialdom, academia (Sovietologists, Kremlinologists, and Russian area specialists), and most of the uncritical media succumbed to and perpetuated the many myths described in this book.

Now for a brief background. Following Stalin's death in 1953 and the resultant conflict in the Kremlin, Moscow's major diplomatic and propaganda drive was for "peaceful coexistence" with the West, a desperately sought breathing period for it to consolidate within both the Soviet Union and its extended empire. Foremost in this campaign was the containment and annihilation of the growing resistance movement so strikingly demonstrated by the successive Ukrainian Insurgent Army (UPA) assaults, the East German uprising, the Polish riots, and the Hungarian revolution. Furthermore, with skillful political warfare in play, Moscow pursued "peaceful coexistence" to destroy the independence of nations in its extended empire while, at the same time, it supported "national liberation" movements for independence in Asia and Africa toward eventual communist party takeovers and dependence on "the socialist motherland."

While at the National War College, I was deeply moved by the free human solidarity underlying these and other national independence phenomena behind the Iron Curtain and well beyond, terribly wasted as lost opportunities short of any direct hot war by a grossly unprepared West. I felt strongly that a concept beyond simple anti-communism, an obscure antibolshevism, an amoral containment, or the insular focus on Central European captive nations was urgently needed. Succinctly, it had to be a concept firmly rooted in history and attuned to the dominant Cold War realities stemming back to 1917, and also conspicuously reflective of our roots and traditions of national independence, democratic government, and societal freedom. In this titanic struggle, for those who lost their independence and for others who would gain it only to revert to servile status again, the title in the resolution had to be toward the first of our traditions—surcease of empire and full-fledged national independence.

Thus, in the spring of 1958, my first attempt on the resolution was directed at the House of Representatives. Rep. Albert Cretella, a Republican from Connecticut, who had cultivated a deep interest in the non-Russian nations in the Soviet Union, was very enthusiastic about it and wanted to lead in its sponsorship. In early July, he submitted it as House Concurrent Resolution 347.[1]

One of the seemingly least objectionable features of the resolution was its call for Captive Nations Days throughout the year in conformance with the national day observances of the once-independent nations. As it turned out, the House Judiciary committee rejected the measure by a deciding vote cast by its chairman. The prime objection was the length of time called for in observances; although, in reality, underlying the objection was the unfamiliarity of several objectors with parts of the resolution's dates. And no time was allotted for authoritative testimony to explain them. Curiously enough, when a year later Congress passed an amended resolution, many critics felt that the yearlong conjunction with the national days of Poland, Lithuania, Ukraine, etc. should have been retained.

So, with more hope than confidence, a second try was made the following year, 1959, but this time in the Senate. Only part of one day that spring was sufficient to make the necessary changes in the resolution. In the mid-afternoon tranquility of Washington's University Club library, I fashioned the text to avoid any unessential objections to its wide-ranging and in part generally unfamiliar contents. At the time, too many commentators and analysts seemed to be obsessed by such subjects as "national communism," "Titoism," and the "nation" of Yugoslavia, not to mention that of the USSR and of mainland

China—all, and more, likely sources of criticism. On a subjective note, believe it or not, the wall of the USSR embassy generated added inspiration as I stared at it during some contemplative pauses between the text's "whereases."

The acceptance of the resolution by key senators wasn't long in the making either. Initially, I turned to Sen. Jacob Javits of New York, whom I had known in Republican circles for many years, and my good friend Dr. Edward O'Connor, a longtime Democrat, assisted by the support of Sen. Paul Douglas, Democrat of Illinois. Both senators already had well-established foreign policy and anticommunist records; both were liberals in a Democrat-controlled Congress; both were highly respected by their colleagues, whether liberal or conservative, for their intellectual prowess and articulate delivery; and both already shared a deep and accurate perception into the nature of the Soviet Union. In connection with the resolution, the law's implementation, and the Captive Nations Week observances since 1959, bipartisanship has always been the rule, strictly observed and applied.

By the end of spring, events moved rapidly. There was general agreement among the original sponsors on the period of a single week rather than "Captive Nations Days" or a "Captive Nations Year" that aimed to serve as a constant reminder of the captivity of nations under communism. A Captive Nations Week was significantly placed in the inspirational light of our own Independence Day, the third week of July. On June 22, for himself and Senator Javits, Senator Douglas introduced the resolution as Senate Joint Resolution 111. His eloquent address dealt with "the very beginnings of the Communist Empire in 1918" and other cognate aspects, but pointedly zeroed in on the issue of issues. Focusing on what he called our narrow "concentration on symptoms—today Berlin, tomorrow something else," the former University of Chicago professor strongly emphasized, "The most basic of issues is the continued enslavement of the captive nations. It is this issue that underlies the so-called Berlin crisis. It is this issue that will be at the foundation of subsequent crises manufactured by Moscow."[2]

In the short time allotted for cosponsorship before its consideration by the Senate Judiciary Committee, seventeen other senators registered their support of the resolution. Numerous other senators, like Everett Dirksen (R-IL) and Strom Thurmond (D-SC), missed the call for formal cosponsorship but had expressed full support of the measure. Sen. James Eastland (D-MS), for example, the chairman of the Judiciary Committee, demonstrated his total support by expediting the committee's favorable consideration of the resolution. Few took seriously the harsh attack launched against the senator by the writer Walter Lippmann, who, as a publicized foreign policy expert, evidently couldn't make up his mind on the resolution, at first writing in favor of it, then opposing it.[3] On July 6, the Senate unanimously passed the measure by voice vote.

Meanwhile, in the other chamber, Rep. Alvin Bentley (D-MI) led the movement for the resolution's adoption by introducing it on June 23 as House Joint Resolution 435. Others soon followed suit. One who played a vital role in advancing the non-Russian concept, Rep. Michael Feighan (D-OH), introduced it on July 8 as H.J.R. 459. But the clincher in the process emerged the following day when Democratic Rep. John McCormack of Massachusetts, buttressed by the Senate's action, introduced the measure on the floor and called for a vote. The distinguished legislator and farseeing speaker had shown his ardent interest in the captive nations several years before with a resolution that unfortunately restricted the concept to those in Central Europe. On firm historical and empirical grounds, this one went far beyond that.

Referring to S.J.R. 111, McCormack prophetically stressed in his remarks, "This is a very important resolution that will have tremendous effect on the minds of men and women throughout the world who are subjected to Communist dictation and who desire to be free under their own law."[4] In a fitting spirit of bipartisanship, representatives Bentley and Walter Judd (R-MN) joined him with similar expressions of thought and feeling, thereby culminating a process begun the year before and marked by ever-growing endorsements of the resolution and its basic ideas.

On that same day, July 9, the House unanimously passed the Captive Nations Week Resolution. Soon thereafter, on July 17, President Eisenhower signed it into law and issued the first proclamation in a succession of highly interesting proclamations by our presidents well into the 1990s.

All of the above formed the legislative part of this brief background. Equally important, and certainly more fundamental, was the analytic and philosophical part extending back to the beginning of the 1950s. To understand this part, which has eluded most Cold War accounts and interpretations, is to realistically grasp the deep conceptual divide that existed on the highest levels of our government on how to meet Moscow's mortal challenge. This divide precipitated intellectual infighting among the various branches of government and, externally, manifested itself publicly by 1951–52.

On one side of this divide were those who viewed the Soviet Union as a monolithic state, even a nation-state, with different ideological ambitions, best frustrated by "containment" in any further expansionism and territorial gains, which could be tamed and accommodated through an evolutionary process into the international community of peaceful states or else would collapse under the corrosive weight of the "Soviet system." On the other side were those who viewed the Soviet Union as a basic empire, driven, in the mode of traditional Russian imperialism, though now masked by utopian communism, to establish via political warfare techniques—and over the walls of "containment"— totalitarian, communist party dictatorships dependent on "the socialist motherland," which itself was supremely vulnerable within (and a prime target for) a well-planned freedom offensive to abolish an empire and not just a "Soviet system."

All of the essential ingredients in the conceptual divide appeared in the official document NSC (National Security Council) 68, which was submitted to President Truman in 1950. The president had called for this interagency study of our national objectives and strategic orientation in the light of the Soviet Union's Cold War thrusts.

A rigorous examination of NSC 68 would show a well-organized and structured presentation of ideas, perspectives, and data—reflective, however, of a broad range of inputs steered by many conflicting concepts and conspicuously marked by the omission of the most fundamental ones. This general condition explains in large measure the aforementioned internal infighting and the subsequent public controversies. For our purposes here, before considering PL 86-90, it is sufficient to highlight the merits and shortcomings of this undoubtedly innovative document ordered by Truman. It overshadows by far the 1949 NSC 58/2 (United States Policy Toward the Soviet Satellite States of Eastern Europe), which originated earlier in the Department of State, with all of its earmarks of limitation in concept and overview and in itself a causal reason for the need of NSC 68.

NSC 68 reflected a compromised balance of different views and inputs, contained no functioning non-Russian and empire concepts relative to the USSR itself, and advanced general freedom and democracy versus totalitarianism. But except for the Central European nations, it played down the specific, galvanizing goal of national independence for those in the evil empire. It also evinced an almost total ignorance of the revolutionary underground and resistance forces in Central and Eastern Europe that were striving to realize such independence, and it showed no appreciation of the non-Russian composition of the Red Army or the massive riots in Moscow's concentration camp system. In short, planning-wise, it contributed little to the methodical disruption of Moscow's consolidation of its inner and expanded empire, and it contributed much to lost opportunities in the initial stage of the Cold War. As for the moral imperative and its accompanying commitment, the call to justify a politico-moral offensive was nonexistent.

All of this formed an additional strand in the background to the Captive Nations Week resolution passed by Congress in 1959. That resolution, signed by President Eisenhower into Public Law 86-90, is included in appendix A.

Even a scanned reading of PL 86-90 will show the supporting principles and concrete elements that caused such vituperative reactions and consistent opposition to it by the former "superpower" and its worldwide communist party mafia. The fourth and fifth "whereases," pointing to the "vast empire" and "the imperialistic policies of Communist Russia," defined the dividing line between the large majority of analysts and the relative few dealing with the Soviet Union. Drawn accurately, it was between those who, with limited historical perspective, viewed the nations in Central Europe as the only captive nations and the Soviet Union as a Soviet monolith, and those who, with a broader perspective and more analytical depth, extended the concept to cover the conquered nations in the empire of the Soviet Union itself, and even, on the basis of political analysis featuring the world communist party network, going beyond all this. In fact, this division of basic thought explains the frenzied outbursts of Moscow and its subordinates against PL 86-90, and, in the free, democratic world, goes a long way decades later to account for the "surprise" and perhaps intellectual shock of that lingering majority over the demise of the Soviet Union.

When it comes to the identification of the captive nations in "whereas" number five, the story has both instructive and entertaining features—instructive in the sense of penetrating intellectual obstacles and entertaining in the mode of types of governmental and private sector reactions to some of the nations cited. On the basis of preceding experiences in different contexts, much of this was foreseen, leaving for subsequent identification other captive nations as circumstances and the course of events allowed and demanded. Succinctly, the phrase "and others" was inserted in "whereas" number five to minimize time-consuming controversy over some of the designations, yet with considerable and reliable evidence to include enough relevant to the Soviet Union, and also, in terms of the underlying premises of the resolution, to keep it open-ended for the inclusion of additional captive nations emerging as the anticipated result of both Moscow's worldwide aggressiveness and the West's policy deficiencies.

Thus, for the period of the law's passage and the week's early observances, a few examples here of penetration and entertainment should suffice. There were no problems in government or the public with the designations of Poland, Hungary, and the other Central European nations as captive nations; these fitted in with generally held conceptions. However, it was not so clear-cut with those of Lithuania, Latvia, and Estonia, despite our official nonrecognition of their forced incorporation into the Soviet Union. For reasons of fait accompli, possible provocation, and even loss of historical memory, their inclusion was widely questioned, so that by the mid-1960s their free representatives in Washington and New York were frightened by the prospect of complete diplomatic nonrecognition. Much to her credit, Virginia Rusk, the wife of our secretary of state, faithfully visited the Lithuanian legation celebrating its independence day in February to buoy up the spirits of all who participated.[5]

Concerning the others, the reception of supposedly new terms gets worse as we travel across the second and first rings of the inner empire. White Ruthenia, for example, tended to be unrecognizable to many who were accustomed to Byelorussia or White Russia and were confused by typical narratives of civil war battles between the Bolshevik Red Russians and the monarchist White Russians. Firmly rooted ethnologically, White Ruthenia was employed in the resolution to avoid such confusion and accurately differentiate the ten million people of former Byelorussia from the ethnic Russians. Little wonder that upon independence in 1991 this nation, still struggling to identify itself in various ways, selected at least the distinguishing term Belarus.

There was no difficulty with Armenia, but Georgia occasionally required a one-sentence explanation because of the state of Georgia in the United States and the parallelist notion of "Georgian Russians." As an aside, foreign minister Andrei Gromyko himself was aware of this confusion when, at a Black Sea dacha meeting with vacationing Khrushchev and visiting Secretary of State Rusk in the early 1960s, he bantered that the secretary shouldn't mistake the Georgian blouse the Russian premier was wearing as a product of his state.[6]

So with several of the other national names. Ukraine, which for the first time was officially recognized in US law as a captive nation, startled those clinging to tsarist fantasies of "Great Russians" and "Little Russians" composing the population of Ukraine—or of "*the* Ukraine," a province of Russia. Vestigial remains of such thinking have continued into the 1990s among both the unreconstructed in Russia and those in the West. The appellations Turkestan and Cossackia didn't fare any better because, it was argued, no official political maps demarcated them. The former territory, strategically split up by communist Moscow into the current five Central Asian republics to extinguish Turkestanian national unity and consciousness, was, however, specified on official military maps; in the 1960s, during Mao's Cultural Revolution, Moscow conspired in the establishment of a Committee for the Liberation of East Turkestan (Sinkiang in the People's Republic of China) populated by kindred Turkic peoples.[7] In the 1990s, the goal of a unified Turkestan has received wider expression on both sides of the PRC curtain. Even before its partial independence, as one analyst accurately stated it, "Among scores of such leaders interviewed in recent months, there is consensus about the future on only one idea: that Central Asia—or Turkestan—should ultimately be independent of the Slavs and unified as much as possible."[8]

Veering into the first ring of the inner empire, namely the Russian Soviet Federative Socialist Republic (RSFSR), mention Cossacks and the spontaneous image is that of a sword-swinging, swashbuckling Russian warrior on a horse in the service of any autocrat or totalitarian. This typical response and its variants immediately suggest an ignorance of the long use of the term Cossackia, Cossack history, its people, and their highly valued customs. On the subject of knowing a people's uncensored history, none of the other captive non-Russian nations have been neglected or ignored as much as the Cossacks have. Yet, in the twentieth century, substantial evidence of their striving for freedom was seen at the end of both world wars: the proclamation of a Cossack republic in August 1991, the formation of a Cossack guard that December, and, in the so-called rehabilitation program sponsored by Moscow as repentance for the mass slaughter of the Cossacks by Lenin's democide in the 1920s, their persistence in demanding self-determination. Another aside for anecdotal insight is an event two months after the passage of PL 86-90, when Khrushchev was escorted on his tour of the United States by Henry Cabot Lodge Jr. In the old Commodore hotel in New York City, the fiction-making Russian leader—operating on all fronts, economics, nuclear weaponry, and nations—staged a well-prepared stunt exhibiting "representatives" of the captive nations, at which the acclaimed Don Cossack writer Mikhail Sholokhov was supposed to have demonstrated their happiness in the Soviet Union. The writer's work stresses Cossack national identity.[9] His absence was explained away on grounds of "illness."

Still within the empire's first ring, Idel-Ural stoked responses based on an astonishing ground of common ignorance shown on the highest levels of government, not to mention other societal spheres. Khrushchev called it a myth, and Secretary of State Rusk confirmed it as such. In his memoirs, describing his attempt re PL 86-90 to quiet the disturbed mind of Moscow's longtime ambassador in Washington, Anatoly Dobrynin, the secretary held it must be a myth because it "cannot be found in the *Encyclopaedia Britannica*."[10] Well, even editors of highly respected publications have to keep abreast of world developments. The term Idel-Ural has openly circulated among freedom-seeking Tatars, Bashkiris, and Kolmarts, the heirs of the Republic of Idel-Ural in the Lenin period. An addendum: Rusk also viewed PL 86-90 as "one of the wildest Cold War documents I ever saw."[11]

The few examples above illustrate the problems that were to confront the implementation of PL 86-90. For this and other reasons, it was necessary to include in the resolution the phrase "and others." The "others" in a growing captive nations list, maintained by a committee overseeing the established annual week and carefully fortified by evidence and definition, would include the Far Eastern Republic, North Caucasia, Mongolia, a detailed "Yugoslavia," Cuba, and areas in Asia, the Middle East, Africa, and Central America.

Before concluding this chapter with President Eisenhower's first proclamation of Captive Nations Week, several preliminary notes are in order as to what is a captive nation, why Russia or the RSFSR was not included, and why the week itself exists.

One of the striking curiosities of the Cold War was the facile, general acceptance of the captive nations concept when applied to the nations in Central Europe, but reluctance and even outright denial with regard to most of the non-Russian nations in the USSR, not to mention the ever-growing list of captive nations beyond these. The ugly presence of foreign force and oppression was duly appreciated in the former; for the latter, in far greater proportions of tyranny, democide, colonialist exploitation, and length of time, this same presence behind the ideological facade of revolutionary bolshevism and communism was virtually ignored. In the 1917–22 period, all of the elements of cold war aggression were employed by the Russian Communist regime against the declared independence and new states of the non-Russian nations—and thereafter their nationalist strivings—long before the Central European experience and the West's full exposure to them in the 1940s and 1950s. In the cases of Poland, Ukraine, and, later, Finland, direct military combat was Moscow's last-resort means of destruction.

The captive nations concept is thus anchored to the earliest experiences with Lenin's perfection of tsarist Russia's established predatory techniques (fully recognized in the nineteenth century by Clausewitz, Marx, and Engels) where a cold war is the very soul and spirit of a hot war, with the formidable body of military forces positioned for cadenced blackmail and reserve in the event of last resort. Succinctly, it is a twilight condition of neither real peace nor a hot war, where all the basic elements of a hot war are present except for open and direct military engagement between the major contending states. Financed by the writer Maxim Gorky, Lenin conducted a small school on this political warfare phenomenon in Italy and France before persuading the German government to surreptitiously transport him to the deteriorating Russian empire during World War I. Such schooling was later elevated to the "university" level under such guises as the Far East university, producing Chinese, Korean, and other revolutionaries, the Patrice Lumumba university attracting African ones, and within the prestigious Charles University in Prague harboring Cuban and Central European revolutionaries. By a historical twist and for freedom objectives, the Republic of China on Taiwan utilized past individual experiences to duplicate the curricula, training, and discipline of the Soviet Russian political warfare schools.

As exclusively employed in PL 86-90, a captive nation is one that, by direct or indirect Soviet Russian intervention—entailing armed imperialist conquest, subversion, "socialist brotherhood" aid and assistance, arms for proliferated aggression, or a variety of other undemocratic means—has fallen under the dominance of a Leninist communist party dictatorship. The so-called motherland of socialism (Soviet Russia per se) was the primary source of inspiration, conspiracy, and abetment for all the totalitarian, communist party dictatorships mushrooming about the globe. In return, Moscow demanded obeisance and degrees of dependence. In effect, the underlying non-Russian populaces became captive in the rational and empirically founded meaning combined in PL 86-90.

The law rests on Lenin's two foremost legacies: the re-creation of the Russian Empire behind the smoke screens of "communism" and "Sovietism" and the Communist Party mechanism of totalitarian rule. The first reinforced such rule within Soviet Russia itself, imperially annexed non-Russian states into the first ring of the new empire (RSFSR, predecessor to today's Russian Federation), and ended with a second ring of captive nations, forcibly incorporating them into the USSR. The clinching, conclusive point here is the initial armed and political aggression by a state—Soviet Russia, ruled by Lenin's Bolshevik/Communist Party dictatorship—against peoples and nations that declared their independence from a disintegrated empire. It took almost seventy-five years for this truth to be generally recognized with the breakup of the Soviet Union.

Lenin's second legacy envisioned—through the communist international, the Comintern—a global syndicate of communist parties aimed at destabilizing existing governments and entrenching their dictatorships, with Moscow, of course, being their directing center. For example, as analyzed in an exceptional, authoritative work, the eventually huge Chinese Communist Party was launched by the Comintern and initially guided by Moscow.[12] Later, the Cominform and other conspiratorial conduits followed, producing Tito, Ho Chi Minh, and others. By 1960, there were eighty-seven communist parties around the globe, but the monolithic syndicate Lenin envisioned, fortunately, did not materialize. Indeed, the free world's thanks are in order to Tito and Mao Zedong, whose individual ambitions and sensitivities irreparably split the syndicate, but no thanks for the captive nations they continued to rule.

The foregoing explication of PL 86-90 should be adequate to answer the question raised now and then, "Why not the inclusion of Russia in the law?" The answer rests plainly in the fact that a government in one state (Soviet Russia) illegally installed and—while professing peaceful coexistence and actual or virtual recognition of neighboring states—resorted to arms and political warfare to destroy the governments and independence of these states (Georgia, Ukraine, etc., later the Baltic states) no matter how short-lived, as a consequence, they had become. The bottom line was the subversion and destruction of independent non-Russian states by a foreign Russian power.

Some analysts, whose perceptions have been altered by the historic events of the 1990s, held during the Cold War that the omission of Russia in the law was an error.[13] To the contrary, given the framework provided here, it couldn't logically be included. Like the imperialist totalitarian regimes of Nazi Germany and Fascist Italy, the Soviet Russian regime cast the Russian nation as a captor nation dominating the captive ones raped by the regime's foreign adventures. As in the imitative Nazi and Fascist cases, the people as a whole, the unvested masses at the base of the system, could never be held morally responsible for the barbaric acts of their government. Just as the Germans, Italians, and others, the Russian people have been greatly victimized by their own regime and institutions. Indeed, historically, the Russian people comprise a sort of "captive nation" subjected to the barbaric excesses of autocratic, authoritarian, and totalitarian rule. It would be sublimely naïve to think, as too many have, that like some Martians implanted in the seats of power, the dictatorships proved for their time to be successful. In fact, they were devoid of deep historical and institutional roots, governing through skillful propaganda, deceit, and bribery, aided by apathy and a lack of sufficient resistance.

On July 17, 1959, President Eisenhower issued the first proclamation of Captive Nations Week.[14] Prepared in the State Department headed by secretary Christian Herter, it modestly set a course of relative disparity between its phraseology and the descriptive specifics of the law. To be sure, "freedom," "national independence," "justice," "individual liberties," and other necessary terms were included, but vague and murky concepts such as "Soviet communism," the presumed cause of "imperialistic and aggressive policies," and "Soviet-dominated nations" obviously diluted the law's meaning. This timid type of diplomacy, pursued at a time when one enjoyed preponderant overall advantages, was not a practical recipe for Cold War victory nor a guarantee of peace.

As in almost all cases, this event, too, had its illuminating, immediate side events. Preceding it was my involvement as a member in the Republican Committee on Program and Progress. The committee, also called "the Committee of 44," was formed by the Republican National Committee with the support of the White House to develop issues analytically for the 1960 presidential race. Chaired by Charles Percy, later a senator from Illinois, it consisted of Senator Dirksen, Robert Taft Jr., John Volpe, and many others slated to play important roles in state and national offices. During its 1959–60 existence, it had full access to, and the cooperation of, all of our national officials. About a week before Eisenhower's proclamation, the committee met to consider the foreign policy sections of a manuscript scheduled for publication the following year. With Vice President Nixon preparing for his trip to Moscow and plans in the works for a Khrushchev visit here, an appeasing mood of "peaceful coexistence" was displayed by several members urging a marked softening of our policy toward the USSR and of observations on the captive nations. Evidently unaware of the passage of PL 86-90 and the president's impending proclamation, they were stunned by the news and my extensive defense of the law. The apparent contradictions were readily underrated, and the proposed sections in the forthcoming book remained substantially the same.[15]

However, contradictions were not so easily avoided in the second event following the president's proclamation. While the proclamation was based on a congressional resolution referring to the inner empire in the USSR and calling for the independence of the non-Russian nations within it, a report on US-USSR relations was submitted to the president by our governors who had toured the USSR, emphasizing that "ways and means can be and must be devised for the people of these two major nations to understand each other better in order to achieve permanent world peace."[16] Under the illusion that they had met their counterparts in the presidents of the presidiums of the Soviet republics, our governors toured, observed—and failed to understand.

We must bear in mind certain essentials pertaining to PL 86-90. First, the law was in total conformance with American principles, values, and rich traditions. Second, the law was the first official recognition by the Eighty-Sixth Congress of the USSR as an empire in itself, sui generis, embodying an official awareness of Russian Communist imperialism and colonialism since 1917–18 and of the non-Russian concept, thus certifying the existence, at the time, of the majority of captive nations in this empire, with no credible, diplomatic "internal affairs" excuse from either side. Third, politically and psychologically, it was hardly comforting for Khrushchev and his successors to have the world know that Soviet Russia's strength, including the military, was built on the parasitic seizure and exploitation of captive nations' resources, with the law promising a basic deterrent against Moscow's Cold War thrusts and a winnable, direct hot war. Fourth, the law's prime implications embodied the rejection of then-existing premises in comparative US-USSR analyses (political, economic, military, cultural) and their replacement by an alternative conceptual framework for implementation in all of these areas. And fifth, until Reagan's administration, understanding of the resolution was sparse and incomplete in the West—yet during the Cold War a year didn't pass without a heavy barrage of communist invective against Captive Nations Week.

Numerous projections can be made from our discussion in this chapter. First, concerning the USSR and the Russian Federation, the written works in the 1990s of both Mikhail Gorbachev and Boris Yeltsin significantly serve to validate several of the major points of the discussion. Gorbachev reveals his conversation with Yeltsin during the unraveling of the USSR: "Remember, our state is held together by two rings. One is the USSR, the other is the Russian Federation. If the first is broken, problems for the other will follow."[17] How profoundly true for one who made every effort to preserve the empire-state.

As a further example of the mindset of Russian leaders in current times, both Gorbachev and Yeltsin, when they appeared together on ABC's *Nightline* in September 1991, unequivocally held that communism was only a failed experiment. It's curious, to say the least, that no query was raised as to why the socioeconomic experiment wasn't confined upon its origin to Soviet Russia but had to be planted on foreign soil by armed conquest and a whole arsenal of political warfare. Was this because the short-lived experiment in human leveling was so attractive to non-Russians?

In its framework, PL 86-90 singularly incorporates the two rings. And in the last decade of the twentieth century, as well as predictably in the twenty-first, self-determination pressures and developments in the first ring (now the Russian Federation, successor of the RSFSR in the Soviet Union, embracing among others Chechnya, Tatarstan, the Far Eastern Republic, and Cossackia) solidly confirm the continuum inherent in the law. For reasons already explained earlier, North Caucasia, consisting of Chechnya, Ingushetia, and others, the Far

Eastern Republic, and even Yugoslavia were presented in the law as "and others." But as the law in its implementation had to be further explicated, these and the anticipated, additional captive nations were appropriately defined in the Captive Nations List maintained by the National Captive Nations Committee in Washington, DC. Originally, there was trouble enough explaining Cossackia and Idel-Ural.

Yeltsin's apologia is no less vulnerable to severe criticism. Examples include his bit on "peoples of Russia" equating Russia and the Russian Federation, his attempt to paint the United States as a failed, empire-seeking power, and the USSR government passing resolutions support-ing communist regimes worldwide merely "to spite the Americans."[18] For one who, in his political rivalry with Gorbachev, played "the non-Russian card" to seize power in the USSR and yet worked with the leader to simply amend the USSR constitution toward a so-called Union of Sovereign States, Yeltsin's attempt to cast an anti-empire image and his representation of "Russia, an independent republic, a new and as yet nonexistent country" in reality discloses the volatile and opportunistic character of Russia's first elected president.[19] Con-sidering alone the supposedly "nonexistent country," his assumption that most readers would not recognize the core base of the previous RSFSR, then through it the Soviet Union, and now the Russian Federa-tion, bespeaks the moral quality of both disposition and views.

Still within the "first ring," and also quite pertinent to the contin-uum potential embedded in PL 86-90, are the absence of any declara-tion of independence blessing Yeltsin's "independent republic," the imposed federal treaty, and, again, indicative events in the 1990s under Yeltsin's tenure in North Caucasia, Cossackia, Idel-Ural, and the Far Eastern Republic. It is significant that while other nations in the crumbling USSR declared their independence after the failed Moscow putsch in August 1991, Russia never did. It had declared its sovereignty in June 1990, as had many others, but sovereignty inher-ent in nationhood is not state independence. All of this confirms that in terms of imperial power control, the USSR was Russia. Thus there was no need for an independence declaration—only an act of succession spelling inheritance. As for the federal treaty founding the Russian Federation, the whole process of its formulation from 1991 to 1993 was marked by Yeltsin's manipulation of the RSFSR's disintegrative tendencies, ending in the revocation of the autonomous republics' special rights, including the right to secede.

Not to be forgotten is the horrible armed massacre of Chechnya in North Caucasia during 1994–96, which clearly attests to a people's long striving for independence, only to be temporarily crushed again by a foreign power. There, as well as in Cossackia (which proclaimed its republic in August 1991 and formed its Cossack accord in December), Idel-Ural, and the Far Eastern Republic, the same political forces—freedom vs. imperial repression—have been in contest, just as during the 1917–22 period. As part of Moscow's "rehabilitation" program, in April 1994 Cossack atamans won their status as "a unique people on its own territory, with its own regional differences and historical traditions." But, with the possible exception of the Terek Cossack Host, they have in the following years resisted Moscow's pressures to draw them into Russian government service as border guards of the Russian Federation by demanding broader self-government on Cossack territory.

Like Khrushchev and others in having no conception of Idel-Ural, Yeltsin virtually writes off the Tatar drive for independence: "Do people want to live in such an 'independent' state, where geographic or cultural or economic independence can never be fully achieved[?]"[20] The cries for independence of the mass rallies in Kazan's Freedom Square in 1991, attacking the Union and RSFSR "centers," have resulted in some autonomy benefits and bilateral economic treaties with Moscow. However, their echoes continue to resound on the beam of truth described by the Russian president: "The former empire will not disappear just like that. It has even more cataclysms in store for us."[21]

As for the Far Eastern Republic, which Lenin destroyed in the early 1920s and Soviet Russian propaganda conjured up as a Lenin-erected barrier between the RSFSR and Japan, pressures in the maritime provinces for decentralization, enhanced politico-economic freedom, a restored independent republic, and integration in the Asian Pacific community have remained persistent.[22] Prior to the collapse of the Soviet Union, both Gorbachev and Yeltsin considered the republic's restoration but failed to act on it. Despite the politically cautious denials of these tendencies by the secretary general of the Far Eastern Society, A. Pantchenko, they have been reinforced by outright disregard of Moscow's orders and revenue demands.

In its elucidation, PL 86-90 pointed to these potential tendencies decades ago, so that for many of its adherents it's refreshing to observe the contemporary studies of several scholars and analysts examining them at the close of the century, not overlooking the overt intent of an independent Siberian republic with its capital in Novosibirsk. Yeltsin, not to speak of Gorbachev, failed to follow the sound advice of his advisor, Galina Starovoitova, on ethnic and nationality questions: allow for as much self-rule as desired, including independence, with long-run politico-economic benefits for Russia itself.[23] She and Yuri Afanasiev fell in the genuine democratic tradition of Andrei Sakharov. The views of Afanasiev (Communist Party member, editor of the party's journal *Kommunist*, influenced by the eminent philosopher Nikolai Berdyaev) are profoundly true: "The state in Russia has always subordinated society to itself"; "The USSR is, in fact, the continuation of the Russian Empire; and Russia is not only the victim of the imperial will but also an imperial force in itself."[24]

Turning to the "second ring"—the once-captive, now-liberated nations—enough has been said to establish the prognostic value of PL 86-90. However, it wasn't that easy thirty or forty years ago to gain acceptance in popular print.

Beyond the Eurasian area of the Soviet Russian empire, two points—Yugoslavia to the west and China to the east—require explanation to appreciate the currency of PL 86-90. Yugoslavia was in 1959 a recognized problem for objective explication because of the general mania about Tito's "natural communism" that gripped the minds of countless observers in government, the media, and academia. Some even viewed it as a prime breakthrough in the Cold War. Confident of the contradiction engendered by such thinking, we temporarily placed the captive nations in the Yugoslavian state in "and others." Individual queries about Yugoslavia could be handled; massive ones would have stalled the passage of the law. Soon after the law was passed, Yugoslavia, not as a captive nation, but as another totalitarian state—indeed, a mini-empire with its center in Belgrade, forming along with Moscow and Prague the imperial triangle—was accurately depicted in the Captive Nations List (CNL) with its captive nations: Serbia, Croatia, Slovenia, etc.

Problems unending? The US Government Printing Office, with its standardized printing rules, in time let this breakdown pass, but for some time resisted the CNL's "Czecho-Slovakia" for Czechoslovakia, or "Romania" for Rumania—again in the end proven wrong. However, more serious by far, as late as 1991 we had to cope with the pronouncements made under convenient covers of "stability," "unity," or "territorial integrity." For example, deputy secretary of state Lawrence Eagleburger asserted, "Each instance of trouble in a multiethnic nation, whether it's Yugoslavia or whatever . . ."[25] At a press conference, Marlin Fitzwater, chief White House spokesman in the George H. W. Bush administration, declared, "The Yugoslav people would be best served by a country that's unified."[26] And after meetings with Belgrade leaders on June 22, 1991, Secretary of State James Baker stated, "We came to Yugoslavia because of our concern about the . . . dangers of a disintegration of this country."[27]

Turning to the People's Republic of China (PRC), we note that the free Republic of China on Taiwan courageously held annual observances of Captive Nations Week. Without doubt, for now and many years ahead, the problem of the PRC will be paramount and fraught with danger. Here, too, although PL 86-90 had concentrated on communist Russian imperialism and now focuses on the eventual liberation of its remaining products of the Cold War, it easily accommodates "China," which conceptually—like the cases of the USSR, the Russian Federation, and the old Yugoslavia—cannot realistically be identified with the PRC empire-state. The law covers the captive nations within that state: mainland China, Tibet, East Turkestan, and Mongolia (Outer and Inner) under "and others" for aforementioned reasons.

In consonance with developments in this midsize empire and sharply critical of misleading and sloppy usages by analysts equating the PRC with "China," or the other captive nations as mere "border-lands" or "autonomous western regions," the Captive Nations List has precisely designated each as a captive nation to obviate old errors repeated in a different context.

As in the other cases, issues that were pointed to in the elaboration of the law three decades ago have evolved in more crystallized form during the 1990s. The Tibetan struggle for independence remains un-remitting. The suppression of pro-independence rallies and under-ground Muslim religious activities in East Turkestan has continued with official dismissals, arrests, and executions reported intermit-tently. Diplomatically cautious concerns are expressed by free Mon-golia for its brethren in Inner Mongolia imprisoned within the PRC.

More on this and other relevant topics as we trace the course of PL 86-90 will appear in succeeding chapters.

CHAPTER 3

# Puncturing Moscow's Central Nerve

I n the wake of PL 86-90, the central nerve in Moscow was obviously punctured. The "superpower" adventurers and their worldwide sycophants exploded in an unprecedented reaction to the law. Most Western observers and analysts were befuddled. Moscow never ceased its intense propaganda onslaught against the law. The West lagged miserably in its understanding of the law. "And others," well anticipated in the law, multiplied during this period.

At a Soviet-Polish Friendship Rally in Moscow prior to Vice President Nixon's arrival, Khrushchev denounced the resolution as "a direct interference in the Soviet Union's internal affairs."[1] When the Russian premier arrived in Washington in 1959, he was haunted by the resolution from Washington to Camp David. Pennsylvania governor William Scranton, attached to the State Department then, accompanied Khrushchev on the tour. Relating his experience with Khrushchev at Camp David, he testified, "I think anybody who was connected with this visit in any way will tell you that this particular resolution made more of an impression on Chairman Khrushchev, and he invected against it at a greater rate almost daily while he was here than any other single thing that America was doing in the ... Cold War."[2] Khrushchev further fulminated against PL 86-90 in the USSR Supreme Soviet and the Soviet Union Communist Party Congress

(1961). In plain fact, Khrushchev and his minions carried on the tirade well into 1964 before his ouster. As for personal credibility, his
later work casts a complete amnesia over these events.

Without overstating the case, thanks to Khrushchev's explosion
and the underlying cause—Moscow's extreme sensitivity to the non-
Russian concept and the illumination of the empire nature of the USSR
per se—worldwide publicity was given to PL 86-90. To begin with,
even before that Soviet-Polish Friendship Rally in Moscow, Khrushchev had initiated his campaign against PL 86-90 while in Warsaw,
declaring, "The only enslaved peoples are in capitalist countries."[3] In
tandem, Radio Moscow screeched and *Pravda* carried a half-page blast
against the United States, claiming a "coincidence of timing" of Eisenhower's proclamation and Nixon's visit and labeling the resolution a
"new provocative anti-Soviet campaign." Meanwhile, one report from
Warsaw stated, "The proclamation of this week as Captive Nations
Week in the United States had hit a raw nerve here."[4] Another quoted
Khrushchev in his scrambled retort decrying this "hysterical campaign
of petty provocation," proving that "panic-stricken monopolists . . .
are losing the faculty of controlling their own actions."[5]

In a prelude to what I call the Moskva River extravaganza, Khrushchev challenged Nixon to "come and have a look at the 'enslaved'
gathered at this stadium."[6] Nixon later confirmed in his book *Six Crises* that the resolution was "the major Soviet irritant throughout my
tour" and a finger-pointing Khrushchev confronted him with "some
earthy four-letter words," also orchestrating for his benefit the Moskva
River boat trip to convince him, as his ally Anastas Mikoyan intimated,
of the absence of any "captives" in the Soviet Union.[7] There's far more
to this Nixon crisis. As the boat proceeded, "crowds gathered around
and Mr. Khrushchev each time pointed to them and said 'captive
people.' They replied, 'No, no, peace and friendship . . .' Mr. Khrushchev poked Mr. Nixon in the ribs in good humor and said: 'Here are
your captives. You can see how happy they are.'"[8] Doubtless, in the
explicit terms of PL 86-90, they were not captives directly victimized
by traditional Russian imperialism and conquest, but the Muscovites

were clearly victims of centuries-long, autocratic authoritarianism magnified into Communist Party totalitarianism. In Communist Party unison, *Pravda* kept assailing the United States for the resolution, denouncing it as "a coarse, dirty venture of American imperialists."

Seizing every possible occasion he could, Mr. Khrushchev, who ranted "this resolution stinks," took to the TV cameras with Nixon, again crying, "I cannot go on without saying it—if you would not take such a decision [proclamation by the United States Government of Captive Nations Week, a week of prayer for peoples enslaved by the Soviet Union] . . . your trip would be excellent." Then the professed atheist, having confused "Captive Peoples" with Captive Nations, ended, "Why this was necessary God only knows. What happened?"[9] Khrushchev knew the thrust of the captive nations concept.

In a prolonged spectacle that significantly overshadowed the overblown "kitchen debate," not only Mikoyan but other officials joined in with Khrushchev to let Nixon know how deeply the Moscow government resented PL 86-90. As another example, meeting with the minister of agriculture, Vladimir Matskevich, a veteran MVD (Ministry of Internal Affairs) hand, Nixon was immediately told, "The Soviet people were surprised and alarmed that the Senate passed the captive peoples' resolution."[10] The fantasies of "Soviet people" and "captive peoples" and the half-truth of Senate passage are obvious. It is important to note, too, that after all this, while Nixon embarked on his tour of other parts of "Russia" (really the Russian Soviet Federative Socialist Republic, or RSFSR) and committed further mistakes, which later I pointed out to him, Khrushchev himself saw fit to make a flying trip to restive Ukraine to deliver a self-assuring address. It wasn't until over a decade later that, upon my urging, President Nixon was the first American president to visit Ukraine—which as vice president he should have demanded of Khrushchev in 1959.

The Russian leader transported his foremost concern to our shores when his article in *Foreign Affairs* preceded his visit in September 1959. Using misleading US-USSR parallelism, Khrushchev writes, "It would be interesting to see, incidentally, how the authors of this resolution would have reacted if the parliament of Mexico, for instance, had passed a resolution demanding that Texas, Arizona, and California be 'liberated from American slavery.'"[11] I prepared a set of questions for Dirksen to ask Khrushchev at a tea given by the Senate Foreign Relations Committee. The senator asked him, "In your article in *Foreign Affairs* you mistakenly compare Texas, Arizona, and California with certain non-Russian nations in the USSR. Would you be willing to stage, under UN auspices and control, free voting conditions to determine whether the nations of Lithuania, Ukraine, and the Caucasus want to remain in the USSR or be independent and whether the residents of comparable Arizona, Texas, and California want to remain in the USA or be completely independent states? Let's compete in ideas and action." Following the closed meeting, Senator Dirksen informed the press that on this and other concrete questions, "Khrushchev took a Fifth Amendment stand."[12]

It shouldn't be surprising to note the arrival in August 1959 of a delegation of USSR writers visiting Washington, DC, at the very moment when the predated copies of the *Foreign Affairs* periodical were released. The editor-in-chief of the *Literary Gazette* magazine, Alexander Chakovsky, filed his complaint against PL 86-90 and "pointedly indicated two or three fellow writers visiting from the Georgian and Lithuanian Soviet Socialist Republics as contented representatives of the 'captive nations.'"[13] On his tour, Khrushchev pulled the same trick in New York. Khrushchev, whose administrative experiences in the non-Russian colonies well surpassed those of all his successors, instinctively knew what had to be done politically.

Apart from the showy orchestrations, the article itself is conclusive evidence of the deep concern shown by Khrushchev and his government. Preceding the specious Mexican parliament comparison, it asserts, "The authors of the resolution call for the 'liberation' of the Ukraine, Byelorussia, Lithuania, Latvia, Estonia, Armenia, Azerbaijan, Georgia, Kazakhstan, Turkmenistan, and even a certain 'Ural Area.'" It continues, "I would not be telling the full truth if I did not say that the adoption of this ill-starred resolution was regarded by the Soviet people as an act of provocation."[14] Factually, from its very inception and to its long-term credit, PL 86-90 referred to the Central Asia republics as Turkestan, avoiding credence given to the brutal Soviet Russian division of the territory. Also, by vaguely raising "a certain Ural area," Khrushchev cagily skirted the other specific identification in the law, "Idel-Ural," an identity with a history to present date in Tatarstan, Bashkiria, etc.

Most interesting at the time was the question raised by many observers: "Why was it that Khrushchev, allegedly sitting on a pile of missiles and nuclear bombs and boasting of economic power progress and history's mystically dictated victory of communism, almost suffered apoplexy over a mere congressional resolution?"

Despite its embraced fallacies and concoctions, Khrushchev's eclectic approach was more in consonance with such organic analysis than was generally displayed by our spokesmen, albeit pinpointing the issue of PL 86-90. Thus in highlighted sequence to his American trip, we observe Khrushchev on October 31, 1959, firing up his own troops in the USSR Supreme Soviet in this vein:

> Now times have changed. Even some of the most active exponents of the "position of strength" policy see its futility. Only the most belligerent Western politicians cannot make up their mind to discard the old formula. In some places one still hears reverberations of the past. Take, for instance, the much-to-be-regretted decision of the American Congress to hold the so-called "Captive Nations Week" and to pray for their liberation. In this case words other than "rolling back" were used, but the gist remained the same, the same appeal for interference in other peoples' affairs.[15]

Khrushchev's next notable opportunity was the UN General Assembly in September 1960, when he tried to appeal to Asian and African delegates by calling for a full debate on Western imperialism and colonialism. Significantly, he delegated Nikolai Podgorny, puppet Ukrainian communist leader and subsequent figurehead president of the USSR, to handle PL 86-90. Permitted by Khrushchev to use for the first time the Ukrainian language, Podgorny, posing as a representative of the "sovereign and free state" of Ukraine, attacked the law and wryly asserted, "Some members of the US Congress, who apparently are not too busy with state affairs, deliver 'moving' speeches, using the same mimeographed crib concerning the so-called 'week of captive nations.'"[16]

Further consequences included sudden publications resulting from Moscow's efforts to downgrade and hopefully erase PL 86-90 from the political scene, particularly its focus on the non-Russian nations in Moscow's inner empire. The first, following the 1959 barrage against the law, was the Moscow-sponsored publication in London of pamphlets titled *The Fifteen Soviet Republics, Today and Tomorrow*, painting in Potemkin village style the "independence and prosperous growth" of each republic.[17] The other, in 1962 and a clear product of Moscow's operations in the United Nations, was the shameless publication of a misleading UNESCO work, *Equality of Rights between Races and Nationalities in the USSR*.[18]

The law troubled the Russian leader well into the last phase of his regime. At the Congress of the Communist Party of the Soviet Union in October 1961, Khrushchev violently inveighed against the law, which—as an indication of Western misunderstanding—the writer Stewart Alsop characterized as one that "Congress passes every year to attract minority votes."[19]

As late as August 1964, two months before his downfall, Khrushchev continued to rail against the law. Shouting to an audience in Czechoslovakia, he exclaimed, "In the United States a farce entitled 'captive nations week' is held every year. The people's democratic system has been in existence for twenty years but the imperialists still ramble on with nonsensical ideas of 'liberating' the nations of Eastern Europe."[20] At least, contradicting the general illusion gripping countless observers in the West, Khrushchev honestly identified himself by recounting a talk with Stalin, saying to him, "It hardly makes sense to send me, a Russian, to the Ukraine."[21]

Predictably, the Moscow explosion had its sequel in the unanimous denunciations of PL 86-90 by puppet regimes in the captive nations, those inside the Soviet Union and the so-called satellite ones outside. As one analyst tracking this for a congressional committee emphasized in a television program, "In Czechoslovakia, Hungary, Bulgaria, Poland, Albania, East Germany, all the official propaganda—radio, the newspapers, controlled press, and so forth—all were extremely vitriolic and loud in their denunciations of the resolution."[22] Following Moscow's line, "interference in internal affairs," "threats to peace," and so forth were the typical themes. With subsequent Captive Nations Week observances, the ideologically servile chorus, in Asia and the Caribbean as well as Eastern Europe, harmonized with Moscow's assaults and persistent prodding in greater intensity and invective.

In the immediate phase of the explosion, the Czechoslovak regime was quick to assail PL 86-90, claiming, "The resolution is a new American provocation and a hostile act."[23] Interestingly, at about the same time, on their diplomatic terrain here, the Romanian legation sponsoring an exposition in New York and the Polish embassy celebrating the fifteenth anniversary of a fake "Manifesto of Independence" expressed their great embarrassment caused by the resolution, while the busy Czechoslovakian embassy condemned the resolution and Eisenhower's proclamation as a "gratuitous insult."[24] Catching up with Moscow the following year, Romania weighed in on PL 86-90 with articles attacking Captive Nations Week as a malicious Cold War event. One, targeting Eisenhower, asserted, "Were it not better if the President, when playing golf, were spared the trouble of signing decrees not worth the paper they are written on? It is one thing to miss the ball, another to hit the barn door."[25] Another, imagining that the previous year's proclamation had been met only with laughs, wrongly predicted that the 1960 proclamation "will meet the same fate, signed as it was in the course of a very interesting game of golf in Newport."[26]

Latvia was brought into play in an overseas radio program titled "People from the Baltic Soviet Republics comment on 'Captive

Nations Week,'" consisting of four presumed Latvians testifying to their "happy life" in the Soviet Union without any repression in Latvia.[27] Another conduit, in East Germany, made for a statement on Ukraine: "When in July of this year American Senators officially shed crocodile tears over the captive nations, they did not forget to cry for Ukraine. . . . It would appear that the Ukrainian people are enslaved."[28]

Meanwhile, for reasons of higher comparative economic standards among the captive nations as well as political ones, Prague continued to be as active as ever: "The US representatives' search for captive people in countries, which in their economic development are today overtaking foremost capitalist countries, is futile. The appeal of Eisenhower is the more dubious as its author is Senator Eastland, one of the most rabid racialists and exponents of racial oppression of the Negro population."[29] Or, for more variation, consider the Czech Home Service's program on "US Fails in 'Captive Week' Plan," July 27, 1960: "What a pity! Captive Nations Week ended ingloriously, and there is no hope that it will be extended. . . . Instead, free nations week could be proclaimed, for instance, for Africa from which all foreign troops would withdraw for one week and for some other countries of the NATO and SEATO pacts—South Korea, Taiwan, South Vietnam." Evidently, no contentious topic was overlooked to obfuscate the essence of the American law.

Moscow kept grinding out its anti–PL 86-90 propaganda. For example, TASS radio teletyped in English to Europe an editorial in the *New Times* magazine, "Captive Nations Week A New Blunder" (July 27, 1960): "It was a week of provocations against the Soviet Union and other socialist countries. Washington should record the anti-Soviet 'Captive Nations Week' in the column of Eisenhower's other political setbacks as a week of personal disgrace."[30] Among diplomats there was complete puzzlement over the totalitarian reaction to a resolution passed by the US Congress that had adopted other revolutions on captive nations and communism without precipitating any such reaction.

I was deeply moved when in 1960 it was a pleasure to address with William Scranton a Captive Nations Week observance assembly in the Pennsylvania city bearing his name. Following it, he graciously invited me to stay over at his home. It was an unforgettable evening spent with him and his charming wife, Mary, discussing in considerable depth the strategic and moral importance of the captive nations in toto for our own national security and the historical dynamics of world freedom and democracy. Displaying a broad knowledge of Eastern Europe and Asia, Scranton evidently was so greatly impressed by what he personally witnessed during the Khrushchev visit that in the following years, as congressman and then governor of Pennsylvania, he ardently supported PL 86-90 in Congress, in his gubernatorial proclamations, and at the Republican National Convention in San Francisco.

On both sides of the Curtains—Iron and PRC—many suspicious voices were raised about the timing of the resolution and Nixon's visit as well as the supposed disadvantage the vice president was subjected to. President Eisenhower quickly dispelled this speculation when in a press conference he plainly declared, "Well, no. I wouldn't think of it in that way. . . . I don't think there is any specific relationship between the two things."[31] In this, he was absolutely correct. There was no linkage between the resolution and the visit. Any disadvantage was to be found in Nixon's gross unpreparedness to cope with Khrushchev's arguments. Soon after that press conference the president participated in the first observance at a Presbyterian church in Gettysburg, Pennsylvania, where the Reverend Robert MacAskill keyed to the president's proclamation.

Most observers and analysts, including myself, agreed that the vice president's performance in the famous kitchen debate with Khrushchev was superb. However, to base an assessment of the total visit as successful on this event alone would be a gross exaggeration. To claim, as many did, that Nixon was severely handicapped by the emergence of the resolution may also be accepted, not for fictitious reasons of timing but rather of a patent unpreparedness to handle the challenge Khrushchev launched. The result was undoubtedly another lost opportunity. One can, without committing simplicity, sum up the situation in a few words—what, later, President Reagan nurtured and skillfully exploited, the vice president conspicuously lacked, namely the decisive empire and non-Russian concepts.

The overwhelming evidence for our appraisal is provided by Nixon himself in his *Six Crises* book and his later ones. First, typical at the time, his conceptual view of the USSR was that of a Soviet "nation" populated by "the Soviets" or "Soviet people," with a population composed chiefly of Russians and other minority nationality groups. Ignoring the latter, Nixon gloated over the fact that he had the opportunity to speak directly to "the Russian people." His publicized comments during the visit and his memoirs later abound with such misleading references lodged in a misplaced ideological context of socialism versus capitalism, your standard of living and ours, and oppression and freedom.

Second, pertinent to the resolution, Nixon had more than adequate time to be briefed on it. Instead, he relied on such misrepresentations that it simply "called for prayers for those behind the Iron Curtain" and that "it was simply the expression of a well-known opinion in the United States, and not a call to action."[32] Almost twenty years later, he wrote, "Shortly before I left for Moscow, Congress passed the Captive Nations resolution, as it had every year since 1950."[33] And third, aside from these erroneous observations and his viewing the resolution as a "major Soviet irritant," he failed to perceive its significance as then expressed. If the excuse of "being a guest" is raised, the very, very least the vice president could have done was to insist upon visiting several of the non-Russian nations in the USSR, one of which he briefly visited when he became president.

It was by chance that I met Herbert Klein, Nixon's press secretary, at the 1959 White House Correspondents dinner in Washington and seized the opportunity to explain the mistakes the vice president had committed in a visit that really touched ground in Russia and not the Soviet Union as such. He asked me to submit a memorandum on the subject. Addressed to the vice president, the memo cited among many points his exclusive concentration on Russia to the neglect of the non-Russian nations, the mythical monolithic concepts of "Soviet people" and "Soviet nation," his reference to Ukraine as the Texas of this "nation," his comparing Novosibirsk, the Siberian hub of slave labor in Moscow's empire, with our own frontier towns, and his rags-to-riches attribution to Khrushchev's rise to power that actually rested on genocidal and political crimes.[34] In his acknowledging letter, dated November 11, 1959, Nixon replied with appreciation, saying in part, "You may be sure that I shall find these suggestions most helpful and I continue my study of the many problems we face in this war with Communism."[35] In some measure, commencing with his *Memoirs* in 1978, his later works indicate such progress.

Democratic Sen. J. W. Fulbright of Arkansas accused the vice president of expressing regrets to Khrushchev on the timing of the resolution and pressed for the release of the official text of the Nixon-Khrushchev conversations pertaining to the resolution.[36] No such release occurred. In the 1960 presidential campaign Sen. John F. Kennedy allegedly challenged him to deny that he had secretly apologized to the Russian leader for Congress's action. There appears to be no evidence of any denial.

Drew Pearson, during Nixon's gubernatorial attempt in California, said that, on the basis of his interview with the Russian leader, Nixon had "actually apologized to Khrushchev for the action of the American Congress." The columnist continued to relate his story of the interview: "'Naturally I know about the resolution,' Khrushchev said, 'but did not plan to mention it since Nixon was our guest. However, much to my surprise Nixon mentioned it himself and said that Congress was foolish to have passed the resolution.' 'Do you mean to say that Members of Congress are fools?' Khrushchev said he asked Nixon. 'Oh, this is just a private conversation between us,' Nixon said quickly."[37] Factually, the sequence of events shows that Khrushchev had already been lambasting the resolution before Nixon's arrival. Pearson, whose comprehension of the resolution was also deficient, persisted in taunting Nixon on this in the 1968 presidential campaign.[38]

On a personal note, regarding the 1968 Soviet Union attack against Czechoslovakia, in July 1972 I had an exchange of views with Senator Dirksen at the Fontainebleau hotel on Miami Beach, the headquarters of the Republican National Convention. My prime purpose was to obtain his support of a strong captive nations plank in the platform, comparable in essence to that of the 1964 platform. Candidly, though agreeing with my points, the senator said that before departing for the convention he had talked with the president about the subject. Both felt that during the pending crisis a "benign" plank would be best in order to avoid provoking Moscow into any rash action.

So it was, but also, so it was a month later, when the Soviet Union led Warsaw Pact troops in an attack against Czechoslovakia. To justify the crime, the contemporary "red tsar" in the Kremlin, Leonid Brezhnev, declared what came to be known as the Brezhnev doctrine: "When a threat to socialism appears in some Socialist country, a threat to the security of the community in general, this becomes no longer a problem of the people of that country but also a common problem for all socialist countries." In reality, the only threat posed by Czechoslovakia was to Soviet Russia's empire both within and outside the USSR.

Captive nations committees mushroomed across the country and also abroad. To say the least, this local and even foreign organizational response to the Moscow explosion and massive reactions on both sides of the Curtains was well beyond my most optimistic expectations. From Massachusetts to California, Washington state to Florida, they emerged, so that by 1965 about seventy-five local committees were in action supporting PL 86-90, calling for its implementation in the range of numerous issues and setting the course for future observances of Captive Nations Week.

Hardly expecting the scope of this development, those in the nation's capital who had participated in advancing PL 86-90 saw clearly that a guiding organization was necessary and had to be instantly formed in order to insure an accurate and legitimate understanding of the law and to prevent its manipulation by extremist anticommunist or infiltrating communist groups. Thus the National Captive Nations Committee was hastily formed, including over 250 leading citizens and with the prime purpose then of guaranteeing a successful observance by all Americans of the second Captive Nations Week in 1960.

The second Captive Nations Week observance was nationally successful, setting the stage for subsequent ones. Khrushchev's right-hand man and long-term chief Communist Party theorist, Mikhail Suslov, ranted, "One must lose his senses to propose that the really free peoples of the Soviet take on the chains of imperialist slavery." *Pravda* lashed out against Eisenhower's second proclamation as "just another insolent and stupid international provocation, spiced, moreover, with unpardonable lies." In the flavor of communist truth, Radio Moscow pontificated that Americans cannot "stomach the fraternal relations of equal cooperation and mutual assistance within the socialist system, for all this is in sharp contrast to their own relations with smaller or weaker countries, a clearcut instance of which are the recent imperialist intrigues, conspiracies, and interventions against Cuba and the Republic of Congo." And, naturally, Moscow's quislings in the so-called satellites goose-stepped in attacking the week as "a slanderous campaign," "a lying campaign," "a provocative act" that could only "make the world public laugh."[39] Interesting how often the theme of imperialism is invoked.

A further highlight was the introduction and compilation of the Captive Nations List (CNL) aiming to focus popular attention on the spreading cancer of global communist party dictatorships. I shall never forget the reaction of CIA Director Allen Dulles when I described it to him at a closed meeting in Georgetown University's Foreign Service building, which the rector, Father Bunn, had convened to discuss the role of a consortium of universities in meeting the crises of the time. He gasped when I enumerated several of the countries at the top of the list. Arguing that the list will continue to grow, I suggested that the CIA might laminate it in respective languages and have it filtered proportionately into threatened areas of the world and behind the Curtains.

He found this intriguing, said he would consider the proposal, but warned that it might be too costly. I never heard from him, doubtlessly because of the change in administrations and outlooks.

The seismic sequel to Moscow's explosion and unrelenting barrage against PL 86-90 was the intense congressional action to establish a Special Committee on the Captive Nations in the House of Representatives. Initiating the proposal in the light of the upheaval of reactions to PL 86-90, Rep. Daniel Flood (D-PA), the able veteran of the farseeing and truth-establishing Katyn massacre commission, advanced the need for such a special committee as the 1960 presidential campaign got under way and references to it mounted affirmatively.[40]

Presidential candidate Kennedy went so far as to declare, "I am, of course, in agreement with the Presidential proclamations. The captive nations should be studied intensively. If a Joint Congressional Committee is the best way to ensure such popular study, I would naturally not be opposed to it."[41]

As a senator, Kennedy had made part of the public record a lecture I presented to a US Army Intelligence conference held at Fort Meade on psychological warfare and the Soviet Union. Kennedy sympathized with its themes.[42] After the lecture appeared in the Congressional Record, numerous organizations and individuals requested reprints for distribution, which the senator approved. Then one day during the 1953 fall semester, as I was lecturing, assistant registrar John Quinn knocked excitedly on the door, motioning me to enter the hallway. Thinking some emergency had arisen, I ran to him and was told, "Professor, Senator Kennedy's secretary is on the phone. The senator wants to talk to you. It's very urgent." Placing my class on hold, I hurried to the phone downstairs, and in seconds Kennedy was on. "Doc," he began, "I'm very sorry to disturb you, but I must know how many copies of your intelligence lecture were printed." I replied, "About 50,000, I believe. Is there a problem?" "Not really," he said, "Well, I'm getting a lot of flak from many on the Harvard faculties. Someone inundated them." Recognizing that almost 100 percent of the reprints were distributed nationally, we agreed on 10,000 the next time.

A joint committee would have been magnificent, at least symbolically, if the new president and the congressional leadership had thrown their combined support behind it. But Rusk evidently was unaware of how deeply influenced he was by fallacious thinking in an area where he was far out of his depth. By his own testimony he couldn't find Idel-Ural in the *Encyclopaedia Britannica*; therefore it never existed, although the independent Republic of Idel-Ural, led by Nur Vakhitov, emerged in November 12, 1917. As to Congress, he deemed its Captive Nations Week resolution "a horrible example," saying, "It was one of the wildest Cold War documents I ever saw." This was published in his memoirs on the very eve of the USSR breakup. Regarding the agitation of Moscow's ambassador Dobrynin, diplomatic sobriety, and intellectual perception, Rusk remembered, "Each year the Soviet ambassador came in to protest the proclamation, and each year I told him, 'Don't get excited. We're not going to war over it.' As actors in this play, Soviet Ambassador Dobrynin and I soberly carried out the roles expected of us." With these feelings and state of knowledge, he sought the efforts of Senator Fulbright, possessed with similar negative assets, to seek a rescission of PL 86-90. Despite several attempts, this never happened.[43]

Before concluding with the last seismic sequel to the Moscow eruptions, a short account has to be taken of additional eye-opening events, now concerning the White House, and the impact of President Kennedy's Captive Nations Week proclamations. When the new Kennedy administration began to establish itself, there was considerable speculation over the prospect of a presidential proclamation of the annual Captive Nations Week. As usual, the National Captive Nations Committee requested one of the president. In response, one of the president's aides called me rather disturbingly to criticize the inclusion of Cuba as a captive nation in the Captive Nations List. He argued, "How could you dub Cuba, which is so far away from Eastern Europe, as a captive nation?" My retort: "Geographical distance is no criterion where Soviet Russian imperio-colonialism is involved." My feeling, shared by others in the movement, was that if this level of thinking reflected the posture of the new administration, we had a serious problem that required immediate attention, tapping others in the White House, including the president's longtime secretary, Evelyn Lincoln, whom I had befriended in her days on Capitol Hill.

As happens so often, sheer fortuity and circumstantial accident played their decisive role in political activism, regardless of the institutional environment. Unbeknown to us was Ambassador George Kennan's attempt to pressure the president into omitting the 1961 Captive Nations Week proclamation. By his account, he raised the question, "Would the new Democratic administration do likewise?" Appointed as the new ambassador to Yugoslavia, Kennan consulted with the president's advisor, McGeorge Bundy, arguing that it seemed "somewhat illogical to go out as ambassador professing to wish to promote good relations with a regime, which, at the same time, I was committed to overthrow."[44] The imagined illogic didn't impede our ambassadors in Moscow, Warsaw, and elsewhere, then or after.

Apparently assured that no proclamation would be issued, the ambassador arrived in Belgrade to predict, rather naively, to the "Yugoslavs, that they need have no worry; things had changed, in this particular year no declaration of Captive Nations Week would be made." When Kennedy did proclaim the week, Khrushchev embarrassingly viewed it as a triumph of domestic policy over foreign policy and lamented years later not knowing "who had twisted the president's arm." The phantom arm-twister was no more than the multiple calls to the White House made largely by Democratic leaders in Congress and across the nation.

Obviously agitated by PL 86-90, Kennan viewed it as "that miserable product of legislative hysteria." He said, "The Captive Nations Resolution has freed no captive nations, nor is it likely to do so"—as though any resolution by itself could do so.[45] Then, regarding the non-Russian nations, Kennan declaimed, "Certain of the national groups whose names appear in the Captive Nations Resolution as those nations thirsting for a lost independence never existed at all in this quality. . . . The Ukraine never was really independent."[46]

Kennan advised, "I can think of nothing more catastrophic than that the policy of our government should be committed to the breakup of the traditional Russian state. Remember that nothing of this sort could be carried forward except at the cost of the violent and total estrangement of the Russian people" (an expression of his fable "the dismemberment of Russia"). The implication that the Russian people as a whole were (or today are) in favor of the retention of the empire at any cost was an untenable assumption that the events of 1991 put to final rest. And his statement about escapers and immigrants from the USSR and the "satellite states" agitating in our country for "a war with Russia," a "war against the Russian people to achieve the final breakup of the traditional Russian state," represented another of his generalizations for which he offered no concrete, legitimate evidence.[47]

In their opposition to PL 86-90, Kennan and some Russian émigrés referred to the law's inclusion of Idel-Ural and Cossackia. Not being precise in handling the two, Kennan vaguely referred to "the 'liberation' of twenty-two 'nations,' two of which had never had any real existence, and the name of one of which appears to have been invented in the Nazi propaganda ministry during the recent war."[48] Both Cossackia and Idel-Ural declared their independence in the 1917–18 period, crystallizing a respective will to secure free statehood for their nationhood that spanned centuries of historical change and turmoil, even before the appearance of Kennan's "traditional Russian territory."

But Kennan didn't stop there in his attack against PL 86-90. He proceeded to inveigh against it for accommodating (via "and others") Yugoslavia and its captive nations with the shallow arguments that in its context, "Yugoslavia figured along with the members of the Communist bloc" and that the president and he as his personal representative were "morally committed to the overthrow of the Yugoslavia government."[49] A candid recognition of the captive nations in the miniempire of Yugoslavia (Slovenia, Croatia, Serbia, etc.) did not figure that state in the "Communist bloc."

In words, if not in adequate policy implementation, President Kennedy rejected these Kennanist misconceptions by consistently issuing the Captive Nations Week proclamations until his tragic assassination. As anticipated, the Communist Party reactions grew increasingly intense and even vile. For some examples: in 1961, *Pravda*, Moscow (July 21): "It is not at all fortuitous that this time the farce presented by the 'Captive Nations Week' should come with the hullabaloo created by American propaganda around the West Berlin question"; in 1962, *Izvestia*, Moscow (July 17): "On the basis of the weeks held in the past, we already know what the ceremonies represent—unbridled anti-Soviet and anticommunist slander. . . . Yes, it is only thanks to American bayonets that oppressors of freedom and blood-thirsty dictators are sustained in power in a number of countries of the Latin American continent and Southeastern Asia"; in 1963, *Pravda* (July 8): "The President of the United States, losing his sense of reality, has declared 'a week of the Captive Nations' and is trying to turn attention away from the struggle of the Negroes for their liberation." Or, to throw in for this year a typical example of the Communist Party chorus: *Pyongyang Radio*, North Korea (July 10): "Kennedy is a third-class clown proclaiming Captive Nations Week, which is a despicable annual campaign of the US ruling circles." A collection of all of these protests from 1959 into the 1990s would make up several substantial volumes.

The final seismic sequel to Moscow's explosion encompassed several layers in 1964: the Republican National Convention in San Francisco, the drive for a Freedom Commission, and a congressional inquiry into the USSR's population. All of these events were intimately related to PL 86-90 and the captive nations.

For the first time in the platforms of either major party, the Republican National Convention in 1964 incorporated a plank on the captive nations along the lines of PL 86-90 and the Captive Nations List. It discarded the myth that the only captive nations were in Central Europe and the Baltic area by specifically listing also those within the USSR (e.g., Armenia, Ukraine), mainland China, Cuba, "and many others."[50] Occurring in the same month as the annual Captive Nations Week, the convention took advantage of the sixth observance, which was marked by a huge assembly that heard both candidates Barry Goldwater and Scranton. Although it had consistently supported the captive nations cause, for reasons of convention timing, incumbency, and perhaps administrative omissions, the Democratic Party didn't follow this course completely. In these matters, the approach of the National Captive Nations Committee has always been rigorously nonpartisan.

One cannot overlook the significance of the long drive for a Freedom Commission and Academy. The basic idea for the commission originated with the Kersten committee in the early 1950s. Formally known as the Select Committee to Investigate Communist Aggression and the Forced Incorporation of the Baltic States into the USSR, it gained a policy assist in May 1955 from "General" David Sarnoff, who in a memorandum to President Eisenhower emphasized in essence the dire need for Cold War education in order to cope with the apparatus operated by Moscow and its Communist Party conspiracy. To counter structurally the advantageous government/Communist Party dualism of our enemies, Senator Douglas of Illinois advanced the idea on the basis of a two-level concept: a commission appointed by the president and responsible to him alone and the level of standard operations by existing executive agencies. Also, an Orlando Committee for the Freedom Academy was already at work for the creation of such an academy offering instruction in psycho-political warfare.

By the time of the Eighty-Sixth and Eighty-Seventh Congresses, the Freedom Commission Bill—sponsored in the Senate by senators Douglas and Karl Mundt (R-SD) and in the House by Walter Judd (R-MN) and A. Sydney Herlong Jr. (D-FL)—called for a Freedom Commission, a Freedom Academy under the wing of the commission, and a Joint Congressional Freedom Committee to oversee both. Hearings on the measure ensued in the Senate Committee on the Judiciary.[51] But with no decisive action taken, the bill's ideas lingered on until they received a salutary boost by the massive reactions to PL 86-90, leading to further hearings in 1964–65.[52] By then, a heavy opposition to the proposal on the part of the executive agencies and the onset of our Vietnam trauma, combined with incipient domestic unrest, placed the project at a standstill and eventual death. Also, to some extent, this confluence of events weakened efforts to strengthen our political warfare capacity in the further development of the Cold War.

The Bill, as it was popularly referred to, essentially sought to institutionalize Cold War education in order for us to cope with and outdo the political warfare techniques of the enemy, to fill in a structural gap within our own government, and to show our determination and will to win the Cold War that had been thrust upon us. Cold War schools and "universities," systematic instruction, and structured strategy and tactics, drawing "Marxists" from all quarters of the globe (Ho Chi Minh, etc.), constituted one of the prime assets serving the other superpower; we possessed nothing comparable to it.

Finally, the last layer in this sequel was an innovative congressional inquiry into the USSR's population by the House Judiciary Committee, which produced its unusual study in 1964.[53] Inspired by its high-ranking member and ardent supporter of PL 86-90, Rep. Michael Feighan, the study consisted of "Nations, Peoples, and Countries in the USSR" and critically examined the assumptions, classifications, and padded statistics of Moscow's outputs that most Western demographers were relying on.

The study was long overdue, as illustrated by the question Senator Fulbright of the Foreign Relations Committee posed in challenging a colleague: "Would we undertake a military occupation of Russia and China and launch a massive program to 're-educate' 200 million Russians and 600 million Chinese in the ways of Western democracy?"[54] Lumping together Russia and the USSR, and China and the PRC, the senator was clearly blinded by the myths of the time. With all due respect to the senator's other accomplishments and apart from any diagnosis in the light of events in the early 1990s, to formulate foreign policy on the basis of such views would be considered hazardous, to say the least. Moreover, the innovative quality and impact of the congressional study can be gleaned from the fact that in the following decade writers and analysts began to seriously question and refute these myths.

When the USSR was crumbling, *Washington Post* journalist Michael Isikoff called me to find out where Idel-Ural was located. Unfortunately, I was away at the time, but my wife took the call. Naturally influenced by my interests, Julie subjected him to a lecture on the media's long-term incompetence in handling the non-Russian concept re the Soviet Union and, without locating the historic area, urged him to research the subject beyond depending on *National Geographic* (as Rusk had on any encyclopedia). Isikoff listened patiently without committing himself to anything. My regret has been that because of other pressing obligations I failed to enlist his interest and resourcefulness in the matter.

On the topic of projections in the historical continuum, the bases of Idel-Ural and Cossackia—similar to that of Turkestan in Central Asia—have burst into full bloom since the overcast of Soviet Russian imperio-colonialism has dissipated. In their respective regions, the terms Idel-Ural, Cossackia, and Turkestan have circulated widely, representing old ideas and past realities, but they have been used discreetly and cautiously with an eye on Moscow's possible reactions and behavior, viz., Caucasian Chechnya.[55] It can be safely predicted that the Moscow center, whatever might be its political nature in the years ahead, will have to deal with a shared national consciousness between the Volga and the Urals—in short, Idel-Ural.

A similar problem for the Moscow center in the twenty-first century is the Cossack national consciousness, even more deeply rooted in history. As in 1918, this passion of nationhood resurged with the breakup of the Soviet Union in declarations of "the historical Cossack territory," "unique Cossack culture," and a "Republic of Cossacks." In the multiethnic Krasnodar Krai region of the Russian Federation, the government's charter declares Krasnodar as a "historical territory of the

Kuban Cossacks." The alleviating Russian Federation's act on the "Rehabilitation of the Cossack nation" may be viewed as being both an act of penance for the horrendous devastation of a people by Lenin's Bolsheviks in the 1920s and of democratic vision for a process of reconciliation. In this promising area, too, future developments within a supposedly southern Russia, in the "near abroad" of independent states, in the Moscow center itself, and in the world at large will partially determine the course of Cossack development. But that there have been a distinctive national Cossack identity and a will toward freedom and independence, there can be no doubt; heavy doubt rests on the opinions and judgments of Cossackia's detractors.

For both further insights and a convenient transition to the next chapter and a trail marked by inevitable curves and turns, the following examples amplify the problems that confronted the application in thought and policy of PL 86-90 in the first half of the 1960s. Arthur Larson, who managed information under Eisenhower and coauthored the work *Propaganda*, sharply criticized the law as "bad" propaganda inciting the peoples of Eastern Europe to overthrow their governments.[56] He publicly joined Kennan, Rusk, Fulbright, and others in a failed attempt to have Congress rescind the law.

Bearing on official information services—in 1962, the popular Benny Goodman band was recruited in a cultural program to impress "the Soviets" with its superb and moving entertainment. All went well in Russia proper. But when the band appeared in Georgia to offer similar renditions in Russian rather than Georgian or English, pandemonium reigned. The press reported, "Angry Georgians hooted and whistled in resentment today when Joya Sherrill, vocalist in Benny Goodman's band, sang a Russian song—'Kativsha.'"[57] She changed quickly to an American song and later said, "I was frightened. They must hate the Russians." The band obviously had not been accurately briefed beforehand by the United States Information Agency that it would be really visiting another country and a proud ancient nation and that the Georgian people don't hate Russians and their culture but rather Soviet Russian domination.

As for thinking in that period, one item among many should suffice. A costly study prepared for the US Arms Control and Disarmament Agency emphasized this warning: "Whether we admit it to ourselves or not, we benefit enormously from the capability of the Soviet police system to keep law and order over 200 million Russians and many additional millions in the satellite states. The breakup of the Russian communist empire today would doubtless be conducive to freedom, but would be a good deal more catastrophic for the world order than was the breakup of the Austro-Hungarian Empire in 1918."[58]

# CHAPTER 4

# A Second Plateau

## *The Reagan Revolution—US Strikes Back*

I ronically, except for the firm supporters of PL 86-90 in government and the private sector, and the huge company of Moscow and its Communist Party proxies who understood the comprehensive meaning of "the evil empire," Western and American analysts largely overlooked the captive nations base of the Reagan Doctrine. Again, little wonder then about their surprise when the Soviet Union collapsed.

A studious reading of Reagan's Captive Nations Week proclamations and his observance remarks in toto clearly shows innovative features that most analysts have overlooked or misunderstood. First, in sharp contrast to all preceding presidents who annually issued their proclamations, Reagan elevated PL 86-90 to its highest peak by signing his proclamations in the assembly of supporters at the White House. As to the assembly factor, one highly significant exception was his observance address at the Ukrainian National Catholic Shrine in Washington in 1987.

Second, unlike his predecessors, he prominently closed the long gap between the spirit and language of previous proclamations and those of PL 86-90. In minor degree, the only exceptions were those by Eisenhower in the waning period of the liberation policy.

The third feature was the precedence of Reagan's 1982 proclamation, based on the empire concept in PL 86-90, to his 1983 pronouncement of the "evil empire" in the oft-quoted Florida address. Magnifying this feature is the fact that, in foreign policy formulation, Reagan was the first president to publicly and truthfully expose the Soviet Union as an evil empire in and of itself.

A fourth unmistakable feature was the emphasis placed on the expansion of Moscow's empire—inner, contiguous, and overseas—founded on armed and subversive conquest. The typical definition of the Reagan Doctrine as an extension of the Truman Doctrine and its goal of thwarting communist takeovers is only partly true. The former clearly was based on discrediting and outing communist party reign, especially in the Soviet Union, with liberation of the captives.

Perhaps the most revealing feature of Reagan's proclamations and observance addresses, which demand reading as a whole, was the format—not just rhetoric—of the developing Reagan foreign policy. Read intently, these addresses provide a framework for the policy applications of the Reagan Doctrine in its full scope and meaning. Doubtlessly, among the many who contributed to the early development of this format were Reagan's national security advisor, Richard Allen; aide John Burgess, later an ambassador; speechwriters Anthony Dolan, later at State, and Dana Rohrabacher, later US representative (R-CA). Later contributors included Katherine Chumachenko, former executive director of the National Captive Nations Committee and White House associate director, Office of Public Liaison, who in 2005 became First Lady of Ukraine as Kateryna Yushchenko.

Richard Allen, who was very familiar with the captive nations movement, deserves highest praise for initiating the action. The 1981–82 Polish crisis sparked by the liberationist workers' Solidarity labor union provided an opportunity for action. The spillover effects of the Solidarity movement, not only in other parts of Soviet Russia's contiguous empire but also, even more importantly, in the inner empire, already had a history of workers' strikes and attempts at free unionism in Estonia, Russia, and Ukraine.[1]

When in 1981, after the John Hinckley assassination attempt, the Reagan administration began to settle in, the president issued his first

Captive Nations Week proclamation honoring the twenty-third observance. Signed without public assembly at the White House, it set in part the tone and content of subsequent ones. It commenced with the vital reminder of the "revolutionary ideal of our Founding Fathers: That governments derive their legitimacy from the consent of the peoples they govern." This basic theme of democracy and self-determination permeated all of the succeeding proclamations. The implied illegitimacy of communist party dictatorships was noted in the very next paragraph, referring to the domination of nations, then and today, by a "foreign military power and an alien Marxist-Leninist ideology."

The succeeding paragraphs pointedly referred to the "broken promises of the Yalta Conference," indicating necessary caution on treaties with Moscow and its long history of treaty violations. Also mentioned were Moscow's attempt to extend, in effect, the empire from Eastern Europe to Africa, Latin America, and Asia, while citing the invasion of Afghanistan and the intimidation of Poland. Reagan proactively advised, "During Captive Nations Week, we Americans must reaffirm our tradition of self-rule and extend to the peoples of the Captive Nations a message of hope," adding that "we cannot be complacent" since Captive Nations Week provides us with an opportunity to "reaffirm publicly our commitment to the ideals of freedom and by so doing maintain a beacon of hope for oppressed peoples everywhere." This cemented the linkage between PL 86-90 and July 4 celebrations of our Declaration of Independence.

By 1982 and the twenty-fourth observance, the administration, now well settled, moved forward with an enlargement of its foreign policy format in the Captive Nations Week proclamations and the president's address to an assembly of PL 86-90 backers in the Rose Garden—the first ever in the tradition of the observance. The media carried the event nationwide, many showing Reagan signing the proclamation with congressional leaders and others who had advocated the law's concrete implementation witnessing the unprecedented act. Here, and throughout Reagan's tenure, the basic themes of his first proclamation resonated in subsequent proclamations and addresses. The emphasis placed on national self-determination and liberty in the 1982 proclamation is seen in this phrase: "This week offers Americans an opportunity to honor our nation's founders whose wisdom and commitment to self-determination and liberty have guided this country for more than two hundred years."

The outstanding element on the non-Russian nations in the Soviet Union was cast in the proclamation's statement that, "Among the oppressed we must also count the peoples of many nationalities within the Soviet Union itself; they are victims of long decades of repression." The following year Reagan accurately defined the area of this element as "the evil empire." Of course, there is considerable background to this (e.g., USIA's special issue of *Problems of Communism, Nationalities and Nationalism in the USSR*, September–October 1967), but none of his predecessors had raised it as Reagan did. By 1984, further research on the subject was in full swing, and it continued well beyond the Reagan years.[2] As the author of an engaging thesis at the Naval Postgraduate School in California observed, "Crafting human rights and democratic self-determination in his 'Evil Empire' strategy, Reagan was the first president to make the annual observance a public event and used it to showcase or announce policy."[3]

In his steady revelation of policy, Reagan, in his address to the assembly, dwelled on points that led to specific action later. He pointed to the Berlin Wall five years before calling upon Gorbachev to tear it down; to the Soviet Union for its "largest military empire in the history of the world"; to Lenin's legacy for its "subterfuges" and "illegal methods" (which would include terrorism, actually investigated by his task force later); to the urgent need for modernizing the Voice of America, Radio Free Europe, and Radio Liberty and the initiation of Radio Martí to Cuba. "We in the West must do more than merely decry attacks on human freedom. The nature of this struggle is ultimately one that will be decided, not by military might, but by spiritual resolve and confidence." These policy points were then discussed at a large luncheon gathering in the Cannon Building of the US Congress and then inserted into the Congressional Record.[4]

On the twenty-fifth observance of the week in 1983, at the White House and public assembly, the stated fundamental truths of the Reagan policy predominated in full force, but with new directions and specificity, as would be the case in all of his later proclamations and addresses down to 1988. In this one, the new direction was the United Nations and its Declaration of Human Rights: "that all human beings are born free and equal in dignity and rights." Properly, the next sentence was a valid historical link: "This reaffirmed an eternal truth that Thomas Jefferson in 1776 wrote into our Declaration of Independence." On this basis, the president reaffirmed our commitment to "the cause of liberty" and, regarding the captive nations, "the United States supports their aspirations for freedom, independence, and national self-determination."

In his address to the White House assembly, Reagan stressed that the subjugation of the Baltic nations was not a permanent condition and that "to every person trapped in tyranny, whether in the Ukraine, Hungary, Czechoslovakia, Cuba, or Vietnam, we send our love and support and tell them they are not alone. Our message must be: Your struggle is our struggle, your dream is our dream. And someday, you, too, will be free."

Deserving of mention on this twenty-fifth observance were the additional events of the International Captive Nations Conference on Capitol Hill, including a congressional luncheon in the House, a further conference in the Senate, and a banquet in the Hyatt Regency hotel. At the luncheon, the address by our representative to the United Nations, Ambassador Jeane Kirkpatrick, elaborated in detail on several of Reagan's points.[5] Covering additional points were the presentations of former national security advisor Richard Allen and representatives Phil Crane (R-IL), Samuel Stratton (D-NY), and Gerald Solomon (R-NY). The conference in the Senate was devoted to communism in regions of the world, featuring ambassador William

Middendorf, US representative to the Organization of American States; Dr. Ku Cheng-kang, chairman of the World Anti-Communist League; British parliamentarian John Wilkinson; and leaders from Afghanistan, Austria, Vietnam, and Angola.

The conference windup at the Hyatt, hosted by Sen. Jeremiah Denton (R-AL) with State Department counselor Edward Derwinski serving as master of ceremonies, highlighted the address by Vice President George H. W. Bush to over 350 guests representing embassies, organizations, and government agencies. A stalwart supporter of PL 86-90, Bush, in advancing Reagan's developing policies, saw fit to remind the audience: "This year, during Captive Nations Week, we mark a grim anniversary—the fiftieth anniversary of the forced famine in the Ukraine, in which five to seven million people lost their lives." For the organization of this unique, tripartite conference, tribute was paid to General John Singlaub, chairman of the US Council for World Freedom, and Katherine Chumachenko, acting chairperson of the National Captive Nations Committee.

A patient examination of Reagan's proclamations and addresses on Captive Nations Week demonstrates the constancy of essential principles, ever-widening foreign policy initiatives, confident leadership, and new directions for both peace and victory. The 1984 proclamation of the twenty-sixth observance mentioned Afghanistan and the "imprisoned Ukrainian Yuri Shukhevych; Lithuania and its religious rights petitioners; Solidarity in Poland and the millions of freedom fighters in Communist-occupied countries" for "it is in their struggle for freedom that we can find the true path to genuine and lasting peace." The proclamation also noted that "it is the duty and privilege of the United States of America to demand that the signatories of the United Nations Charter and the Helsinki Accords live up to their pledges and obligations." This drive for legitimate demands on UN members has continued into the period of post-9/11, including the demand for democratization and UN reform.

Before the signing ceremony, ambassador Max Kampelman, who had led the Helsinki review conference in Madrid, addressed the

White House assembly, saying, "In areas like the Ukraine, Latvia, Lithuania, Estonia, and Caucasian republics, smoldering yearnings for self-determination continue to exist." Presciently, he stated that "the greatest threat to the leadership of the Soviet Union probably lies within its own borders."

After the signing, Reagan's remarks ran true to form and substance: religious freedom for Muslims, Jews, and Christians; the persecution of Andrei Sakharov and his wife, Elena Bonner, both firm advocates of democracy and national self-determination; aid for "freedom fighters" in Nicaragua; a working budget for Voice of America, Radio Free Europe, and Radio Liberty; and the establishment of Radio Martí. As always, congressional members participated in the event. Later, Rep. Frank Annunzio (D-IL) kept score by placing the Captive Nations List in the Congressional Record.[6] Soon thereafter, the president extended the proclamation's message with a speech at the United Nations on September 24, emphasizing the relationship between human rights and peace, the UN Charter's goals on peace and human dignity, the moral basis of US policy objectives, and "constructive negotiations" with the Soviet Union.

Entering into Reagan's second term, the proper question of negotiations was raised by his critics, both left and right. In the liberationist mode, the president had been eager for a summit meeting for some time in his first term. As he creditably and aptly put it to close friends, Moscow's leaders "kept dying on me": Leonid Brezhnev in 1982, Yuri Andropov in 1984, and Konstantin Chernenko in 1985. The posture of his administration, shown in part by the Captive Nations Week proclamations and speeches, as well as presidential documents on national security issues, rested on three pillars—realism, strength, and dialogue.[7] Realism appeared in the proclamations; strength in Reagan's dealings with Mikhail Gorbachev; and dialogue in the confident mode of "trust but verify," "deeds not words."

The Captive Nations Week proclamations and remarks continued for Reagan's second term with further elaboration and the addition of new elements providing a still more comprehensive view of

Reagan's farsighted leadership. Thus, on the twenty-seventh observance in 1985, the longest yet proclamation dwelled again on the UN
Charter and the Helsinki Accords, Eastern Europe, Afghanistan, and
freedom struggles in Asia and Latin America. But it focused now on
the uniqueness of our vision of liberty worldwide, the oppression of
women, and the organic relationships of liberty, humanity, and justice to the political freedom of all peoples and nations, implying huge
alterations of social policies.

Relevant to the proclamations were the deeds, not just words and
rhetoric. Underlined earlier were the issues of illegal methods, the illegitimacy of communist party dictatorships, and treaties. In his 1982
Captive Nations Week remarks, the president specifically pivoted to
Lenin's legacy of illegal methods that included terrorism. Stefan
Possony's study on terrorism, published in 1978, was not without
influence on this, and its coverage of Soviet Russian franchises and
alliances provided a perspective on al-Qaeda's operations in the 2000s.
Sparked by the terrorist attack on the US Marine Corps barracks
in Beirut in October 1983, official studies of the problem ensued in
1984–86, and a cabinet-level Task Force on Combating Terrorism
was formed, headed by Vice President Bush.[8] In 1984, Secretary of
State George Shultz summarized the situation in this vein: "When the
Soviet Union and its clients provide financial, logistic, and training
support for terrorists worldwide . . . they hope to shake the West's
self-confidence." He added, "We must be willing to use military
force . . . to combat international terrorism." In hindsight, some
might argue that this development should have been broadened, but
the far broader picture of US-Soviet Union relations and the stakes
involved would nullify the argument. In short, keep focused on the
forest and attend in deeds to its trees as conditions permit.

Reagan demonstrated his awareness of the direction of Moscow's
global political warfare, not just in successive Captive Nations Week
proclamations and addresses, but also in concrete actions. The pre-
ventive strike in Grenada in October 1983 illustrated the ignorance
and foolishness shown in this area of political warfare. Many viewed

it as a bully's show of force. Fortunately, the president saw it as Moscow's attempt to create additional captive nations, specific checkpoints on shipping lanes, as in Africa, and a Caribbean domino, plus one in Central America via Nicaragua. Centered on Nicaragua, his speech in June 1986 incorporated these points, preceded by official studies on Soviet/Cuban plans after Grenada and the Soviet Union's connection with Cuba.[9]

The Bolsheviks' long history of broken treaties and subversive and aggressive activities requires only a brief overview. These segments of the Leninist legacy date back to December 1917, when Soviet Russia as such recognized the independence of Ukraine and then subverted and invaded it. Soon Georgia and others met the same fate. After the establishment of the Soviet Union more than a hundred treaties were violated.[10] The whole saga of conspiracy and stealth via the US Communist Party rings with names such as John Reed, financed by the Kremlin in 1920; the decrypted Venona cables; Julius Rosenberg stealing atomic secrets during World War II; and the party still being financed into the Gorbachev period.[11] It was with this background that Reagan seized upon "the broken promises of the Yalta Conference" in his first Captive Nations Week proclamation in 1981 and extended his favorite theme, "Dovorey no provorey" (trust but verify), throughout his tenure.

Evidently, 1985 was a year of further revelations strikingly pertinent to PL 86 90 and Reagan's Captive Nations Week proclamations and addresses. For example, Thomas O'Neill, Jr., Speaker of the House of Representatives, led a congressional delegation to Moscow and was confronted by Gorbachev who, fearing the breakup of the Soviet Union, raised the subject of the "evil empire." The Speaker reported, "It seemed to upset him more than anything else."[12] Also revealing was the impact made on Reagan by a briefing book released by the Heritage Foundation prior to the president's meeting in November with Gorbachev in Geneva, the first summit of four. Covering many of the subjects we have been discussing, the book was unique then as other think tanks and sources were urging concessions to the Soviet Union.

In the meeting the president held fast on what was nonnegotiable. Gorbachev later railed against the foundation in the Supreme Soviet. The scholarly and proactive media released in this policy area were well vindicated by the outcomes only a few years later.

In 1986, at the twenty-eighth observance, proclamation, and address following the signing ceremony in the Roosevelt Room, Reagan intensified his dual concerns for individual persons and states, with characteristic, verbal panache in each category. In more detailed remarks to the audience, he elaborated on his pride in keeping "faith with the people of the Captive Nations" since the first proclamation through his talk with Anatoly Sharansky, the former Soviet Union prisoner, citing a letter from ten imprisoned women that had been smuggled out of the Soviet Union. He brought up his meeting with Gorbachev in Geneva and his proposal for the reduction of restrictions on travel and personal contacts between the United States and the Soviet Union, injecting again "deeds now, not words"; his concern about the Soviet Union's massive, military buildup since the early 1970s; and the meaning of Captive Nations Week, primarily freedom for all in Eastern Europe.

In his sweeping address, the president expressed his additional pride that during his term of office "there have been no new Captive Nations" and that he had brought one small country, Grenada, "back into the family of free people." Anecdotally, offered the privilege and honor to address the assembly, I was deeply moved by the president's personal reference.

Overlooked by most analysts and the media were the extraordinary changes in direction that the presidential-led twenty-ninth Captive Nations Week observance in 1987 represented. Yet this was understandable since they, from the time of the first proclamation, were oblivious to the unfolding of Reagan's foreign policy. The proclamation in 1987 clearly cited the struggle against Soviet imperialism—"a struggle that began in Ukraine seventy years ago is taking place throughout the Soviet empire"—in, among other places, Kazakhstan, Latvia, Lithuania, and Estonia. It mentioned the persecutions of

Gunars Astra, Lev Lukyanenko, Mart Niklus, and Viktoras Petkus. And, of course, the persistent pressure for deeds under the UN Charter and the Helsinki Accords continued.

Another change was the unusual staging of the assembly for luncheon at the Ukrainian Catholic National Shrine of the Holy Family in Washington, DC. The president, who was accompanied by Howard Baker, his chief of staff, appeared before three hundred invited guests and sixty journalists. In his televised speech, Reagan raised his appeal to Gorbachev the previous month: "Tear down the Berlin Wall and give freedom to the Ukrainian Catholic and Orthodox churches." The speech continued his demands for the renunciation of the Brezhnev Doctrine; freedom for prisoner Petro Ruba, who made a wooden replica of the Statue of Liberty and satirized the Soviet Union's invasion of Afghanistan; and support for the contras in Nicaragua.[13]

At the time, and well into 1988, a widely pondered question was, "Why was the Captive Nations Week assembly held at the Ukrainian National Catholic Shrine and not the White House?" Did it symbolize a new policy direction, a message for the Kremlin? Judging by the expansive content in the proclamations, it would seem not. Factually, however, the move was certainly buttressed by Lenin's basic, political axiom—Soviet Union–Ukraine=0—upheld by every Kremlin leader down to Gorbachev, who strove desperately to save the Soviet Union and imputed along the way the so-called brotherly relationship between Russians and Ukrainians and a common history. Also, in fact, despite his more democratic stance, heroism, and stand on national sovereignty across the breadth of the Soviet Union, Yeltsin shared with Gorbachev a great surprise over Ukraine's secession. This concept has continued into the Putin reign among those seeking the revival of the Soviet Union or the alternative Commonwealth of Independent States with, of course, Moscow as its center. For everyone else, Ukraine's historic Orange Revolution in 2004 put an end to both ignorance and ambivalence on the subject.

The 1988 proclamation and presidential address in the Rose Garden for the thirtieth Captive Nations Week can be viewed as the summit of Reagan's declarations. The proclamation specifically pointed to the republics of the Soviet Union: "Across continents and seas, the cry for freedom rings out and the struggle for its blessings continues, in the republics of the Soviet Union, in the Baltic States and throughout Eastern Europe, in Cuba and Nicaragua, in Ethiopia and Angola, and in Vietnam, Laos, and Cambodia. It also continues in Afghanistan . . ." It mentioned specific, persecuted individuals in Lithuania, Ukraine, Poland, Latvia, and Estonia and persisted with demands on the United Nations. The president's lengthy address to the assembly deserves careful reading for its reach and specifics, such as Reagan's talks with Angolan Jonas Savimbi, Nicaraguan Dr. Henry Zelaya, and Natan Sharansky (who altered his first name after being freed from Soviet incarceration). The following year the Berlin Wall fell, and Moscow's empire began unraveling.

The Kremlin's reactions to Reagan's 1983 "evil empire" remark and his Captive Nations Week proclamations and addresses were downright volcanic. Reminiscent of the Khrushchev explosion over the passage of PL 86-90, TASS, the Russian news agency, in 1982 berated Reagan for his "interference in the internal affairs of the Soviet Union" pleasing "the most reactionary forces of imperialism" and blithely extolled Moscow's "equal rights for nationalists and ethnic groups in the USSR." These and other attacks were repeated over Radio Moscow and the Kremlin's international broadcasts. In fact, *Pravda* suggested my remarks were "hysterical" and, offensively, the work of an intellectual "pygmy."[14]

In the captive nations, the communist parties followed suit. In Ukraine, *Radyanska Ukraine* attacked not only the president but also his cabinet members in an air of scandal, while conveying the Kremlin-stamped stereotypes on "interference in internal affairs." Radio Kiev in English to North America aired the "Week of Provocation Against Nations," charging an "anti-Soviet plot."[15] From Poland, General Jaruzelski's advisor, Wieslaw Gornicki, assailed Reagan: "The speech is insulting to the Polish state and people. . . . It is

beneath the acceptance level of civilized countries maintaining diplomatic relations."[16]

The Kremlin's psychological warfare continued with its international network and institutes. A striking example was the intellectual peregrinator Georgi Arbatov, director of the Institute on
American and Canadian Affairs (a KGB facade) and then an advisor
to Gorbachev. In February 1982, he appeared before the Canadian
Parliamentary Committee on Exterior and Defense Affairs, attacking the Captive Nations Week in the United States: "As you know, in
the United States there exists an organization—what's its name? The
Captive Nations, which observes the Captive Nations Week, and the
President supports it, and the Congress does likewise." With a map of
the Soviet Union, he deceitfully argued, "It appears that our country
(Russia) is allowed to have only the areas around Moscow and Leningrad and perhaps between Smolensk and Gorky. . . . We will never
allow this to happen."[17]

In 1984, Arbatov was interviewed by Ted Koppel on ABC's *Nightline*. Asked why Moscow withdrew from the Olympics in Los Ange-
les, he answered that the climate was not good because of the Captive
Nations Week demonstrations. At the end of 1986, the roving Kremlin ambassador smeared Reagan as a "provincial ideologist" feeding
on anticommunist falsehoods and repeating Nazi propaganda.[18]

In 1984, Vilen Ivanov, director of the Moscow Institute of
Sociological Research, raised the notion of "ethnographic warfare"
against the Soviet Union, arguing that setting the Russian people
against the non-Russian population of the national republics had
become a fundamental thesis of Western propaganda.[19] Another
piece, out of Azerbaijan and with a pan-Slavist tinge, contended, "Our
ideological opponents are reconstructing their propaganda arsenal in
order to set non-Slavic groups against the Russian, Ukrainian, and
Byelorussian peoples."[20]

Journalists missed many opportunities to raise appropriate and
pointed questions. For example, before the Washington summit

between Reagan and Gorbachev in December 1987, and later at the Soviet Union embassy, Tom Brokaw of NBC was told by Gorbachev that the Soviet Union is "a whole conglomeration of over a hundred nations and nationalities" and also at the embassy made the point, "We cannot leave our relations as they are, the relations between our peoples, between our two nations," meaning the United States and the Soviet Union. This sounded like a mix of apples and peanuts and presented an opportunity for a deeper inquiry, but unfortunately it was passed by.

Even after the Reagan years, new versions continued to emerge. An editorial, "A Soviet Disunion," in the *New York Times* (February 9, 1990) related the Soviet Union crisis to our Cold War experience, asserting that "the principles at stake have torn Americans ever since Abraham Lincoln fought against separation."[21] In the realm of academia, where critical research and empirical exposition are primary standards, a dark cloud reigned for decades in university history textbooks treating "Russia."[22] Reversing academic trends on the Soviet Union was a slow process.

Far more worrisome were the outlandish conceptions of distinguished economists and Sovietologists on conditions and trends in the Soviet Union. In 1981, for example, Seweryn Bialer, a Sovietologist at Columbia University, held that, "The Soviet Union is not now, nor will it be during the next decade, in the throes of a true systemic crisis." Paul Samuelson of Harvard University, in the 1985 edition of his popular Econ-101 textbook, firmly stated, "What counts is results, and there can be no doubt that the Soviet planning system has been a powerful engine for economic growth." At the time, that growth was already on a downside to reach new lows. As late as 1989, sharing in the Samuelson misconception, Lester Thurow of the Massachusetts Institute of Technology opined, "Today it is a country whose economic achievements bear comparison with those of the United States." These were the perspectives of numerous Sovietologists in the West for a crassly distorted, hybrid political economy, cancerously overmilitarized and largely neglectful of citizen needs.

Obviously, the debate over "captive nations" was still ongoing, decades after passage of the original resolution. In the next chapters, we will delve more deeply into these nations whose freedoms and identities Moscow's imperial system worked so hard to destroy, with particular attention to Ukraine. But first, we will provide an insider's view of some fascinating but almost-forgotten events in the early 1950s and 1990s—events that are strikingly relevant to today's situation concerning Russia, Ukraine, and NATO.

# CHAPTER 5

# Support for Freedom Fighters in the Soviet Empire

R ussia's invasion of Ukraine in 2022 turned the spotlight on NATO and its role in securing the country's sovereignty.[1] This question echoes debates dating back to the early days of the alliance as to whether NATO should play a purely deterrent role or a more active role in the face of Russian expansionism. The latter would involve direct coordination with freedom fighters in the captive nations.

For the present and future, there couldn't be a more striking confluence of issues than what was provided by the evolving mini-paths of the 1950s—in capsule form, NATO, nationalism, and strategy.

Shortly after the North Atlantic Treaty Organization was founded in 1949, questions arose as to whether it should adopt a liberation policy. Should NATO just militarily deter or react to a possible Soviet Russian aggression in Western Europe? Or, more positively, should it provide politico-moral support for existing anticommunist freedom fighters in the vast Soviet Russian empire? Was this idea radical, diplomatically impossible, or perilously disadvantageous? Typical "evolutionists," self-serving revisionists, familiar appeasers, and other breeds would maintain that all three applied, pointing to our involvement in the Korean War and domestic problems. Actually, from a realistic political warfare perspective and comparing holistically our strong position vis-à-vis the thoroughly weak state of the Soviet

Union then, the only sensible adjective would be the first: "radical" in the sense of getting to the root of things.

In 1951, joint hearings of the Senate Foreign Relations and Armed Services committees regarding the Wherry Resolution (S.R. 8) were the setting for the injection of the above orientation. Sponsored by Republican Sen. Kenneth S. Wherry of Nebraska, the resolution essentially aimed to restrict sending troops abroad without Congress determining policy covering it, in this case to NATO. Many salient aspects were considered by the combined committees. But as Sen. Tom Connally (D-TX), chairman of the Foreign Relations committee, candidly admitted in response to my testimony, his committee had not adequately considered the specific area it covered—NATO and its natural allies behind the Iron Curtain.[2]

To fully appreciate the opportunities open to us, one must constantly bear in mind the context of political warfare as practiced by the Soviet Russians, not to mention the Chinese Communists and others. Weak as they were politically, economically, and militarily, they nevertheless pressed on ideologically, propaganda-wise, conspiratorially, and so forth in zigzag movements and were always ready to retreat a step or two backward if challenged directly.

Only in this framework can the Cold War be intelligently understood with all of its pieces—nuclear arms and threats, military blackmail, diplomatic tirades and conciliations, cultural exchanges, etc.—fitting in accordingly. A blatantly disproportionate amount of resources was poured by Moscow into "universities," schools, and fraternal conferences training its own "revolutionaries" from all continents in systematic political warfare.

The example on NATO and freedom fighters behind the Iron Curtain illustrates what could have been achieved at the lowest conceivable risk at a time of maximum comparative advantage enjoyed by the West. Widespread resistance to imperialist Soviet Russian consolidation, Siberian separatism, massive concentration camp strikes, and the reality of underground groups and actual systems in the Ukrainian Insurgent Army and armed groups in Slovakia, Lithuania,

Poland, and elsewhere constituted our objective assets, our natural allies, in this type of warfare. They furnished evidence on the increasing efficacy of the Voice of America and performed many different operations and deeds that, with adequate assistance, would have gone a long way in interrupting and stifling Moscow's long-range plans for the consolidating of its expanded empire and subversive operations worldwide. They would have demonstrated objectively the myth of Russian invincibility with desertions from the Red Army, which consisted of over 40 percent non-Russian nationals. Including freedom-seeking Russians, this phenomenon occurred in the past and was repeated only several years later in the Hungarian Revolution. In the 1990s the fragile and emasculated state of the Red Army's remnants brilliantly reflected its deep-rooted and longstanding weaknesses.

Sen. Alexander Wiley (R-WI) depicted my proposal in this vein as a "new atomic bomb" that should be sold to the executive branch. However you may interpret this characterization, the process would have been based on least-risk courses of action, a judicious calculation of forces at play, and a readied seizure of likely opportunities in pursuit of the basic goals. Nothing precipitous nor crusading, but, in chessboard manner, a one-upmanship toward the realization of our goals.

Sen. William Knowland (R-CA) understood all of this quite well. I accepted his invitation to visit him that afternoon of the hearing day. It proved to be a most productive and pleasurable first meeting. At this session, the beginning of numerous such visits, we reviewed the main points of my testimony and their political possibilities. In what developed as a warm relationship, he offered the support of his office for all projects we would agree on. One significant project was the advancement of the liberation policy at the 1952 Republican National Convention in Chicago. His support and influence in the party were crucial in making possible the wide distribution of a pamphlet on liberation vs. containment. Truly, for me he was a source of great inspiration and political wisdom.

As to NATO then and now, a communist-ruled Russia/Russian Federation in some alliance with Beijing would revive across-the-board national underground resistance systems similar to those that existed at the time of the Wherry deliberations. One system lasted more than ten years in the face of overwhelming Nazi and communist forces. Most of the anti-Soviet Russian operations were in the western part of the primary empire and its extension in contiguous Central Europe, ranging from propaganda to armed resistance and high-level assassinations.

In Russia itself, there was no systemic underground resistance—a fact well attested by individual Russian democrats. The Vlasov army desertions to the Nazi military during World War II do not wholly apply here. True, the general and his officers were anticommunist, but, much to the annoyance of Hitler, they plugged for the retention of the territorial empire.

Also during the war, most Western observers failed to distinguish between the Ukrainian freedom fighters in the Ukrainian Insurgent Army (UPA), which was formed in the fall of 1942, and the Red Russian partisans. Ironically, the UPA, opposing both the Soviet Russian and Nazi German forces, contributed more behind the lines to Hitler's defeat in Stalingrad than the communist partisans. In Ukraine, UPA members severed lines of communication and demolished main routes of transport heading east, severely impeding the flow of supplies. After the war, and on a necessarily lower scale, their chief targets were Red Army general leadership, political commissars, depots, and the like.

Regarding so-called Titoism in the postwar period, the rise of "national communism" represented nothing more than calculated national assertions against Soviet Russian domination and Moscow's bossism. On record, one of the earliest but unsuccessful expressions of this was furnished in the 1930s by Mykola Skripnik in Ukraine, a former associate of Lenin. As to Yugoslavia's Tito, his transformations of character are important to know for an understanding of the captive nations concept with reference to the Yugoslavian state.

Politically bred and trained in Moscow, Josep Broz, known as Tito, was assigned the tasks of leading the communist partisan fight against the Axis forces in Yugoslavia, undermining the democratic partisans, and eventually seizing political power in the region. Having achieved all three, he later launched a five-year plan that promised to outmatch in rates of economic growth and development any that Moscow had produced. In this he failed miserably. What grew markedly instead was Belgrade's conflict with Moscow, monumentally highlighted by its divorce from Moscow control and the irreparable cleavage in Lenin's worldwide dream apparatus, Comintern, which Stalin expediently camouflaged as Cominform to satisfy his allies during the war.

The split between Belgrade and Moscow, followed later by Beijing, cannot be overemphasized. It was a mortal blow to the Kremlin's direction of the world communist movement. In addition, it had a meaning for the captive nations concept with respect to both Yugoslavia and mainland China. Simply put, because of Moscow's loss of control over both, were they then no longer made up of captive nations? Hardly. Tito's ability to maintain the unity of Yugoslavia through dictatorial Communist Party control in no way erased the freedom aspirations of the respective nations in that state framework, although it had produced the illusion of a Yugoslav nation that misguided one of our own administrations. The same applies to the other communist deviator, mainland China and its various national entities imprisoned in the mini-empire.

Little imagination is required to envision the consequences resulting from a second Russian attempt to re-create the empire. In magnitude and depth, Bosnia and Chechnya would appear as microscopic previews. Considering the historic changes of the late 1980s and early 1990s, it is noteworthy that in sharp contrast to the barbarities and carnage in the Balkans, caused by imperial Serbian expansionism, those in the former Soviet Union, with the exception of Chechnya, weathered the transition to freedom with a spectacular minimum of violence, conflagration, and needless deaths.

From a strategic as well as cultural viewpoint, it should be noted, too, that following World War II, a close, collaborative relationship developed between the Ukrainian Insurgent Army and Polish underground resistance forces. This collaboration signaled a long step forward from the dark days of irreconcilability and endless tension in Polish-Ukrainian relations to now a period of amity and friendship. Significantly, when Ukraine declared its independence in 1991, Poland was the first to recognize it.

In light of persistent Russian political pressures for another empire in the 1990s, the proclamations of the UPA bear unique credibility and certain relevancy in our time. One is worth repeating in part: "In no wise are we fighting against the Russian people, but we do fight against the Russian Bolshevik imperialism, that is those Russian elements as well as other nationalities which are relying upon Moscow as the center of their empire."[3] The elements of confirmation: the long Cold War itself and the resurgence of Russian imperialism, with or without the communist smokescreen.

An important figure who recognized and deeply appreciated this whole phenomenon of anti-Soviet Russian resistance was General William Donovan, the former head of the wartime Office of Strategic Services (OSS), which originated in 1942 and was the predecessor of the Central Intelligence Agency. I was introduced to him by Evron Kirkpatrick, later the husband of our prominent ambassador to the United Nations, Jeane Kirkpatrick. My friendship with the general began in 1950 with a visit to his Wall Street office in New York, followed by almost monthly visits—always Saturdays at 10:30 a.m.—in his apartment on Sutton Place.

If Donovan earned by successful deeds the reputation of "Wild Bill," he undoubtedly was enthusiastically wild about the political warfare potentialities of the resistance groups and systems. Our discussions were lively and concrete, my amiable host consistently displaying a propensity to raise questions aimed at the most detailed explanations. In answering them, I could go only so far, not being in the underground network. For his side interest in the empire economy of the USSR, I was able to answer his questions in abundance, but here, too, within realistic limits because of Moscow's statistical acrobatics and gross distortions.

Aside from my memorable conversations and social amenities with the general, a bridge of communication with the leading resistance organ behind the Iron Curtain had to be established for purposes of further information and the possibility of practical assistance. This was accomplished, leading to the formulation by the UPA leadership of a three-stage plan that Donovan submitted to the director of the CIA. The first stage was informational in detailed but cautious form; dependent on a mutual acceptance of the first, the second stage concerned meetings between representatives of the CIA and the UPA for logistical preparations; the third involved the transmission of material aid.

In the end, both Donovan and I were dismayed that the plan never went beyond the first step because of endless dillydallying and a lack of seriousness by the CIA. We sought a breakthrough but also anticipated the outcome in view of the state of affairs at the time—policy indecision and defects, bureaucratic bungling in the Voice of America, and the like. Notwithstanding all this, the general maintained an optimistic attitude and a faith in America's resourcefulness to win the Cold War. With an extraordinary breadth of political warfare knowledge, he had an appreciative understanding of the inimitable power of legitimate nationalism and the strategic position of Ukraine. Aware of my other involvement at the time, Donovan favored the positive implementation of the Kersten Amendment to the Mutual Security Act of 1952. But here, too, he banked on a fortuitous breakthrough rather than any result of farseeing policy.

The Kersten Amendment proposed to set aside $100 million to people who were living behind the Iron Curtain or had escaped from there in order to support anticommunist military forces. Its linkage with NATO and the resistance underground is obvious. Yet, it represented in part another facet of what could have been accomplished in our active acceptance of Moscow's political warfare challenge. If engineered properly and skillfully, its program would have caused Moscow and its satraps complications galore in attempting to seal the Iron Curtain and to consolidate Moscow's extended empire.

Debate on the amendment was extensive, with the expected lineup of the usual inactive or reactive "evolutionists" waiting for things to happen and those cognizant of Moscow's deepest weaknesses and its political warfare tactics. For example, all the essential aspects of the amendment were crisply treated in radio and TV programs at Georgetown University.[4] A subsequent program on the same subject and facilities featured Averell Harriman who, in opposition, defended the administration's position.

As I viewed it, there were four essential features in the program as envisioned by the amendment's author and its supporters. First, it had the inherent quality of forging a desperately needed unity of anticommunist groups and forces, here and abroad. For there could be no question about the range of information and conveyance of reality in the entire empire that would have been transmitted by those escaping from it. This kind of real focus was lacking; thus all the contradictory and even slanted reporting in the West. Our natural allies behind the Iron Curtain, especially those who knew and suffered under Soviet Russian domination for decades, extended from the Danube to the Pacific and could have been tapped in various supportive ways.

Second, the amendment aimed to attract young, able-bodied men and women in their escape through the porous Curtain. At the time, well over a thousand per month made their way through the pores (some estimated ten thousand).[5] The attraction would have been a most influential and powerful one, admittedly at higher levels of risk but not necessarily self-depleting considering the boundless obstacles and impediments posed to the border guards and their likely reinforcements. This second factor could not have been satisfactorily placed in operation without the underground at work.

The third feature of the amendment's program was the formation of these young escapees into military units attached to NATO. These were to be according to nationality and the flags of their respective, once-independent nations. No matter how large or small at first they may have been, the striking symbolization of alliance for the defense of Western Europe, the restoration of freedom for the captive nations, indeed, the preservation of civilization itself, would have been electrifying across the entire expanse of Moscow's empire and its Communist Party quisling fiefdoms.

Fourth, the link with the underground systems and groups was indispensable to the whole projected program. Material aid of all sorts— arms, medical equipment, money, propaganda technology, and so forth—would have been on the agenda. The predominant human element was there, more widespread and agile than most observers in the West knew or understood in its entirety. For our time and well beyond, institutional allowances for free archival research in the former captive nations and their captor will uncover massive data and assessments on the personages and operations of the freedom fighters in the cold/hot war behind the Iron Curtain.

Several months later the subject was again discussed on the Georgetown University TV/Radio Forum. This time the panel composed of Harriman, O'Connor, and myself. By then it became evident that the administration wasn't prepared to undertake the outlined program. Harriman indicated as much—escapees were transformed into refugees. The escapees would fall into a program of refugee assistance.

One interesting aspect of that Georgetown University event was the beginning of my acquaintance with Harriman. We seemed to discover a warm rapport at this first meeting. Following the radio portion of the program and on our way to the Channel 5 TV station downtown, he surprisingly broached the idea of my joining his campaign for the Democratic presidential nomination. To say the least, I was taken aback by the offer. Skeptically, I informed him of my connection with the Republican National Committee. He replied, "I used to be a Republican, and back in the mid-1920s I changed to the Democratic Party." Unaware of my heavy involvement in the RNC, the ambassador nevertheless pressed on. Our paths crossed many times but, as he and I knew, our positions on the USSR, the captive nations, and domestic economic policy were far apart. Nonetheless, I respected his views, valued his public service to our country, and, above all, admired his gracious character with all of his fine human traits. However, like countless others given to the false promises of economic determinism, Harriman unfortunately fell short of seeing the total picture of political warfare, particularly on the power of nationalism and strategic thinking in the Cold War.

I recall that when in the early 1960s, following Congress's Captive Nations Week Resolution, we strove to have a Select House Committee on the Captive Nations, Speaker John McCormack told me that the most sustained criticism of the House Un-American Activities Committee was its unintended length of existence, a factor that militated against the proposed committee.

With reference to the former Soviet Union, the concept of non-Russian nationalism was a very effective one. During the Cold War, it served to differentiate the non-Russian nations from the Russian, particularly for the vast majority of people in the West and elsewhere who confused the Soviet Union with Russia. In addition, it pinpointed a force that was the most powerful and invincible in opposition to Soviet Russian imperialism and totalitarian command rule. Also, in sharp contrast to the relatively superficial and transient targets like "Trotskyism," "Bukharinism," and so forth, it tenaciously withstood Moscow's incessant denunciations against "bourgeois nationalism," a favorite (supposedly Marxian) Kremlin concoction. With the incorporation of Central Europe into the empire, the non-Russian concept gained additional significance and potency, as was demonstrated by the combined resistance efforts of the underground forces that were capable of penetrating the Iron Curtain to the west.

As further proof of the validity and efficacy of the non-Russian concept, it fit into a whole series of political power plays—before the forced creation of the Soviet Union, during its existence, and after it. For example, Lenin played with it in his liberations appeal to the "oppressed nationalities" in the tsarist Russian Empire. Upon the death of Stalin, and in a terrorist tradition, the spy- and prison-master, Lavrenti Beria, sought non-Russian backing in his attempt to seize Kremlin leadership. In the 1956 blast against Stalin's heinous record, it was the Armenian Anastas Mikoyan, with the support of other non-Russian representatives at the party congress, who launched the attack. Khrushchev followed and maximized it. Parenthetically, another Western illusion conjured Khrushchev as a Ukrainian, though he openly admitted being Russian. In Ukraine he was widely known as "the hangman of Ukraine." On the demise of the Soviet Union in the early 1990s, Boris Yeltsin in his power play against Gorbachev is seen racing throughout the non-Russian region promising "sovereignty" to all. But this latest example is just the beginning of another story—the scheme of the Commonwealth of Independent States, exercises in Russian pressure-building, and the pursuit of Russian political dominance.

How the developments in the Russian Federation will turn out, only the future will tell. The salient point here is the concept's provision of a structure of thought that accommodates both the continuance of rule by the imperial center or enhanced freedom and self-determination, even to the extent of independent republics. Genuine Russian democrats of the stature of the late Andrei Sakharov and his wife, Elena Bonner, have strongly supported the principle of self-determination and free political choice in all of the mentioned areas. They courageously denounced the Yeltsin-declared war against independent Chechnya.

The Caucasian cauldron of endless strife has a centuries-long history of struggle by its various nations for independence from the Russian Empire. North Caucasia, a federation of these nations, emerged after World War I, only to be destroyed by Lenin's Soviet Russia. One doesn't have to be steeped in the history of this region to sense that the cauldron of boiling issues will remain to measure the political character and integrity of Moscow.

Statism has been an institutional virus in Russia from its very origin in the state of Muscovy to the present. The degree of virulence has remained stable throughout, regardless of the intermittent liberalization programs undertaken by the tsars or commissars. Interwoven with the omnipotent power of the state and its glorification has been the sanctification of its father-leader, or *vozhd*, the patrimonial dispenser, be he a Romanov or a Stalin. When the Mikoyan/Khrushchev blast against Stalin occurred, a desanctification of the renegade

Georgian set in. Western analysts in large measure hailed it as the beginning of a liberalization era. Subsequent events proved otherwise.

In the 1990s, the streets of Moscow and elsewhere continued to be
contaminated by large Communist Party rallies, clamoring for Stalin's resanctification and the maintenance of overall state power and
control. And, naturally, associated with this clamor was not only the
unquestioned rule by the center over the entire Russian Federation
but also the re-creation of the Soviet Union.

Democracy, with all its rules of law and politico-economic institutions, necessarily requires time and supportive forces for its eventual
fruition. Particularly is this true in the case of Russia, which, since its
Muscovy origins, has never known democratic life. Statism, imperial
dominance, politico-economic authoritarianism or totalitarianism,
leader and cult worship, and so forth are influences that will in greater
or lesser degree continue to obstruct Russian democratic development. It will take years into the next millennium for democracy to
become firmly rooted there.

Completing the series of interrelated subjects in this chapter, I
handed a letter to Secretary of State John Foster Dulles in October 1956 at a meeting in his office.[6] In a sense, it was both a calling
card and a ground for discussion. I was privileged to head a delegation of four representing the Ukrainian Congress Committee of
America to discuss Cold War strategy and Ukraine with the secretary.
Incorporating some additional data, the letter summarized partial
contents of a lengthy memorandum presented in July 1955 to President Eisenhower at a similar meeting in the White House.

Emphasis was placed in the letter on the empire nature of the Soviet Union; however, in this setting with Dulles it called also for a
courageous specification of the captive nations in the Soviet Union as
par for the course of executive policy. Another, a polite commenda-
tion on the progress of the policy of peaceful liberation was made, yet
with a justified reference to the much-needed changes effected in the
Voice of America as concerned the Ukrainian and other desks.

Turning now to our time, it is not inconceivable that these themes would cement the past into the present. The scourge of a re-created empire, for instance, with all of its accompanying institutional baggage would undoubtedly revive on the Eurasian stage many familiar themes and catchwords: containment, liberation, peaceful coexistence, captive nations, even "the Soviet people." The last has been an illusion that persisted well into the 1980s and 1990s, so much so that former national security advisor Zbigniew Brzezinski suggested, "The West . . . should support . . . a program that truly is meant to give the various nations that inhabit the Soviet Union (and President [H. W.] Bush would do well to stop speaking of 'the Soviet people'—a phrase from the odious past) an opportunity to join the modern world."[7]

If such a disastrous outcome were to recur, the mode, if not the specific contents, of the strategic operations recommended in the letter would be in order. The sheer passage of time has not obliterated the real possibilities facing us today, and it certainly has not erased the strategic importance of Ukraine to our own national interests. This was the chief thrust of the letter and the conference call with Dulles. Briefly, Ukraine's strategic posture is the same today as it had been throughout the entire Cold War era. It couldn't be otherwise: the largest non-Russian nation within the Soviet Union and in Central/ Eastern Europe, by its declared independence, was the crucial igniter of the cremation of the Soviet Union. Ukraine stands apart with its compact geographical area endowed with rich mineral, agricultural, and industrial assets; a long and exceptional record of resistance and struggle against Russian imperialism and communist totalitarianism; a distinctive national culture with a forward-looking intelligentsia; and a determination to preserve its freedom while reconciling its dominant Western orientation with friendship and peace toward Russia and other neighbors.

While the Franco-German democratic alliance constitutes a veritable anchor of peace, stability, and prosperity in Western Europe, Ukraine in similar alliance with Poland would with the latter serve as the anchor in Central/Eastern Europe. NATO's extension eastward would guarantee these conditions. And, beyond any doubt, a democratic and non-imperial Russia, whether in or out of NATO, would inaugurate a veritably new Europe.

In the letter to Dulles, the formula of liberation, independence, and federation was advanced. This formula applies practically today: liberation from an empire has taken place, but the process perforce continues in the form of institutional release from all the basic totalitarian structures and behavioral constraints of that framework. National independence has in the main been won. But what was won can be lost, and it has to be conserved and justified through democratic change. Always presupposing independence and free choice, federation lends itself to many forms and—given the fruition of widespread democracy—European trends in the mid-1990s were favoring economic union.

Lastly, the letter recommended a "studied capitalization of the Ukrainian and Byelorussian representation in the United States," which was backed by *Newsweek* correspondent Edward Weintal and others in the media. In the waging of political warfare it directed attention to the diplomatic arena—another mini-path in the formation of the central trail, another area of cultivation for the future.

In 1952, I had been working with Republican senators H. Alexander Smith of New Jersey and Lawrence Smith of Wisconsin on an idea that would open another mini-path on the road to the central trail.

The potential zig was in essence the extension of diplomatic relations with the republics of Ukraine and Byelorussia. It presented a direct challenge to Moscow's pretensions and constitutional masquerade. And its values and advantages to us in the political warfare of the Cold War were boundless, an estimation that can only be arrived at by seeing things in toto.

Underpinning the eventual resolution (H.C.R. 58 proposed in Congress by Wisconsin Rep. Smith) were two pillars: (1) Article 18a of the USSR constitution; and (2) the original memberships of Ukraine and Byelorussia in the United Nations. The first stipulated, "Each

Union Republic has the right to enter into direct relations with foreign states and to conclude agreements and exchange diplomatic and consular representatives with them." Significantly, this provision was added to the constitution in February 1944, in the course of World War II, ostensibly reinforcing Article 17, whereby, "The right freely to secede from the USSR is reserved to every Union Republic." Actually, the implementation of Article 17 was restricted to Ukraine and Byelorussia with their miniscule foreign ministries; the other fourteen republics, including the Russian Soviet Federative Socialist Republic (RSFSR), had only the USSR foreign ministry in Moscow. The membership of the two republics in the United Nations ensued later after Stalin's brazen attempt to gain sixteen votes in the UN failed.

A hearing on the resolution didn't come about until July 15, 1953. The timing couldn't have been better: Beria had been disgraced and executed; Moscow continued to zig for "peace"; in the light of international law, we were already recognizing Ukraine and Byelorussia by virtue of their presence in the United Nations. And in these circumstances, the proposed resolution, as a test of Moscow's "peace" intentions and for our own strategic reasons, pointed to direct, bilateral relations with Ukraine and Byelorussia. However, the yearlong background to the hearing is most revealing, featuring the State Department's feeble and disingenuous treatment of the subject.

A preliminary inquiry into the State Department's position on the resolution was made in June 1952 by Sen. H. Alexander Smith. A memorandum on the subject, which I had prepared, was attached to his letter. State's negative response of untenable arguments and the length of time between the exchange of letters (June 11 and 13 until June 26, 1952) indicated that little studied consideration was devoted to the subject. Nine months later, the chairman of the House Foreign Affairs Committee, Rep. Robert Chiperfield (R-IL), also dispatched a written inquiry into State's attitude in light of a change of administration following Eisenhower's victory in November. The reply—most of it extracted verbatim from the previous response—arrived in March.

Several foreign affairs analysts and journalists proceeded to investigate this situation. Felix Morley, writing in *Barron's*, April 13, 1953, had this to say: "But two months after the introduction of the resolution it has been discovered by the State Department. And several alert officials there are of the opinion that the proposal should be seriously pressed." He continued, "Without the present Soviet 'peace offensive' the Smith Resolution would probably still be slumbering undisturbed. Now policy planners at the State Department are saying: 'Why didn't we think of that ourselves.'" The widely respected analyst viewed the resolution as "a clever legislative proposal, well calculated to create difficulties for Soviet Russia."[8] Remember, there was a change in administration and the question was, "Who was handling what?" Prime aspects of this whole affair with State were treated in my July 1953 testimony to the House Foreign Affairs Committee on "Favoring Extension of Diplomatic Relations with the Republics of Ukraine and Byelorussia."[9]

Adding further insight into the drift of general thought and bias during the period, Commissioner Edward O'Connor of the Displaced Persons Commission delivered an address on "The Tragedy of the Ukrainian Nation," which Sen. George Smathers (D-FL) sponsored in the Congressional Record.[10] In it, the commissioner made this observation: "I have noted with interest and great pleasure that there has been formed in the United States an organization known as the Free Russia Fund, Inc. It is encouraging to know that some good Americans have recognized the plight of the Russian people and are planning to do something to bring about their well-deserved freedom from the tyranny of Communism. On the other hand, I find myself seriously disturbed that no one appears to have done anything about the cause of the non-Russian people of the Soviet Union who make up the majority, and who clearly comprise a group of nations who want their freedom and liberties just as much as any other people."[11] With this kind of prevailing bias, the Smith resolution was faced only by another layer of impediments.

On the other hand, largely due to the influential knowledge and understanding of Dr. Harry Schwartz, the *New York Times* produced during the period editorials and articles showing the plight of the non-Russian nations. In the early period, the *New York Times* was consistently on target in respect to the fundamental issues. I had frequent telephone contacts with Schwartz, a former OSS analyst, professor, and distinguished economist who was then on the publication's editorial board, and I have no doubt about his constructive influence and output concerning these issues. Like others, these were annexed to my testimony. For example, one on "Rationalizing Imperialism" (February 29, 1952) concentrated on Russian imperialism in Central Asia and the oppression of Muslims, pointing out, "The correct teaching, they are told, is that this imperialist aggression was a most 'progressive' event, since Czarist Russia in the nineteenth century had the germs of the Bolshevik Revolution and was 'the center of the world revolutionary movement.'" This obviously relates to Ukraine and Byelorussia and to the rest of the Smith resolution.

For the purpose of presenting the broadest picture to ensure a favorable consideration of the resolution, other additions to the testimony included a *New York Times* editorial on "The Russian Purge Resumes" (June 14, 1953) depicting the zigzag nature of Kremlin politics and an illuminating, comparative address by Secretary of the Interior Oscar Chapman on "The Spirit of Independence: America and Ukraine" (July 5, 1952), which was inserted in the Congressional Record by Sen. Blair Moody of Michigan.[12]

In our day, Ukraine declared independence in 1991—the very key to the collapse of the Soviet Union—and established its Washington embassy in 1992. A parallel development embraced Byelorussia, now named Belarus. What was vigorously advocated in the area of diplomatic relations nearly forty years ago has come to pass in the 1990s. In reality, it didn't matter that both nations were not independent and sovereign then, for the invincible forces at work were the identical forces that eventually led to the outcome we have witnessed in our time.

Undoubtedly, the Cold War demanded our tapping these forces of enlightened nationalism, which in combination with other necessary requirements could have hastened our victory and spared ourselves and our allies the human sacrifices and real costs suffered over a period of four decades. Naturally, many critics will be quick to assert that this assessment cannot be proven, which objectively it cannot. But, albeit subjectively, the patent fact is that the heavy burden of proof rests with them and those who grossly underestimated these forces, particularly in the Soviet Union, and pursued policies of misdirection and failed opportunities. Little wonder the surprise and bewilderment in the century's last decade.

Before concluding this section on the diplomatic front, a number of engaging aspects deserve mention and further elaboration, points that were alluded to in testimony before the special House committee and others. Although these are numerous, covering about three years, a few examples will suffice.

In the private sector, the popular columnist Bob Considine supported H.C.R. 58, highlighting the fact that "The Kremlin likes to boast that the Ukraine and Byelorussia are independent republics. . . . If Russia won't let the 'independent' republics accept ambassadors from the United States, their slavery will be illuminated for all the world to see and all the anti-Communist factions inside the countries to feed upon."[13] The writer observed, "Conservatives in Congress went in for a bit of jowl-shaking indignation at the thought of sending an ambassador to these apparent enemies." Actually, this reaction was ephemeral. Once the rationale of the resolution was grasped, initial indignation gave way to enthusiastic support. The resolution was hardly an appeasement gesture.

Reference in the testimony to Georgetown students and two ambassadors to the United Nations evoked curiosity on the part of the special committee members and spectators in the audience. The letters addressed to the Ukrainian and Byelorussian representatives at the UN were written by Robert Shafter and A. X. Bader, respectively president and vice president of the International Relations Club at

Georgetown University. They sought answers to three specific questions: their awareness of H.C.R. 58, their position on direct diplomatic relations, and their evaluation of the resolution's practical aims in furthering the widely publicized intentions of the Soviet Union and its neighboring states to lessen tension and improve amity and friendship with the United States. The letters were dated April 20, 1953. Almost three months later, those attending the July 15 hearing were naturally curious to know how ambassadors A. M. Baranovsky of Ukraine and K. V. Kiselyov of Byelorussia replied. Absolute silence, no reply. For what it's worth, I had nothing to do with these letters. The letters and similar inputs were purely voluntary and the result of congressional notices and information, as well as a growing public interest in the subject.

In the pre-hearing period, editorials and commentaries appeared. One editorial commenting on H.C.R. 58 struck the right chord: "It deserves a better fate than to be laid on the shelf. It should be studied on its merits."[14] Factually, it was studied on the congressional side; it wasn't on the State side.

Preconceived notions dominated those in the State Department planning to offer a negative view based on an array of vulnerable arguments that only suggested a responsive consideration of the resolution in vacuo. In the mode of staid diplomacy, two State letters treated in the testimony showed no sensitivity to the total politico-economic context in the early 1950s or to the reality of Moscow's permanent political warfare. The writers of the letters displayed also a blindness to the unique opportunities provided by Moscow's multiple troubles, which its "peace offensive" aimed to conceal, and they were clearly short on knowledge and understanding with respect to conditions and developments in Ukraine and Byelorussia. "Heads We Win—Tails They Lose," the banner of the resolution, completely eluded them.

The conflict surrounding the resolution had its political reverberations. For our purposes, only two need be cited. One was the alignment against the resolution. This consisted of fellow-traveling and Communist Ukrainians, the amorphous anticommunist Russian groups, and the Kennan adherents in and out of State.[15] The other was the diplomatic dilemma that confronted the State Department under simultaneous pressures of (1) nonrecognition of Red China; (2) Senate Resolution 247, proposing a complete severance of diplomatic relations with all communist party–dominated governments; and (3) H.C.R. 58. A bit of reflection on each would show that (2) and (3) were not mutually exclusive, and (1) stood on its own empirical ground, for as Secretary Dulles emphasized then, "The Chinese Communist regime has been consistently and viciously hostile to the United States."[16]

In the end, the special committee under chairperson Rep. Frances Bolton voted unanimously in favor of extending direct diplomatic relations to Ukraine and Byelorussia. Under heavy pressure from the State Department, including the secretary of state, H.C.R. 58 never reached the floor of the House. As conveyed to Chairman Chiperfield of House Foreign Affairs and the Special Committee, the administration was engrossed with other pressing issues, like the aftermath of the Korean War and brewing trouble in Vietnam, and it wasn't confident that it possessed the resources to engage in poker diplomacy.

To say the least, this denouement was disappointing to all who supported the resolution and viewed it as a valuable asset for an unfolding liberation policy. The secretary of state called for new and different methods in diplomacy: this unquestionably was. For those who became instantly skeptical about the implementation of the liberation policy, the solid contribution of the administration in backing the Kersten committee and its monumental works then had to be underscored. You win some, you lose some.

However, the lasting significance of the Smith resolution in pinpointing Ukraine and Byelorussia is enshrined in the independence they achieved in the early 1990s and in their embassies in Washington, as well as ours in Kyiv and Minsk. In the critical post–Cold War period, begun with an insular Russia First approach by two administrations and featuring political vagaries and uncertainties in the Russian Federation, these gains in themselves bear tremendous strategic significance, especially as concerns Ukraine. A more balanced and even-handed policy would capitalize on these gains for our long-run security and the avoidance of a tragic déjà vu. Such a policy would of course consider seriously the utilities of their representation in the United Nations—original members, but now free. All of which, in concluding this chapter, leads into another mini-path of the forming central trail: the United Nations and the two republics.

The stage for this additional path was set up in 1955 by the Senate Foreign Relations Committee. It commissioned a subcommittee to examine "proposals to amend or otherwise modify existing peace and security organizations, including the United Nations." Regarding the United Nations, one such proposal was the elimination of Ukraine and Byelorussia from the world organization. It had the backing of several senators. Based on a letter to Sen. Alexander Wiley the year before, an invitation to testify was extended, and I accepted for myself and as a representative of the Ukrainian Congress Committee of America, which was agitated by the proposal.[17]

The testimony requires only a few additional comments. In striking at the sources of the misconceptions and false comparisons and interpretations used in the promotion of the revisionist proposal, it successfully prevented any further official consideration of this misleading idea. In the Cold War, Moscow would have had a propaganda bonanza, a field day multiplied by years, had the proposal advanced legislatively and gained any popular momentum, this in the wake of the Asian-African Conference in Bandung, Indonesia, where colonialism and imperialism were the chief topics.

The statements by senators Wiley and Lodge, as well as others, comparing Ukraine and Byelorussia with Texas, Massachusetts, or New York and by implication equating an empire with our nation were out of order in the light of history, international law, and the demands of political warfare competition. A year before the hearing, my letter to Wiley, whom I personally admired, emphasized the falsity of such comparisons.[18] At the United Nations, the Ukrainian delegates evidently irritated him with their repetitive harangues. But this type of reaction plus the superficial political glamour of three votes and triple speaking powers are surely not bases for serious maneuvers during a Cold War or afterward. Actually, on this superficial plane the Soviet Union with its veto power didn't need more votes. Had our UN representatives been properly prepared and equipped with the enormous factual data assembled by the Kersten committee, all three of the Slavic representatives would have been placed under permanent pressure, even in a state of apoplexy.

At the time, Sen. Margaret Chase Smith (R-ME) voiced the appropriate theme in connection with the Bandung conference: "seize the initiative" and demonstrate to the less developed nations our dedicated opposition to colonialism and imperialism and our equal dedication to national sovereignty and independent statehood. The revisionist proposal tended to negate this; the reasons for opposing the proposal fully affirmed it.

In that period, I was awed by what I called "the Smith triad," equipped with anvil and hammer to forge the truth in its concern for our foreign policy directions: Sen. H. Alexander Smith of New Jersey, Rep. Lawrence Smith of Wisconsin, and now the inspiring Sen. Margaret Chase Smith of Maine. My relationship with the first two was rather close, working on ideas we mutually shared and attending functions in Washington and elsewhere that were related to our interests.

The senator from New Jersey was the go-between for Eisenhower and Robert Taft Jr. after the Chicago Republican convention in 1952, centering their attention on the meaning of the liberation policy. When I served as an assistant to the chairman at the stirring convention, I had the pleasure of sitting beside him in the chair area throughout all the proceedings, and this opportunity afforded discussions covering a broad range of foreign and domestic issues. We hit if off nicely. My association with Rep. Lawrence Smith was mainly restricted to Washington, entailing frequent consultations, development of issues, and politico-social events. Both men were highly principled, intellectually resourceful, incisive in their thinking, and passionately devoted to the exemplary greatness of our nation. However, in this

Smith triad, a closer relationship with the keen and charming senator from Maine unfortunately eluded me. But over the years her support of a more skillful foreign policy and of the captive nations was unstinting. She was in every respect a forward-looking legislator and a stalwart lady gracing the Senate.

It became clear that the arguments for the revisionist proposal were thoroughly untenable. The characterization of Ukraine and Byelorussia as "territorial entities of questionable sovereignty" was totally invalid since, as detailed in an appended memorandum, the sovereignty of Ukraine reaches in the modern era as far back as the seventeenth century, reasserting itself in various forms down to the very present.[19] Skilled in international law, the author aptly quotes for his introduction Justice George Sutherland in the 1936 case *United States v. Curtiss Wright Export Corp.*: "Rulers come and go; governments and forms of government change; but sovereignty survives." With a firm knowledge of Ukraine's history, the author methodically demonstrates in terms of informational law the nation-person-sovereignty-state conceptual integration applicable to Ukraine. In pointed fact, referring to the Montevideo Convention (1933), the San Francisco Conference (1945), and other recent sources, these arguments fortified by international law opinion turned the whole subject around to justify the one state/one vote principle (and thus speaking power) for Ukraine and also Byelorussia.

As said, win some, lose some. In this case, it was a win as the revisionist proposal fortunately was rendered dead and unceremoniously buried.

In our time, most of the UN seats that were occupied by illegitimate communist delegates are now occupied by representatives of free nations. It was emphasized above that for our strategic planning those ambassadors (especially the Ukrainian one for reasons of Ukraine's geography, size, resources, and proven history) can play vital roles toward the good of their nations and our collective security.

What transpired over forty years ago has application today to the many entities in the Russian Federation to which Yeltsin has already ascribed sovereignty. In the 1950s, tightly secreted in the RSFSR, they yielded sparse information. More votes, more speaking power for Russia in the United Nations? Yes, but in the new Eurasian picture with its enormous politico-economic possibilities for a free, democratic, non-imperial, and economically prosperous world, these multiple votes and enhanced speaking power would have the same value as the threesome of the Soviet Union. The power of information will not be suppressed as it was out of ignorance in the interwoven case of the UN, the Kersten committee, and Ukraine and Byelorussia.

Speaking of politico-economic possibilities and the power of information, it's time to consider these in the next chapter, along two more mini-paths that offer additional insights into policy directions during the Cold War and lessons for the future—and, at this juncture, the concrescence of the central trail itself.

# CHAPTER 6

# Non-Russian Revolutions

The guiding principle behind the Captive Nations Week resolution was the time-honored American belief in national self-determination. This principle presupposes a state of independence from an empire, without foreign intimidation, manipulation, and coercion. Historically and empirically, it fit in perfectly with the non-Russian experience of a lost independence when Lenin and his Soviet Russia re-created the Russian empire under the guise of communism. Its recovery was crucial to the thinking, dedication, and very existence of the non-Russian émigré organizations, operating in a center sponsored in the final analysis by our government.

Inertia, habit, disinclination to view things critically, and an intellectually slavish dependence on history in Russian textbooks, which in turn depended heavily on imperial Russian state-approved sources, accounted for the miasma of misconceptions, each breeding another.

In the 1990s, the reemergence of independent states in the Baltic region, Belarus, Ukraine, Georgia, Armenia, and so forth exploded empirically misleading notions held in the preceding decades. Even as late as 1992, President George H. W. Bush, for ostensible personal and tactical reasons, viewed the independence drive in Ukraine as "suicidal nationalism." Others—columnists, analysts, etc.—still find it difficult to detach themselves from such imaginary concepts as "the Soviets," "the Soviet people," "ethnics," "nationalities," and the like. As late as the mid-1990s, as one example among many, a writer chairing a post-Soviet studies group ascribed to "the Soviet people themselves, that brought about the collapse of communism."[1] Empire, distinct nations, real totalitarianism, and American-inspired movements for self-determination and independence escape their lexicon. The current myth—Russia equals the Russian Federation—simply transfers to the present configuration the same terminological blunders we struggled with in connection with the USSR.

For perspective and meaning at this juncture, some essential notes on the institutional background to all of this are in order. Considering the imposing features of the tsarist and communist pasts, probably no definition of the Russian state surpasses the one offered by Secretary of State Dean Acheson on June 26, 1951, before the House Foreign Affairs Committee:

> Historically, the Russian state has had three great drives—to the west into Europe, to the south into the Middle East, and to the east into Asia. . . . Historically also the Russian state has displayed considerable caution in carrying out these drives. . . . The Politburo has acted in this same way. It has carried on and built on the imperialist tradition. What it has added consists mainly of new weapons and new tactics. . . . The ruling power in Moscow has long been an imperial power and now rules a greatly extended empire. . . . This is the challenge our foreign policy is required to meet. It is clear that this process of encroachment and consolidation by which Russia has grown in the last 500 years from the Duchy of Muscovy to a vast empire has got to be stopped.[2]

With our fixed orientation of utility in the present and the future, one should underscore the Acheson quote, truly a defining classic and a precipitant of sharp argument at the time. In our period, if so-called

Russian ultranationalists (really imperialists) were to gain control of Moscow's government, its profile would be perfect in application.

Moreover, when during my tenure Acheson visited the National War College to discuss the Mideast situation, I had occasion, in private and off the college's record, to congratulate him warmly on the 1951 statement and ask him why it had not become integrated in overall policy during the Truman administration. Based on his reply, my insights were sharpened as to the inchoate state of affairs in this earliest phase of the Cold War, characterized by conflicting agency tendencies and the burdens of the Korean War. As anyone who has served at a sufficiently high level in government knows, turf struggles and adamantine thoughts are not uncommon. A glaring example of this was the departmental struggle over the recognition of independent Ukraine in 1991, not to mention a protracted hesitancy in regard to the Baltic nations. In short, the bottom line for all of this is strong but also sound and accurate presidential leadership, such as the Reagan Doctrine provided.

Another point requiring some perspective and meaning is the distinction between totalitarianism and authoritarianism. Long before the 1980s, those involved in Russian history and its basic imperial development grappled with the parameters of rule and control of each, the consensual bent leaning toward authoritarianism (autocracy for the tsarist stages and totalitarianism for the Bolshevik and communist period). Briefly, it can be argued that the Communist Party was above God and could do anything, whereas the tsar was below and only anointed by God, thus under a set of moral constraints. However, despite admitted differences in scope and magnitude, the nature and types of barbarity are similar, differing by the state of technology, communications, transportation, and so forth. My usage in the text of the Naval War College lecture signified largely a continuum. Given our current state of the arts and global telecommunications, not to emphasize the politico-economic forces at work in the broad Eurasian context, the likelihood of a communist-type totalitarianism in Russia is virtually nil. Authoritarianism? With far less repression than a

Communist Party totalitarianism, more likely—if Russia's democratic forces are not sufficiently strengthened within and also from without.

Let's look at a historic episode which is indispensable to understanding the revolutionary changes in the 1990s. Déjà vu is the only fitting expression for one's mental leap from the 1917–18 events to those in 1991. The Russian attempt at democracy and the non-Russian one at independence have repeated themselves—the past vibrating in the present. In our time, the politico-economic burdens on the Russian people and its genuine, democratic leaders to achieve structural reforms and an entrenched democracy are unquestionably enormous. The same applies to the once-again independent non-Russian nations to sustain their independence and democracy, given the time and the additional, essential condition of non-interference by Russia. In neither case is spontaneity possible where institutional processes of change and methodical development dominate.

The fact that over the decades most scholars, writers, and others omitted the significant non-Russian revolution for independence should be cause for wonder. For a long time, a virtual hiatus existed in Western scholarship and reporting in respect to this crucial event. Most portrayals of Russia and its two revolutions submerged it under a mass of socioeconomic issues related to bolshevism, communism, socialism, and the like. Even in the 1990s, when the objective truth confused them, countless writers and commentators simply referred to the earlier independence as "short-lived" and accidental, giving little or no recognition to the fact that that historic event had been preceded by an authenticated history of movement toward independence down to the present, including North Caucasia, Idel-Ural, and others harbored now in the Russian Federation.

In our time, what should also be firmly borne in mind is that the imperial base carved out by Lenin's Soviet Russia still exists in the form of the present Russian Federation. No sooner had Lenin seized power in Soviet Russia proper, in March 1918, than he embarked on the contrivance of a federated state built on the suppression and armed conquest of areas in the former tsarist empire that opted for freedom and independence. Idel-Ural, consisting of Tatarstan, Bashkeria, etc., was one of the first to be forcibly incorporated—or should one say "federated," like Chechnya in the 1990s. It was only a few years later, following the solidification of this first layer of the resurrected empire, that Soviet Russia succeeded in forming the second layer by destroying the independence of Byelorussia, Ukraine, Georgia, Armenia, Turkestan, and the Far Eastern Republic, and then, by 1921–22, debating among its Russian Bolshevik and quisling victors whether to legalistically federate these more visible "national areas" into the Russian Soviet Federative Socialist Republic (RSFSR). With an uncanny instinct for future operations, Lenin shrewdly persuaded the debaters to opt for a Union of Soviet Socialist Republics, with Moscow, of course, as the power center.

Customary in the writings of the 1990s is the misidentification of Russia and the Russian Federation. Remember—steadfastly—as we pursue the trail, that the current federation is founded on Lenin's RSFSR. This historical fact will go a long way to an understanding of the persistent pressures for freedom within the supposedly new federation.

The fundamental question for us today is whether another déjà vu is in the making of another Russian empire. The importance of the 1917–22 lessons can hardly be overlooked. For there are numerous possible scenarios entailing a resurrected empire and its tragic long-run consequences for us and our democratic allies within Russia, the Russian Federation, in the West, and beyond.

One outstanding problem that has plagued the analyses long used by most Western analysts, governmental and private, is the continuing inability to distinguish between a state and a nation. For example, in our time, our ambassador to the United Nations slipped on this thorny road, comparing the United States and Russia as nations of different nations because "we are two huge continental powers which are really nations of nations."[3]

Surely the observations on populations in the former USSR are enough to arouse one's intellectual curiosity. For a spell its disclosures shook the Kremlin. Long before some Western observers began in the late 1970s and 1980s to question the majority status of Russians in the USSR, a pioneering demographic study of the subject was undertaken by the Displaced Persons Commission in the 1950s. Inspired by the work of the commission, Dr. Edward M. O'Connor, who was one of the three commissioners and later served on the Psychological Strategy Board and other government bodies, spearheaded the study with official demographers. At the time, he was one of the scant few in government who grasped the non-Russian concept and played crucial roles in its advancement.

This critical line was pursued thirteen years later by the House Judiciary Committee, further laying the groundwork for skepticism and rejection in the late 1970s of Moscow's manipulated statistics. As for today, the overblown emphasis on the "107 nationalities" in the Russian Federation, the absence of the Siberyak distinction, the suppression of Cossack national identity, and other uncorrected data surely warrant the questions and criticisms raised in the past.

The economic resources and their locations in the former Soviet Union also suggest the fragmentation of the remaining imperial base of that ersatz state. From 1991 on, "the greatness of Russia" and its world power have been repeatedly exclaimed not only by the misnamed ultranationalists but also by Yeltsin and innumerable social democrats. As the long imperial history of Russia unmistakably shows, this "greatness" has rested on the conquest, subjugation, and coercion of other nations and peoples, including Russians and other Siberyaks. The drive for self-determination and independence by the Siberyaks in the Far East is over a century long, highlighted, for example, by their campaign for US support after World War I.[4] A national "greatness" predicated on the backs and real cultivated properties and wealth of others has been a longtime illusion in imperial Russian politics. Indeed, the legitimate greatness of the Russian nation resides in its oft-displayed scientific, technological, entrepreneurial, artistic, and multicultural creativity and accomplishments.

Unquestionably, the Muslim factor, increasingly important during the USSR's existence, will become even more important in the years ahead. No sooner had the USSR collapsed than Moscow and analysts in the West pointed to the Muslim threat, encompassing Muslim fundamentalism, Iran, Afghanistan, terrorism, etc., and their infiltration in Central Asia and the Russian Federation. From the viewpoint of our national interest, some see Russia as a necessary buffer against this threat, regardless of its actions in Tajikistan, Azerbaijan, Chechnya, and other Muslim-populated areas. Complicated as the subject may seem to be, our sights, attuned to basic principles and capabilities, must remain fixed on the necessity of supporting the independence and reforms of the Central Asian states as well as the aspirations of the millions of Muslims in the Russian Federation. And certainly we should be on guard against any political manipulation of the issue by Moscow, exaggerating *radical* Islamic fundamentalism (which we must also guard against) and posing as a defender of Western civilization's values.

What the non-Russian concept required, foremost, was a dramatic event, which actually occurred in the passage of the congressional Captive Nations Week resolution. The event furnished a tremendous boost to the concept, but it also opened up a broad range of debate and activist undertakings with the widening of the paper trail.

Prior to 1959, there were numerous, unconnected, and formative paths in the trail. For example, my 1953 article titled "The Soviet Centrifuge" embodied in full the non-Russian concept.[5] The title in itself is suggestive; by the beginning of the 1990s, "centrifuge" and "centrifugal forces" in the USSR became standard usages in the free world.

Following the 1959 congressional event, many other paths emerged with their attendant misconceptions and misperceptions, but these were now suitably integrated and connected with the established central direction and tendency of the trail. For instance, on the path of Russia area studies in the United States and abroad, I wrote an article in 1963 for a prestigious organ under the title "The Roots of Russia."[6]

Its initial paragraph alone sets the tone and the continuation of the basic, conceptual framework in the next chapter:

> Perhaps no subject is fraught with as many basic misconceptions and errors as that of Russia. What so often happens is that on the basis of these fundamental errors, misleading analyses are constructed, and invariably a number of false conclusions are drawn. Then in time, the popularization of these conclusions only helps to reinforce and perpetuate the original erroneous premises. The cycle repeats itself on higher levels of assembled information, while the malformed perspectives spun about the subject become more entrenched than ever. At no risk of exaggeration, this is the general state of our so-called Russian studies in this country.[7]

# CHAPTER 7

# The Semantics of Liberation

A serious conflict developed in 1951–53 between the American Committee for the Liberation of the Peoples of Russia and the Ukrainian Congress Committee of America (UCCA), which I headed.

The American Committee's commendable objectives were (1) the formation of a center in Munich unifying all anticommunist groups from the Soviet Union in a common effort against bolshevism; (2) the launching of scholarly and sundry programs dealing with the Soviet Union; and (3) broadcasting through Radio Liberation to the respective regions in the Soviet Union.

Despite largely amicable personal relations, working agreements, and understandings between the two, the conflict became so intense that UCCA was forced to go public on the issues involved. However, as a good result of this step, it avoided the desperate position of revealing that the American Committee was the recipient of funding by the Central Intelligence Agency. This fact reached the public's ear much later when Congress relegated what was then Radio Liberty to a new international broadcasting arrangement.

Viewed in toto, those who were engaged in the conflict saw the net result as salutary and productive because, beyond doubt, substantial and well-managed progress ensued under the leadership of Howland Sargeant. The output of the reorganized Munich center (in

part following the lead of the Kersten committee) was truthful and
formidable, and the broadcasting to the Soviet Union, though limited,
became increasingly effective. Surveys of listeners during the Cold
War and after have amply confirmed this.

The renowned Admiral Alan G. Kirk chaired the American Committee for, unfortunately, too short a time after the committee's shake-
up in the spring of 1952 and before he was appointed chairman of the
Psychological Strategy Board in Washington. This was unfortunate
solely because the sudden change enhanced the burden already carried
by the Congress Committee. The UCCA, an American organization
with strong cultural ties to Ukraine and its people, for over a year had
been receiving protests and complaints from Ukrainian and other
non-Russian organizations in Western Europe and Turkey about the
American Committee's operations. For this and other reasons, the
UCCA became in effect an intermediary between the American Committee and those concerned organizations. A point that cannot be too
strongly stressed was the vital and strategic position of Ukraine in all
of this. Without its bona fide émigré representatives in the programs
of the American Committee and its CIA backers, the entire undertak-
ing would have been baldly lopsided and a source for magnified fric-
tion and ridicule.

Happily, to become publicly entangled with the CIA wasn't necessary. What transpired was for the long run beneficial, chiefly because
there were, in addition to UCCA and other American organizations,
many concerned people like James Burnham, O'Connor, and Kirk in
government, as well as individuals in the private sector. All were viv-
idly aware of the vital significance of Radio Liberation in the Cold
War and the need for unity among the émigré organizations. As in the
steps taken to establish an effective Voice of America during the Truman administration, those launched under the banner of liberation
found an equally effective Radio Liberation. However, the lack of a
coherent overall foreign policy, which was widely debated in the
presidential campaign, remained a primary and disturbing concern
affecting the construction of these vital operational instruments.

At its very origin the American Committee signaled its main direction by naming itself as one for "the Liberation of the *Peoples of Russia*" (the old USSR = Russia myth) and one totally indifferent to the concept of empire. Later, as criticism mounted, a tactical shift to "liberation from bolshevism" scarcely improved either its image or the quality of its thinking, now concealing its chief direction with a term outdated by "communism" and, in reality, imperialist Russian communist totalitarianism.

What was intended to be an effective propaganda campaign against Moscow's massive machine was actually a product in line with the superficial anticommunist writings of Eugene Lyons and Isaac Don Levine. Both had vehemently criticized the Acheson statement on traditional Russian imperialism. This in itself indicated the confusion on policy that prevailed then: a secretary of state with one position and CIA operatives with another and subsidizing a venture led by two strangely appointed writers virtually in control of the American Committee. Because of the largely outside but persistent opposition in 1951–52, the two were actually dumped. The misleading observation by Richard Gid Powers in his pioneering work that the two "stepped down because of sniping by anti-Semitic Russian nationalists" is one among many examples of the work's serious shortcomings.[1]

Brilliantly reflecting the policy confusion was the dilemma the American Committee carved for itself as given in the core statement of a charging letter exchange with the UCCA: "The committee did not want to be put in a position of taking action which might be interpreted by the Soviet Government to the Great Russian peoples that the committee was seeking to fractionalize the Soviet Union, or which, from the point of view of the non-Russian nationalities, would make it appear that the committee was striving to continue a system under which the rulers of the Soviet Union can hold, against their will, for all time, many differing peoples by undemocratic methods."[2] In short, "non-predetermination" was the murky operational principle offered by Adlai Stevenson.

Taken at its face value, the above statement and its elaborations would appear to be a fair and unbiased approach in the task of unifying Russian and non-Russian émigré organizations in a center dedicated to fighting against bolshevism and for liberation, all under the rule of non-predetermination. What it hides from the reader and observer is a whole array of vital facts and questions: the committee's own dilemma, non-predetermination over self-determination, the absence of empire focus and candid recognition of Soviet Russian conquests, the practical matter of equality and distributive equity among all the groups, and, of fundamental importance, the nature and substance of the propaganda directed at the enemy.

It is obvious that the American Committee sought to bury its dilemma of organizing those Russian groups dedicated to the sanctity of the Russian empire, whatever its name, with those non-Russian entities seeking national independence from the empire. For operations at the center, non-predetermination—the neutralization of the fundamental and consummate issue—was to be the rule, the presumed impartial path in a fight against the sparsely used bolshevism. Adding to this feeble projection were, first, the fear that the Kremlin would manipulate the prospect of "fractionalizing the Soviet Union" on the untenable assumption that the Russian people as a whole supported the Russian empire and, second, the committee's blatant avoidance of the empire concept and nonrecognition of the original Soviet Russian conquests of the non-Russian nations.

Burnham, who played an important role in this case, encapsulated the whole affair in his penetrating foreign policy work: "If Russians who claim to be anticommunists refuse to extend the goal of freedom to non-Russians, then we must wonder whose side such Russians will be on when a showdown comes."[3] This capsule of thought has accurately applied from the 1950s into the 1990s to some politically motivated Russian émigrés here and countless Russian "democrats" during the 1990s in Russia itself.

With all this in mind, one cannot but seriously question the type of propaganda that would have been meted out to the respective nationals in the Soviet Union. Yes, of course, the horrible events and tragedies under communist totalitarianism, the forced deprivations and real costs incurred in the Kremlin's global adventures, and the countless other heinous phenomena would have been transmitted over Radio Liberation, along with the hope of freedom once liberation from bolshevism was achieved. In a Cold War context of political warfare, however, this course was scarcely a prescription for victory. Concrete "fors" more than the general "againsts" and "antis"; the historical glories and heroes of each nation for freedom; the soulful resistance of the underground Ukrainian Insurgent Army as well as other resistance forces—these and other specifics constituted the meat of our role in the political warfare.

A month after the presidential election, the American Committee sponsored a mission to Europe. Significantly, by then the American Committee was rethinking its misleading and ominous reference to the "Peoples of Russia." The delegation that I had the privilege of leading in December and January 1952–53 had a mission that was unmistakably clear and precise. Its objectives were: (1) equality among all the bona fide émigré groups entering the planned Coordination Centre of the Anti-Bolshevik Campaign (CCAC); (2) distributive equity in support of programs initiated by the participating groups; (3) the determination of meaningful and effective messages to the respective nations and peoples in the USSR; and (4) a formulation of policy unambiguously reflective of American values, principles, and traditions.

The American Committee was well aware of my position when, after its reorganization, it decided to subsidize this mission. It was fully cognizant of my specific objections to its ineffectual neutralist stance, its feeble anti-Bolshevik axis (including the CCAC), and the techniques employed to influence the non-Russian groups to join the hybrid center.

From the very beginning of this intensive mission, we concentrated on fact-finding, information analysis, and daily conferences and investigations of all interested non-Russian émigré organizations, as well as talks with individual Russians like Boris Nicolaevsky. Even the dramatics of Levine, the American Committee's European operator, didn't escape our notice. For example, at a meeting with non-Russian representatives in Karlsruhe, West Germany, he outrightly threatened them to accept the committee's rules by pulling out a US dollar and characterizing it as a symbol of world power that would be used discriminately against them should they continue to resist and object to the rules.

The delegation's open inquiries drew the attention of interested foreign governments (Germany, Italy, Spain, the Vatican, and Great Britain) followed by meetings with their designated representatives. Each had radio broadcast interests regarding the nations in the Soviet Union. Our work also stimulated the interest of other non-Russian émigré organizations, such as the Azerbaijan National Center, the new Union of Fighters for the Independence of Idel-Ural, and the North Caucasian National Committee.

The mission began to bear fruit after the first week of operations. All of the participating non-Russian representatives enthusiastically accepted our proposed changes in the statutes, guaranteeing equal votes and distributive equity among all the groups. The American Committee's predication of such basics on the population division of the Soviet Union between Russians and non-Russians in itself was subject to strong criticism and implicitly suggested a retention of that artificial political framework.

The working delegation arrived at an acceptable formula, which was later successfully applied in both the Voice of America and Radio Liberty, differentiating the Russian and non-Russian components by dividing the center into these two sections and thereby guaranteeing appropriate messages to the respective nations and peoples. An American supervisor and coordinator would oversee their operations, ensuring economy in effort and funds. While all of this was occurring, the American Committee, in recognizing the strategic position of the Ukrainian representation in this process, singled it out by forming a Temporary Working Committee for Ukrainian Groups to engage in direct negotiations with the American Committee. The committee's intent at this stage was subject to speculation.

Shortly thereafter, in the midst of all this progress, a bombshell in the form of an official release from the American Committee exploded in our faces. In an obvious attempt to appease the Russian émigré groups, the release called for the inclusion of Ukrainian federalists in the center. Plainly, this maneuver was a typical Russian and Leninist divide-and-conquer tactic aimed at the breakup of the united Ukrainian front in its struggle for sovereignty and independence. The tactic has been used so often that it seemed rather foolhardy and amateurish for the committee to have accommodated it, particularly in the course of our mission. For the bold fact was that no such group of federalists even existed in the widespread Ukrainian community in Western Europe.

The activist, political directions taken by Russian émigrés were often supported by naïve individuals and institutions in the West. One émigré, a priest connected with a group at Fordham University, went so far as to rally Catholic representatives in Congress to safeguard the sanctity of the empire on the basis of the Fátima revelations.[4] In the American Committee case we witnessed the capacity of Russian émigrés in semi-official operations to concoct an artificial organization with opportunists always at hand for the purpose of dividing their opposition. At the same time, we should take note and bear in mind their long-term Cold War incapacity to organize anywhere in the free world, and in the natural mode of all other nationals from the empire, a Russian Committee for the Independence of Russia from the Soviet Union.

After this torpedoing of the mission, it was evident that no further progress could be made with the American Committee despite its reorganizations. Going public was the only recourse, only without involving the CIA directly or staging hearings and so forth. In consequence, the committee fell under a new, informed leadership. Radio Liberation, later called Radio Liberty, became a highly effective instrument of penetration among the various nations in the Soviet Union, and the policy technique of reporting only events and developments in the USSR and other parts of the given nation forcefully supplemented the external world news reporting and editorializing of the Voice of America. Thus, endless Soviet reactions to our annual presidential proclamations and White House observances (above all during the Reagan years) neatly predicated such internal reporting that allowed, as in the case of Radio Free Europe, the utilization of the Captive Nations Week resolution and all of its concepts on empire, independence, democracy, and human rights.

Viewing this Cold War case overall, was it shy of the natural theme of national independence from an empire? Yes, of course, and needlessly so as the historic events of the late 1980s and early 1990s have proven. Also clearly unnecessary was the appeasing move to change the active name of Radio Liberation to the more passive Radio Liberty (one of many shortsighted contributions by our "evolutionist" policymakers, some of whom even contemplated the illusion of politico-economic convergence with the Soviet Union and Central Europe). In political warfare terms, the change reserved a monopoly use of *liberation* to the enemy or, as some preferred, our adversary.

# CHAPTER 8

# Human Rights and the Faith Community

The dark clouds of the 1960s and 1970s were not without their silver linings. The undoubted silver linings in the intermix of the national and international forces were both the revisit to the Genocide Convention and the elevation of human rights to the core of US foreign policy. Predominantly, the former related to Nixon, the latter to President Carter.

Briefly, Nixon strongly backed the long-delayed ratification of the UN Convention on the Prevention and Punishment of the Crime of Genocide more than twenty years after the United States helped in drafting the convention, organizing support in the United Nations for its adoption, heralding the document with President Truman's summons to the Senate for appropriate ratification, and staging early hearings toward that end. I testified in favor of ratification twenty years later, and again during the Carter administration.

Buttressed by the genocidal evidence of World War II, the UN General Assembly passed on December 11, 1946, a resolution declaring genocide a crime and calling for an international treaty; it unanimously adopted (55 to 0) the drafted convention on December 9, 1948, the United States signing it on December 11 (the treaty's fiftieth anniversary was observed in 1998); Truman submitted it to the Senate on June 16, 1949; in January and February 1950, a Senate

Foreign Relations subcommittee reported favorably on it, but no action was taken by the full committee.

To be sure, each of Truman's successors over two decades was supportive of its ratification but didn't press hard enough to realize it. Notwithstanding, the Senate Foreign Relations Committee approved the treaty five times, but only once did it reach the Senate floor, where it was blocked by filibuster.

Antiquated arguments against the convention, advanced by the American Bar Association and aggravated by other organizations in a pool of public misunderstanding, still held sway when President Nixon in 1970 pressed for ratification. As one ABA representative six years later wistfully observed, the Genocide Convention "is eligible in the Guinness Book of World Records as being the oldest treaty pending before the United States Senate."[1] By then, the ABA began to see the light.

The convention, after thorough scrutiny in the Department of Justice for constitutional obstacles, received the support of Secretary of State William Rogers, who on February 5, 1970, recommended to the president its submission to the Senate for ratification. Two weeks later, on February 19, Nixon submitted it in a message emphasizing, "We should delay no longer in taking the final convincing step which would reaffirm that the United States remains as strongly opposed to the crime of genocide as ever."[2] He declared also that it was necessary to "demonstrate unequivocally our country's desire to participate in the building of international order based on law and justice." The result: after twenty years, new hearings on the treaty.

I plunged into this second round of hearings—not without some eerie feelings, since many who testified on the subject in the 1950s, whether pro or con, had already passed on. I expected that opposing newcomers would present only retreads. My first testimony had covered sufficient empirical evidence of genocide. This one had to focus on the definition and meaning of the crime itself and certain paramount legal points that my mentor Raphael Lemkin had taught me.

With the new administration under President Carter settling in, the advancement of human rights in our foreign policy resounded and, naturally, a powerful executive pressure was exerted for the treaty's ratification. Another round of hearings ensued—a third one of participation for me. My condensed statement on May 27, 1977, highlighted the structural nexus between a human rights policy and the Genocide Convention, emphasizing the somewhat overlooked generic categories of human rights.[3] At the time, eighty-three countries had ratified the treaty; here, it remained in deep freeze, but not for long.

Victory was finally realized under the Reagan administration. The succession of events was fairly rapid. Like Nixon and Carter, President Reagan pressed for ratification in September 1984 and again in 1985.

In this final effort, it was my privilege to be called again to participate while serving as ambassador to the Bahamas. Responding to a call from Assistant Secretary of State Elliot Abrams, who was very instrumental in the effort, I telegraphed on September 24, 1984, my support to Sen. Howard Baker Jr. (R-TN), the majority leader, and also a message of readiness to testify again to Sen. Charles Percy (R-IL), who was chairing hearings on the treaty.[4] The overall plan didn't need my further testimony.

The consolidated effort paid off well, for in the following month the Senate agreed 87–2 to support the convention's principles. By February 1986 it rendered its advice and consent, 83–11, laying a legislative base for the treaty. This in turn led in 1987 to the Senate's Genocide Convention Implementation Act, and by October 1988 the Senate gave final legislative approval.

At long last, on November 4, 1988, President Reagan signed the act (properly designated "the Proxmire Act") with appropriate remarks on "horrors this century: in the Ukraine, in Cambodia, in Ethiopia." The convention became our national law in 1989—after forty years, and nine years before its fiftieth anniversary—with the final overwhelming push provided by the Reagan administration in alliance with Sen. William Proxmire (D-WI) and bipartisan supporters.

The unrelenting drive for ratification of the convention weighed heavily in the emergence of human rights as a core of American policy. Indeed, it represented the most basic connection between the two. In the sub-context of the conflicts in the 1970s, the human rights projection was old hat for the Captive Nations Week Resolution, and the Captive Nations Week observances in 1974–76 figured prominently in it.

Unfortunately, with the policy straitjacket of détente, the challenge for human rights was not sufficiently pursued by the Ford administration. A special congressional Commission on Security and Cooperation in Europe (CSCE) took up the cudgels in 1976. The Carter administration in 1977, with its emphasis on human rights in foreign policy, provided the necessary, though unstructured, impetus to the movement. And in a structured doctrinal format, the Reagan administration advanced it stridently and immeasurably. The Helsinki Final Act Conference in 1975 gave birth to the structure of the CSCE, and the subsequent review meetings in Belgrade and Madrid developed this structure further with the heightened interest shown by the Carter and Reagan administrations. Although faced by many difficulties in consummating decisions by consensus, it grew in practical, institutional importance, changing its name to the Organization for Security and Cooperation in Europe (OSCE) in 1995, expanding with over fifty members, and expressing a vital role in the post–Cold War period.

The Helsinki Accords consisted of four "baskets." Basket I covered security, inviolability of borders, natural self-determination, and noninterference in internal affairs; Basket II, cooperation in areas of economics, science, technology, and the environment; Basket III, cooperation on freedom of movement for people, ideas, and information, and humanitarian and other areas. The fourth provided for follow-up review action in Belgrade in 1977.

Moscow viewed Basket I as the most important and no longer subject to negotiations, stressing noninterference in internal affairs and the inviolability of present borders. Contrary to provisions in the Soviet constitution, operation of foreign ministries, and de jure recognition in the United Nations, Ukraine and Byelorussia were denied direct access to the Accords. Concerning dissidents in the Soviet Union, Moscow failed to foresee the voluntary human rights groups emerging in Russia, Ukraine, Lithuania, Georgia, and Armenia (Russia's Helsinki Monitoring Group, the Ukrainian Public Group to Promote Implementation of the Helsinki Accords, and so on).

It is imperative to keep in mind the successful drive for the structured integration of human rights as a paramount component of American foreign policy. President Carter deserves prime political credit for this phenomenal change.

The years 1976–82 marked an intensive legislative process that finally resulted in the passage of a congressional resolution on religious freedom in Ukraine and "the attempted genocide—the absolute physical extermination—of both the Ukrainian Orthodox and Catholic Churches." In 1982, S.C.R. 18 was readily incorporated in President Reagan's implementation of PL 86-90, including a later appearance at the Ukrainian Catholic National Shrine in Washington, DC. Undoubtedly, it strengthened the position taken by the Vatican in the unusual advances made by Mikhail Gorbachev. And the pope's visit to independent Ukraine in 2001 may properly be viewed as the historic culmination of the entire campaign for the resurrection and freedom of the two churches.

The realities of Ukraine as the largest non-Russian nation in both the Soviet Union and Eastern Europe, the Russifying genocide of its two national churches, and the strategic, geopolitical importance of the country in our struggle for victory in the Cold War held sway in congressional thinking. Indeed, this importance has been steadily reflected in US foreign policy since the collapse of the Soviet Union.

Clearly, it was only natural for the Vatican to defend and aid in a variety of ways the Ukrainian Catholic Church. The Uniate Church emerged in the historic year of 1596 when, resisting Muscovite hegemony, bishops and laity of part of the Ukrainian Orthodox Church accepted at the Conference of Brest the leadership of the pope while retaining all rights and customs of the Eastern rite. At the time of Stalin's genocidal crimes following the annexation of western Ukraine, the Vatican became deeply involved in circulating the truths of the subject. In his encyclical *Orientales ecclesias* (1952) Pope Pius XII, with reference to the Russian Patriarch Alexius, went so far as to suggest the bizarre role of a Christian Church (the Russian Orthodox) serving an anti-Christian government to destroy another Christian church (the Ukrainian Catholic).

Extreme as Moscow's action was in institutionally obliterating the Ukrainian Catholic Church, the scope of the Vatican's concern and involvement expanded greatly to protect as much as possible Roman Catholic and other churches subject to communist persecution in Central Europe and the Soviet Union. By the 1960s, with the sweeping Vatican Councils, Pope John XXIII's encyclical *Pacem in Terris*, and other reformative events, an Eastern policy was in the making. Brilliantly sculpted by Cardinal Agostino Casaroli (who served under four popes and under Pope John Paul II was elevated to the cardinalate and also to the post of secretary of state), the Ostpolitik resulted in a series of outstanding breakthroughs with communist regimes, especially in the end—and on a condition related to the Ukrainian Catholic issue—with the unprecedented meeting between the pope and Kremlin leader Mikhail Gorbachev in December 1989.

An interesting anecdote involves two persons who first met at a Washington function in 1960. Both were deeply immersed in foreign policy issues but neither was connected with the National Captive Nations Committee until years later. At that initial meeting, Donald Miller, a former naval intelligence officer, Korean War veteran, and writer on Cold War subjects,[5] queried Dr. Edward O'Connor about national security matters. To the question about PL 86-90 raised by Miller, O'Connor answered that Eisenhower's security advisors rejected it because the American people did not have the discipline and persistence to make it work. Their conclusion was that "only one institution has the discipline and persistence to do it—the Vatican."

When Miller asked further if the Captive Nations policy, based on PL 86-90, had been presented to the Vatican, O'Connor replied, "Of course."

Fifteen years later, Miller was in Rome to receive a Knight of Europe award tendered by the Associazione Premio Internazionale Cavalieri della Nuova Europa, and was inducted into the International Circle of Knights of Europe. Before the ceremony on December 16, 1975, several priests from the Vatican appeared at the hotel to meet with the awardees. As Miller relates it, one of the priests was introduced to him as a member of the Foreign Service at the Vatican. With diplomatic diffidence, he said, "I did not know the Vatican had a Foreign Service," and asked "What is your policy?" "Well," the priest said, "it is hard to describe." He continued, "In the States you have something called the Captive Nations Committee. Do you know it?" To which Miller responded, "Yes, I have," and the priest asserted, "That's our policy. Do you understand?"[6]

When on October 16, 1978, Cardinal Karol Wojtyla was elected to the papacy and assumed the enormous moral authority of the office as Pope John Paul II, he wisely elevated Casaroli to secretary of state and in the following year, with his first visit to Poland and intimate knowledge of both Nazi German and Soviet Russian totalitarianism, as well as the non-Russian nations in the Soviet Union, initiated an unprecedented, dynamic global mission of historic proportions. It was indeed providential that in 1978 Margaret Thatcher became prime minister of Great Britain and, in 1980, Ronald Reagan was elected president of the United States. Truly, with the new pope, an articulate triad for freedom was formed, each member pursuing it in respective ways.

CHAPTER 9

# Captive Nations—Who's Next?

The impressive twenty-second Captive Nations Week observance accommodated by the 1980 Republican National Convention in Detroit made an indelible imprint for significant changes and differences between the Carter and Reagan administrations. Despite the pivotal contributions of numerous Democrats to the passage of PL 86-90 and observances of the week, planners of the Democratic National Convention, overabsorbed with domestic concerns, showed indifference to the annual observance. The emergence of three more captive nations—Ethiopia in 1977, Afghanistan in 1978, and Nicaragua in 1979—in the Carter period reinforced the haunting question, "Who's next?" while demanding a policy aimed at preventing the further expansion of Moscow's multilayered empire and seeking the liberation of the long-ensnared ones.

The year 1980 leads to the second plateau of our Cold War policy and actions, primarily against Moscow and its communist party allies around the globe. It signals for us a return from the more individual paths we've pursued to the broad avenue of events featured in the 1980s. It represents a cumulation of political steps toward the eventual integration of PL 86-90 into the Reagan Doctrine—a fundamental fact often overlooked or merely referred to in accounts of the Reagan legacy.

In 1980 the vast majority of Cold War analysts in government and the private sector clung to the notion that the Soviet Union was here to stay and sought at best a change in government, authoritarian rather than totalitarian—in most instances, simply because the Soviet Union is Russia.

When over a decade later the Soviet Union did implode, most in this majority seized upon selected factors in the complex of fast-moving events to causally explain the Soviet Union's collapse. The picks covered economic stagnation, ideological putrefaction, societal degradation, our policy of containment, rapid military rebuilding, Star Wars (SDI), Afghanistan, and so forth. None of these sufficiently accounts for the historic event. Richard Pipes, the distinguished Harvard historian, has raised the question, "Why then did experts on the Soviet Union—practitioners of so-called Sovietology—not foresee its fall?"[1] Apart from the non-Sovietological advocates of PL 86-90, some of them did, but not for any of these reasons.

To repeat with additional examples, the differences in policy substance as well as operational applications marked the transition from the Carter to the Reagan administration. Openly recognizing the Soviet Union as an empire in itself was a change in substance, for it established a new context of perception, thinking, and developed action than what had prevailed before. No previous administration had elevated PL 86-90 by staging the annual Captive Nations Week at the White House as did the Reagan one. And if one compares the annual presidential proclamations of the week, those issued by President Reagan reflect best the contents of PL 86-90 and this new policy course of his administration. Most observers and analysts failed to comprehend the significance of these changes.

For a composite overview to appreciate the manifest import of "the second plateau," a concatenation of the basic themes and trends portrayed in previous chapters is now in order. On the subject of genocide, definitely most relevant to the captive nations, it is curious that so little attention has been devoted to the successful Reagan pursuit of the ratification of the Genocide Convention after three decades of excessive delay and in consideration of the enormity of the genocide crime, no matter where perpetrated or how numerous the victims.

The crucial difference between the Carter and Reagan administrations was the structuring by the latter of the human rights standard and criteria not only in the template of anticommunism but also that of anti-imperialism and anticolonialism. Evidence of this marked shift in thought and policy action emerged early in Reagan's nomination and presidential campaigns. The projections of this structuring of human rights and integration in the Reagan Doctrine can be readily delineated in the 1980s, 1990s, and the first decade of the new millennium. The forces of religion and nationalism, which were repeatedly stressed in congressional testimonies, were primarily formidable in the advancement of human rights, not just individual and civil but also national and international. As one example, the combination of the two reigned in the efforts of Pope John Paul II and the Solidarity movement in Poland.

Interwoven with human rights is the spread of democracy. During the 1980s and 1990s, the rise of new democracies in Latin America, Europe, Asia, and elsewhere exemplified the powerful trend. A yearning for freedom even manifested itself throughout the People's Republic of China and the Russian Federation. The growth of human rights organizations both inside and outside the Iron Curtain has attested to the sturdy nature of the issue.

More democratic nations reflecting the will of the people means a larger community of democracies in the world. If properly institutionalized, this community idea could have multiple uses, such as preventing regional and civil wars and facilitating expanded trade and concourse, in addition to revamping the United Nations. Looking backward and constantly forward on these vital subjects of human rights, democracy, and genocide (all rooted in captive nations experience), our former representative to the UN, Ambassador Richard Holbrooke, summed it up in these words: "It is sad to think that the enormous cruelty and suffering caused by the leaders of the Communist world have been ignored and yet the irony is that today's conflicts and crises can all be traced back to this era of massive violations of human rights."[2] This was written in 2000 with regard to the idea of a UN Year of Remembrance of Over 100 Million Victims of Communism, which he enthusiastically supported.

The spheres of religion, terrorism, and US-Soviet politico-economic trends shed further light on the captive nations movement and its elevation in the Reagan period. The religious factor was a powerful force in the Cold War. Aside from theological grounds for national faith, it was a unifying shield against robotic communist party doctrine and propaganda on atheism. The perseverance of the majority Sunnis in the Muslim nations within the inner empire, the Kremlin's onslaught against the two Ukrainian churches and its perversion and manipulation of the Russian Orthodox Church, and numerous other examples of religious repression and genocide were presented in abundance in congressional hearings.

Now for the meaningful perspective that bids us return to the late 1970s and the 1980s. The cardinal fact is that the global terrorism that emerged with spectacular report in the new century—brazenly aimed at American power and leadership—has its firm roots in Soviet Moscow's international terrorist network built in the 1960–80 period. Aside from the illusions of communism and theocratic Islamist utopianism, the basic pattern of global terrorism is the same.

In characteristic terms of spurious ideology, techniques, franchises, and state support, the revolutionary groundwork was laid by the earlier global political warriors. The Kremlin's imprints have remained in the new chapter of global terrorism, extending from Libya and the Middle East to North Korea and even Cuba. The extent of communist influence is well exemplified, among countless others, by Saddam Hussein, former terrorist leader of Iraq, who glorified the century's prime genocidal practitioner, Josef Stalin, and also acquired the design and engineering of Tito's bunker system.

Back in 1978, Dr. Stefan Possony, a colleague of mine and an associate of the National Captive Nations Committee (NCNC) and the American Council for World Freedom (ACWF), which I was privileged then to serve as president, coauthored the seminal study, "International Terrorism: The Communist Connection." Carefully and in scholarly fashion the analysis defined terrorism as "the use of murder and violence against noncombatants, for the purpose of intimidating enemies, paralyzing their authorities and institutions, and spreading chaos within target societies." It specifically did not claim the existence of some "terrorism international" with a controlling and directing central authority, but it did "recognize—and will show—that a significant degree of coordination of terrorist activities does exist, and that it is mainly communists who are doing the coordinating."[3] Terrorism had predated the rise of Lenin, but the Bolshevik leader underwrote its use as an instrument for advancing revolutions. The linkages cited in the work included the Palestine Liberation Organization and others in the Middle East.

The truth-blazing study went largely unheeded as concerns official policy. It stimulated further works on terrorism in the following decade, but it drew little serious consideration in the CIA and other parts of government at the time of its release. However, the major subject of international terrorism was advanced in the 1980 Reagan campaign, strongly ordered for critical review by the new CIA director, William Casey, and placed under the first congressional inquiry and hearings in the Senate.

Unfortunately, the momentum this created fell short of a public awareness leading to official policy and farsighted legislation in dealing with the problem. The bottom line reason for this regrettable outcome was that the successful strategy of proactive public diplomacy underlying the Captive Nations movement was not applied to the scourge of international terrorism. Vigorous advocates in the movement, like Possony, Herbert Romerstein, and many others, were also advocates of this strategy concerning international terrorism. The NCNC was totally engrossed with the further implementation of PL 86-90; the ACWF lacked the necessary resources to counter those behind the drive for US-Soviet nuclear arms limitations and "peaceful coexistence."

The three additional captive nations that emerged in the Carter period—Ethiopia, Afghanistan, and Nicaragua—were hailed by most communist party dictatorships and sympathizers in the free world as evidence of the success of Moscow's national liberation policy and the historical spread and inevitability of communism. The additions supplemented the other five that had surfaced in the decade: South Vietnam, Cambodia, Laos, Angola, and Mozambique. The policies under the Nixon and Ford administrations failed to prevent the extension of the Captive Nations List (CNL).

On the eve of the Reagan administration, with regard to the understanding of the Soviet Union and the captive nations, the preconceptions and mindset of most analysts in government, the media, and academia remained the same as described in previous chapters. The complete CNL was largely ignored by them. But the trend of CNL acceptance, though still uneven and with minority status, was an upward one to justify the radical policy change under Reagan. The thousands marching during the annual Captive Nations Week in Chicago, St. Louis, New York, and elsewhere in the 1960s and early 1970s receded in favor of other activities involving churches, state and local governments, and journalists. Taking an exceptional cue from Lenin: "Ideas are much more fatal than guns."[4]

A look now at the updated CNL should deepen your appreciation of the radical policy alteration under the Reagan administration. For the 1980 CNL (see appendix B), the definition was generally restricted to what more loosely was called "Soviet expansionism," "Soviet proxies," "Soviet satellites," "the spread of communism," "Communist imperialism," and the like. Historically and logically, the more precise definition of a captive nation is one that, by direct or indirect imperialist Soviet Russian force and through a variety of undemocratic means, has fallen under the domination and monopoly control of a Leninist Communist Party dictatorship.

As depicted in the Captive Nations Week Resolution (Public Law 86-90 and its adjunct CNL), the evolution of captive nations dates back to 1920 with the first international military conquests by imperialist Russian Bolshevik communism (more specifically, the state of Soviet Russia). From its empire base in the forced USSR, the controlling Soviet Russia forged additional captive nations, from the Baltic nations in the 1940s to Nicaragua at the end of the 1970s, by means of armed occupation, indigenous communist party support, subversion, incitement of civil war, diplomatic and propaganda duplicity, and other political warfare techniques, including terrorism. In this evolution, subsequent feuds and differences with communist party–dominated states did not diminish in any fundamental way the basic captivity of the nations as such.

A Department of State publication on the USSR viewed the Soviet Union as "a nation," with a stress placed on "more than 170 separate ethnic groups living there."[5] The publication was referred to well into the 1970s. To offset this erroneous orientation, which reemerged in the otherwise excellent curriculum of the prestigious National War College, I submitted to the commandant in mid-1969 a critical evaluation of its relevant contents, urging the substitution, "The Empire-State of the USSR."[6]

As far back as President Eisenhower's signing of PL 86-90 in July 1959, the empire theme became the dominant theme in the work of the National Captive Nations Committee. Spurred on by friends in the media, I sent a telegram on July 30, 1959, to the president expressing "gratitude for your well-worded Proclamation and also for your personal participation in a prayerful observance of the Week in Gettysburg, PA," in addition to highlighting "the empire character of the USSR itself."[7]

The preconception of the Soviet Union as a single nation was an obstacle to the implementation of PL 86-90, one that was hard to crack in the period before and after the 1980s. The highly reputable Freedom House, for example, in 1978 continued to list the USSR in its column of "Not Free Nations," a release reproduced by the media nationwide.[8] Even after the Reagan change, the myth of

USSR = Russia, and thus a nation, persisted to the end of the twentieth century, fortunately on a declining trend line.

Another obstacle to understanding the law was the quarter-baked conception that the communist party–ruled captive nations resided only in Central Europe. If the writers, speakers, analysts, etc., hadn't suffered the lapse of memory exhibited by many, they included the Baltic nations. The causes of this condition were the impact of the disillusioning results of World War II in Poland, Romania, and elsewhere, the lack of objective knowledge about the non-Russian nations in the Soviet Union, and an equal lack of understanding of Moscow's global political warfare and its aim of creating additional captive nations.

Notably associated with these impediments was the imputation of an ethnic equivalence between the United States and the Soviet Union, the latter also a nation of ethnic groups, if not immigrants. For decades, the ethnic components or "nationalities" in the Soviet Union had been overplayed, but by the mid-1980s the Moscow Institute of Ethnography disclosed that most of the 103 nationalities were very small. Only twenty-two of them numbered more than a million members. Forty-nine nationalities had fewer than one hundred thousand members—and twelve of them were below two thousand (the Negidals at 504, Aleuts at 546, and so on). The concept of non-Russian nations sufficiently dispels this muddle. An American of German heritage is an American; a Georgian in Georgia is a Georgian, but an ethnic in Russia.

Complicating the situation, argued on radio and TV shows during the period, was another "equivalency" fantasy. In a naïve endeavor to show the Soviet Union governmental system resembled ours, the federalist proponents even suggested a similar division of powers, checks and balances, and a genuine rule of law. Thus, in the 1980s, three fantasies of equivalence floated about in comparisons between an imperial, totalitarian state and an outstanding democratic one: ethnic, federalist, and, astonishingly, moral.

The Yugoslav and Chinese splits with Moscow were viewed hopefully by countless observers as the beginning of a check on communist power and the development of "national communism," leading to a decline in Moscow's imperial domination of the captive nations and its threat to the free world. When writing the congressional resolution, I had to weigh the impact of the Yugoslav separation and concluded by placing the captive nations in Yugoslavia under "and others." Events themselves would demonstrate the illusion of Tito's "national communism" and its adoption in the so-called satellite region. This in time quickly came to pass, though the illusion of a "national communism" within the mini-empire of Yugoslavia, made up of several captive nations, should have been obliterated by its intrinsic contradiction. Tito, trained in Moscow, lent support to Moscow via the non-aligned nations in the Cold War.

Judging the murky drifts in our foreign policy, the phrase "and others" was premised on expectations of more captive nations arising in the future. Anecdotes galore surrounded the media's inquiries about Idel-Ural and Cossackia in PL 86-90. The problem of having to explain each continued down to the end of the century. For example, the superb article written in 1998 by the astute analyst, Dr. Paul Goble, sub-titled "A List Without an End," left unresolved the connector issue by neglecting the necessity for the law's adjunct, the CNL.[9] As for the later Chinese split with Moscow, the problem scarcely existed since the list in PL 86-90 covered at least three large captive nations—"and others"—in the PRC, dominated by a communist party that Moscow had created and taught its original members the smokescreen of Marxism.

Muddying the waters for many observers were references to other captive nations resolutions passed by Congress before PL 86-90. A comparative analysis of the preceding resolutions would show a marked difference in essence, scope, and effect between those earlier ones and PL 86-90. The earlier ones focused essentially on the captive nations in Central and Eastern Europe and the Baltic countries, oblivious to the empire nature of the Soviet Union and indifferent to the other captive non-Russian nations in that empire (and the PRC). They reflected the policy that established the government-subsidized body, the Assembly of Captive Nations, composed of émigré representatives from the indicated areas. And none of the preceding resolutions produced any political explosion comparable to Khrushchev's reaction case or moved other governments in the noncommunist world to support an American law, as in the case of PL 86-90.

Lev E. Dobriansky, author of the Captive Nations Resolution (undated).
*Georgetown University Manuscripts, Lev E. Dobriansky Papers, box 1, folder 61*

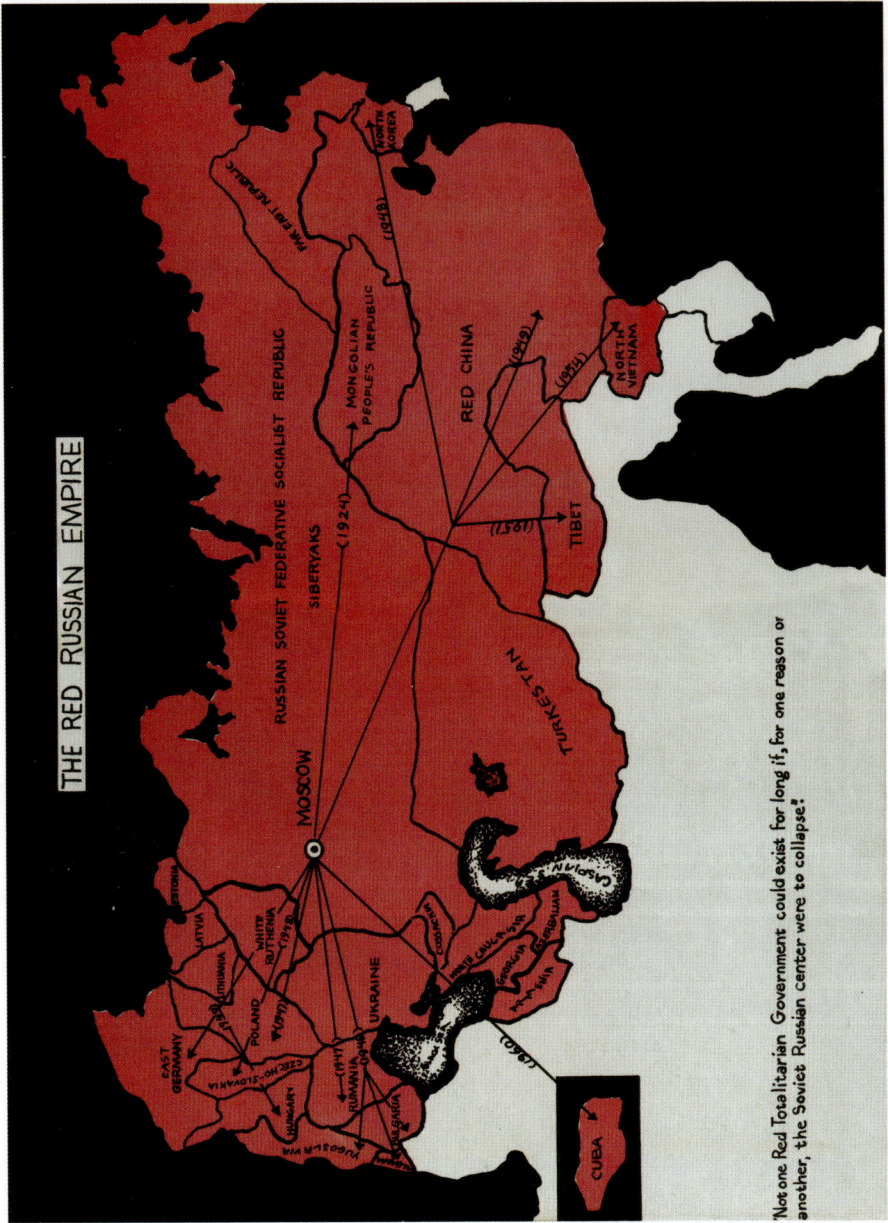

Map reproduced from Lev E. Dobriansky's 1967 book *The Vulnerable Russians.*

Lev E. Dobriansky on Chinese border (undated).
*Georgetown University Manuscripts, Lev E. Dobriansky Papers, box 1, folder 59*

Lev E. Dobriansky conferring with staunch Captive Nations supporters
Congressman Daniel J. Flood, Reverend Dr. Chas W. Lowry, and
Congressman Edward J. Derwinski.
*Hoover Institution Library & Archives, Lev E. Dobriansky Papers, box 10, folder 40*

Quadrennial convention of the Congress of Ukrainians in America, New York (undated).
*Courtesy of Ukrainian Congress Committee of America*

Ukrainian Congress Committee of America event on Capitol Hill, Washington, DC (undated). At center is Speaker of the House Tip O'Neill, with Lev E. and Julia Dobriansky to the left and future first lady of Ukraine Kateryna Yushchenko at the right. Judge Bohdan Futey is at far left.
*Courtesy of Ukrainian Congress Committee of America*

The Taras Shevchenko Memorial, Washington, DC. President Dwight D. Eisenhower signed Public Law 86-749 authorizing the erection of the monument.
*ID 276917128 © Rzyotova | Dreamstime.com*

National Captive Nations Committee flyer, 1977.
*Hoover Institution Library & Archives, Lev E. Dobriansky Papers, box 6, folder 27*

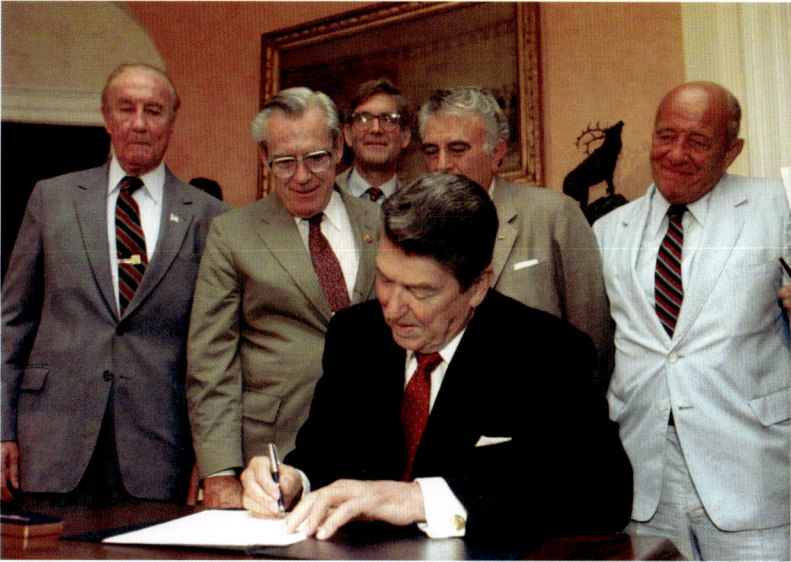

Ronald Reagan signs the Captive Nations proclamation at the White House on July 21, 1986. Behind Reagan, left to right, are Strom Thurmond, William Broomfield, Warren Zimmermann, Benjamin Gilman, and Lev E. Dobriansky. Reagan was the first to sign the proclamation in a public White House ceremony, in 1982.
*Courtesy of Ronald Reagan Presidential Library*

Captive Nations event hosted by the Heritage Foundation (undated). From left to right are Lee Edwards, Ian Brzezinski, Armando Valladares, Christina Arriaga, Lev E. Dobriansky, and Hongda Harry Wu.
*Courtesy of Ukrainian Congress Committee of America*

# Captive Nations Week, 1981

*By the President of the United States of America*

**A Proclamation**

Twenty-two years ago, by a joint resolution approved July 17, 1959 (73 Stat. 212), the Congress authorized and requested the President to proclaim the third week in July as Captive Nations Week.

Last January 20 saw again a change in Administration under our Constitution, the oldest written document of its type in continuous force in the world. The peaceful and orderly transfer of power in response to the sovereign will of our people is sometimes taken for granted by Americans. Yet events in some other areas of the world should remind us all of the vital, revolutionary ideal of our Founding Fathers: that governments derive their legitimacy from the consent of the peoples they govern.

During Captive Nations Week, Americans should realize our devotion to the ideal of government by consent, a devotion that is shared by millions who live in nations dominated today by a foreign military power and an alien Marxist-Leninist ideology.

This week, Americans should recall the series of historical tragedies—beginning with the broken promises of the Yalta Conference—that led to the denial of the most elementary forms of personal freedom and human dignity to millions in Eastern Europe and Asia.

In recent years, we have seen successful attempts to extend this oppression to Africa, Latin America and Asia—most recently in the brutal suppression of national sovereignty in Afghanistan and attempts to intimidate Poland.

During Captive Nations Week, we Americans must reaffirm our own tradition of self-rule and extend to the peoples of the Captive Nations a message of hope—hope founded in our belief that free men and women will ultimately prevail over those who deny individual rights and preach the supremacy of the state; hope in our conviction that the human spirit will ultimately triumph over the cult of the state.

While we can be justly proud of a government that is responsive to our people, we cannot be complacent. Captive Nations Week provides us with an opportunity to reaffirm publicly our commitment to the ideals of freedom and by so doing maintain a beacon of hope for oppressed peoples everywhere.

NOW, THEREFORE, I, RONALD REAGAN, President of the United States of America, do hereby designate the week beginning on July 19, 1981, as Captive Nations Week.

I invite the people of the United States to observe this week with appropriate ceremonies and activities and to reaffirm their dedication to the ideals which unite us and inspire others.

IN WITNESS WHEREOF, I have hereunto set my hand this 30th day of June, in the year of our Lord nineteen hundred and eighty-one, and of the Independence of the United States of America the two hundred and fifth.

*Ronald Reagan*

Captive Nations Week Proclamation, 1981, signed by President Ronald Reagan.
*Hoover Institution Library & Archives, Lev E. Dobriansky Papers, box 11, folder 2*

CHAPTER 10

# The Novelist and the Poet

Two writers—a twentieth-century Russian author and a nineteenth-century Ukrainian poet—played important roles in Captive Nations Week. Here we take a brief detour to examine their stories.

A sorry episode in the implementation of PL 86-90—centered on Aleksandr Solzhenitsyn—was most unexpected. It is regrettable in several ways that the famous Russian writer in his campaign against communism and the Communist Party dictatorship in Moscow found it necessary to attack the law in the mode of a corollary mini-campaign unleashed during his stay in Vermont and continued upon his return to the current Russian Federation.

Solzhenitsyn was a profoundly religious man who had openly criticized Patriarch Pimen of the Russian Orthodox Church for subservience to the Kremlin. The courageous novelist soon thereafter, on September 5, 1973, dispatched his historic "A Letter to the Soviet Leaders." Among other items, it decried Marxism, called for the withdrawal of Russian forces from the non-Russian areas of the Soviet Union back to the ethnological territory of Russia, and with authoritarian overtones urged a revival of the cultural environment of old Russia. Solzhenitsyn's sensational book, *The Gulag Archipelago, 1918–1956*, smuggled abroad and published in Paris in

December 1973, led to his arrest on February 12, 1974, and expulsion from the Soviet Union the next day.

Except for several examples of criticism in his role as publicist following his short stay in Europe and a longer one in the United States, there is no need to trace here the novelist's thoughts and attacks outside the context dealing with PL 86-90. In general, his attack against the law followed the pattern of some Russian émigrés in Europe and the United States, extending back to Alexander Kerensky, David J. Dallin, and others. For example, writing in the same journal (*Foreign Affairs*) that had afforded Khrushchev the opportunity to lambaste the law decades before, the Nobel Prize winner characterized the law as "notorious" and denied the existence of Idel-Ural and Cossackia.[1]

In addition, still pertinent to PL 86-90, the writer raised the question of why the law doesn't include Russia as a captive nation, thus implying some sort of anti-Russian bias.[2] The plain fact is that the law is riveted in the historical reality of the first wave of Soviet Russian imperialist conquest of independently declared non-Russian nations— Armenia, Byelorussia, Ukraine, and so forth. No one, including Solzhenitsyn, has been aware of any foreign army having invaded and subjugated the people of Russia in 1917–18. In the implementation of PL 86-90, the captive plight of the Russian nation and its longing for independence, democracy, and freedom from traditional arbitrary rule have been consistently underscored. The National Captive Nations Committee was one of the first to hail the promising declaration of independence by the Russian leader Boris Yeltsin in 1991, and Americans of Russian heritage have participated in the annual Captive Nations Week.

Outside of the PL 86-90 context per se, Solzhenitsyn roamed over subjects that unmistakably proved his departure from the spirit and contents of his pristine letter to the Kremlin in 1973. His emotion-ridden article in *Time* magazine (February 18, 1980) on needed American respect for Russian nationalism, as though this means a blind acceptance of Soviet Russian imperialism, revealed strains of the old "Holy Mother Russia" refrain. One can very much engage in

Russian nationalism (preferably patriotism) and glorify the accumu-
lated cultural goods of the nation without embarking on an imperialist course of subjugating other nations.

Further tarnishing Solzhenitsyn's image were conspicuous omissions in his historical research concerning the non-Russian nations in
the Soviet Union, a curious interpretation of a practiced technique of
cultural subversion, and an unbridled criticism of Western intellectuals and scholars. Somewhat contrary to one element in his historic
letter to the Kremlin, Solzhenitsyn overlooked the first wave of Soviet
Russian imperialism against the independent non-Russian nations in
the 1917–20 period. His view of the genocidal Russification technique, practiced by the tsars and magnified by the red ones in the
sweeps of cultural erosion and political homogenization of these subjugated nations, hardly sustained his initial image in the United States.
To interpret the imposition of the Russian language, educational curricula, and different patterns of cultural life as merely "a mechanical
device" revealed the hollow depth of his political knowledge, not to
speak of acuity. And as to his broad, temperamental assault against
Western scholars—a description of this would take us far afield from
PL 86-90. However, one example of justifiable retaliation should suffice here, in addition to rendering further insights into this unfortunate interlude.

After Solzhenitsyn's tirade of attacks and his apologizing for it by
an admission that he's "an artist, not a social scientist or scholar," the
distinguished Harvard historian, Richard Pipes, who had been singled out in the attack, continued his coverage of the artist's romanti-
cism. For instance, seizing the opportunity to address the Russian
audience of Radio Liberty, the novelist conveyed what Pipes described
as this "eccentric political message to Russian audiences—such that
democracy means self-destructive chaos, that the United States is not
a reliable ally of Japan; or that US generals are planning a genocidal
nuclear attack against the Great Russian population—he is in fact
lending support to communist propaganda with the assistance of the
US taxpayer's money."[3] Pipes found "no less damaging" the novelist's

concoction that the Russian revolutions resulted from external forces, such as "Western ideas and machinations, in which Jews played a prominent role."

Indeed, it was regrettable that Solzhenitsyn blemished his own stature as a literary artist. Countless Americans rightfully applauded him for his *Gulag Archipelago* (which reawakened many on the barbarities of Soviet Russian rule that the congressional Kersten committee detailed in scholarly fashion thirty years earlier) and for his anticommunism. But when much of the above surfaced, his appeal began to evaporate. In obdurate form, he nevertheless persisted with his polemicizing, taking a swipe at PL 86-90 for promoting the idea of "the Russians" rather than Soviet Russian rulers for having seized China and Tibet, another example of his lack of understanding of Soviet Russian political warfare.[4]

As his publicist performance began to fade away, Solzhenitsyn, not surprisingly, called for a "Russian Union" consisting of Russia, Ukraine, Belarus, and parts of Slavic-populated Kazakhstan. For the first three respectively, the washed-out pan-Slavist notion of the past was presented as Great Russia, Little Russia, and White Russia. Before the Soviet Union's collapse, Gorbachev accurately characterized the novelist, "He is all in the past, the Russia of the past, the Tsarist monarchy."[5] After the writer's return, officialdom in Moscow properly recognized him for his literary achievements but exhibited deaf ears to his outdated views. In the end, what has been the vision in PL 86-90 has been realized in the historic changes in Eastern and Central Europe and Central America.

Enough about the novelist—what about the poet?

A statue of Taras Shevchenko, Ukraine's venerated poet laureate, was erected in June 1964 in the 2200 block of P Street NW in Washington, DC. This event was preceded by a turbulent controversy involving scores of detractors, solid congressional and journalistic support, a resourceful reporter, and a disagreeing but determined editor of the *Washington Post*. Shevchenko projected a vision that exceeded the oft-quoted: "When will we receive our Washington, with a new and righteous law? And receive him we will some day!" He said this and more in the spirit of our Declaration of Independence and our Founding Fathers.

In the spirit of the poet's vision, former President Eisenhower unveiled the enormously symbolic statue. His stirring address to an assembly of one hundred thousand, which the Washington Board of Trade estimated to be the largest at an unveiling event, significantly advanced the captive nations movement in line with PL 86-90. Earlier, President Kennedy recognized Shevchenko on March 25, 1961: "I am pleased to add my voice to those honoring the great Ukrainian Poet, Taras Shevchenko. We honor him for his rich contribution to the culture not only of Ukraine, which he loved and described so eloquently, but of the world. His is a noble part of our historical heritage." Later, President Nixon, on his trip to the Soviet Union, opened the gate of official recognition of the largest non-Russian nation in the Soviet Union and Eastern Europe, but because of his policy constraints failed to follow through on the Shevchenko vision. Two decades hence, in Ukraine itself, President George H. W. Bush, President Clinton, and First Lady Hillary Clinton did follow through, as did President George W. Bush in an address given close to Ukraine.

The congressional publication, "Shevchenko: A Monument to the Liberation, Freedom and Independence of All Captive Nations," covers the event in detail.[6] The essence of the timely effort was threefold: paying tribute to the poems and farseeing vision of Shevchenko on the centennial occasion of his death in 1861; illuminating for our citizenry the meaning of his thought in the captive nations movement and its impact on future US captive nations policies; and crystallizing the event's integral role in the Cold War.

Shevchenko's poem "Kavkaz" (The Caucasus), written in 1845, supporting the Caucasian nations in their struggle for independence from Russian rule, is strikingly applicable to this day with the Russian ravage of Chechnya and repressions in Dagestan and Ingushetia (covered in PL 86-90 as North Caucasia). Symbolizing the spirit of freedom for all captive nations, Prometheus is appropriately featured on the monument. And in the Cold War, the erection of the statue effectively countered the Soviet Russian attempt to exploit the centenary by unveiling a Shevchenko monument in Moscow, causing Khrushchev to shorten a Scandinavian trip in order to unveil it before Eisenhower's unveiling in Washington.

From the first time of advancing the idea of the statue in the nation's capital to its fruition, the development was fraught with intra-organization intrigue, reportorial laudation deflated by editorial derogation, and an attempted official communist penetration. Well before the passage of PL 86-90 in 1959, the Ukrainian Congress Committee of America (UCCA), an umbrella organization of Americans of Ukrainian heritage, which I was then privileged to head, formed a cooperative agreement with the Shevchenko Scientific Society to realize the idea. The society is an international entity, established in Ukraine in 1873 and comprised of scholars and savants, including Albert Einstein, Abram Joffe, Max Planck, and many others. Roman Smal-Stocki, an outstanding ethnologist, professor at Marquette University, and president of the society, served as the chief link in this bond, later becoming the head of the Shevchenko Memorial Committee of America, commissioned to monitor the statue's construction after the passage of PL 86-749.[7]

The legislative phase in 1960 was relatively short but intriguing. Observers raised the question, "How can it be, a measure rejected in the Senate, then passed by the House and the Congress, ending up as PL 86-749?" A rogue leadership of a member organization had urged aides of Senator Javits, an original sponsor of PL 86-90, to funnel a statue measure (S.J.R. 54), which was tabled because of Department of Interior objections. Despite this internal chicanery and with little difficulty, the UCCA turned to Rep. Alvin Bentley of Michigan to introduce a more legitimate measure (H.J.R. 311), which was passed in the House, then in Congress, and resulted in PL 86-749, signed by President Eisenhower on September 13, 1960, authorizing the erection of the statue.

Similar to the reaction of Moscow and its puppets against PL 86-90, opposition to PL 86-749 was equally vituperative and coarse. The *Washington Post* reported in "Reds Decry Ukraine's Statue Here" (March 7, 1961) that over a period of eight months Moscow and its quislings railed against Washington for taking Shevchenko as one of its own. A few examples: an elite Moscow periodical on culture, *Sovietskaya Kultura*, in an article on "Taras Shevchenko and Champions of the 'Cold War,'" denounced "the murky part" played by American Cold Warriors in honoring the poet.[8] The theoretical and political journal of the Central Committee of the Communist Party of the Soviet Union, *Kommunist*, painted Congress's work as one of "the most incredible and filthy distortions."[9] With Soviet Ukraine dragged into the onslaught on a large scale, *Robitnycha Hazeta* ridiculed Senator Javits as a "reactionary-minded uncle" for his part in the passage of the law.[10] This went on and on while Moscow propagandized Shevchenko throughout the empire, in China, Poland, Bulgaria, and even North Vietnam.[11] Not strangely, but tactically, toward the close of the controversy here, Moscow and its minions shifted gears.

Throughout this phase and the controversy later, the bipartisan basis of the law remained steadfast and solid. In the passage of the law, the pivotal roles played by Democratic representatives Paul Jones of Missouri and John Lesinski of Michigan were momentous—the former for steering H.J.R. 311 in the House, the latter for his wisdom and prescience in sponsoring a resolution (H.R. 524) for the publication of a biographical account of Shevchenko's life and character, which was extremely useful in the controversy three years later. "Europe's Freedom Fighter, Taras Shevchenko 1814–1861" was distributed nationwide to the media, universities, cultural centers, churches, and national organizations.[12]

This publication received a favorable public reaction. On its first page, with a photo of the poet, the *Evening Star* in Washington carried the article, "Free Man Or Slave? Cold War Warming Up Over Obscure Poet." Writer John McKelway accurately pointed out, "As far as the West is concerned, Shevchenko's poetry reflects man's aspirations for liberty and national independence."[13] A little prematurely, an article in the *New York Herald Tribune* grasped the Cold War significance of the statue, asserting, "Next year will see a new trial in the East-West Cold War."[14] In the *Chicago Sunday Tribune*, an extensive article by Robert Young expressed similar thoughts: "Dead Poet Now a Live Issue."[15] Others followed suit, not knowing the full ramifications of the statue's erection, both here and abroad, both in the twentieth century and the twenty-first.

Given all of the above, relative calm reigned in the ensuing three years as work progressed on the statue. Endorsements by the Fine Arts Commission, the National Capital Planning Commission, and other agencies were obtained, and all aspects of the project were in order for a spring unveiling in 1964. Then, in 1963, a tumultuous confrontation arose, portrayed best as an initial conflict of knowledge and judgment between a reportorial account of the project and then an editorial derogation of it within the *Washington Post*, the latter lasting acrimoniously for several months into 1964.

The article by reporter Stephen Rosenfeld was written while the editor in chief, James Russell Wiggins, was commencing his months-long editorials opposing PL 86-749, remarkably similar in depth of knowledge and understanding to his earlier opposition to PL 86-90. Fair, informative, and objective, Rosenfeld's lengthy article addressed Shevchenko's life, the impact of his poems—"Two non-Ukrainian Washingtonians familiar with his work speak of him 'as Pushkin and more,' 'ah, a Shakespeare'"—the congressional highlights, the September groundbreaking and banquet, and the Cold War feature of the campaign.[16] The reporter continued this interest with numerous commentaries on the captive nations movement following his assignment to Moscow as the paper's correspondent and subsequent elevation to editorial status.

Whatever were the personal motivations and backing of the *Post's* editor, the muddled campaign Wiggins launched to prevent the National Capital Planning Commission from accepting the statue (in itself legally beyond the commission's bounds) produced overwhelming, countervailing reactions in Congress, the media, and the public sector. The barrage of protesting letters to the editor reflected a broad diversity of organizations and individuals. Most were not published, but the referenced congressional material on "Shevchenko: A Monument to the Liberation, Freedom and Independence of All Captive Nations" contains adequate examples of the letters and reactions that raised questions circulating then on matters of cultural insularity, arrogant ignorance, and criteria of responsible journalism.

With all things going well, the groundbreaking for the statue was staged on September 21, 1963, highlighted by addresses by Sen. Thomas J. Dodd (D-CT) and others and followed by a large banquet in the Mayflower Hotel. Two days later, the first of Wiggins's editorials appeared, mild compared to what followed. Titled "Poetic Injustice," he acknowledged having "never read a line of Mr. Shevchenko's verse," but complained: Why not substitute a monument of Shakespeare instead?

It was obvious the editor didn't understand the message to be conveyed by the statue in this critical period of the Cold War. Shevchenko's poems and writings—already translated into scores of languages—were already on the immortal scale of poetic artistry and justice. Moscow understood this for its propaganda. Wiggins and others didn't.

Bombarded by criticisms from every quarter, both Ukrainian and non-Ukrainian Americans, the editor became virulent and desperate in his next editorial, "The Shevchenko Affair" (October 18, 1963). It labeled Shevchenko as being "offensive in various ways" to other Americans, thus contributing "to a disunity and recrimination among Americans," and appealed to congressmen "to reverse their earlier error." Zeroing in on its Ukrainian American sponsors conceiving the statue as "a blunt weapon in a fierce cold war propaganda campaign against the Soviet Union," Wiggins opined, "They are using it to advance their own peculiar notion of how to fight communism and their own implausible goal of Ukrainian nationhood."

Apart from the divisive nature of the editorial, the goal was not the one cited, since Ukrainian nationhood has existed for centuries, but rather the independent statehood of Ukraine and other captive non-Russian nations in the Soviet Union. Here, too, Rosenfeld clearly comprehended the message; the editor apparently took a leaf from some indivisible Holy Mother Russia source. Also, by mentioning Poles and Jews among the Americans who would be offended by the statue, the editor set the stage for his next editorial.

Gracelessly titled "Monument to Ignorance" (November 1), it consisted of conflicting charges engendering anti-Semitism, communist party colonization, a "flaming nationalism" affronting Polish Americans, and the fear of a Khrushchevian intervention—along with an honest admission of the *Post* receiving "a great many letters" protesting his editorials. Each of these points is amply examined in "Shevchenko: A Monument to the Liberation, Freedom and Independence of All Captive Nations." On notes of factual and logical contradictions, the balanced Rosenfeld article depicted Shevchenko, in person, signing "a petition against anti-Semitism, a brave act for the time." The poet's humanism also embraced the African American Shakespearean actor Ira Aldridge, whom he met and befriended in Moscow in 1858, a relationship that affected the statue's development in Washington over a century later.

The editorial onslaught finally ended when the National Capital Planning Commission issued its final approval of the statue on December 6, 1963.

To complete this phase of an open-ended chapter beyond the Cold War, a day before the commission's final, decisive decision, an attempt to turn the tide was made by reporting a basically irrelevant incident in New Jersey's Hamilton Township, where a proposal to rename a street Shevchenko Boulevard was rejected. The report cynically commented, "Washington no longer has company in its misery over Taras Shevchenko."[17] On the serious side, however, and totally relevant, was the calculated but naïve solicitation of views by the Ukrainian representation at the United Nations. The *Post*'s request was sent four weeks before receiving the representation's reply at the end of December.

Although the full statement by Soviet Ukraine's envoy, L. Y. Kizya, was not released, it was not surprising to read in the report, head-lined "Communists Love Shevchenko," the following excerpts: "he favors a statue here of the 19th century Ukrainian poet"; "he protests . . . to use it 'to fan up animosity toward the Soviet Ukraine, and all the more to aggravate the cold war'"; "Kizya portrayed him as a man with deep ties to the Russians and revolutionaries of his day"; and "commemorating the 150th anniversary of Shevchenko's birth in 1964, Kizya said it 'will be marked in the Soviet Union by nationwide festivities,' including erection of a monument in Mos-cow."[18] Apart from the "nationwide" fiction, one need only compare this approving stance on the statue with the absolute disapproval expressed by Moscow, Kyiv, and other communist capitals in 1961. Also, the headline "Communists Love Shevchenko" failed to attract any anticommunist American opposition to the statue.

The trail of disturbances continued well into 1964. For example, now funneled through the Russian-controlled USSR embassy in Washington, a five-page letter signed by thirty-six "prominent Ukrai-nian public figures" supported the statue. Adding to its dubious allies, the *Post* reported in "Red Embassy Joins Row on Shevchenko" (Jan-uary 7, 1964) that the signers offered to participate in the statue's unveiling and to bring "some sacred soil" from Ukraine, although, "We are resolutely against the malicious attempts of the enemies of the Soviet Union to use the poet's works against our country, against the cause of all humanity—the struggle for peace." The report con-cluded with another appeal to the planning commission for a review of its approval at its February meeting. As was anticipated, nothing came of it, but the disturbance via private letters persisted.

Several additional notes indicate the multidimensional aspects of the Wiggins effort and its aftermath. First, the *Washington Star* joined the battle with articles, editorials, and published letters to the editor favoring the statue, many contained in the congressional *Shevchenko* product.[19] Second, also included in that product were supporting articles and statements by distinguished Americans, such as the chaplain of the US Senate, Frederick Brown Harris, and former representative Charlie Kersten, head of that famous House Select Committee on communist aggression.[20]

Third, articles published in English on Shevchenko were more than plentiful then. One inspired by PL 86-749, for instance, was written by Pauline Bentley for national and international readership under the title, "Taras Shevchenko: Ukraine's Poet of Freedom," in the *UNESCO Courier* (July–August 1961), not to mention other media accessible to Americans.[21]

And fourth, upon his retirement from the *Post* in 1968, Wiggins was nominated to represent the United States in the United Nations, causing widespread speculation in Washington as to the reasons for the move by the Johnson administration. One theory was that this was political payback for his support of the administration's Vietnam policy; another his campaign against the statue; other theories centered on his friendship with the president and the value of the media for the upcoming presidential election.

Nevertheless, the Senate confirmation hearing on September 30 consisted only of Wiggins's testimony and of mine in opposition to the nomination, recounting essentially segments of the facts described above.[22] As a throw-in nomination succeeding Ambassador Ball's sudden resignation after earlier confirmation, Wiggins's stay at the United Nations was generally predicted to be no more than six months. Short term it was. But, as we shall see, the *Post*'s policies and content eventually changed, even with acknowledgments of error concerning the captive nations.

The defining moment, of course, was the unveiling of the Shevchenko statue by former president Dwight D. Eisenhower on June 27, 1964. His moving address to the one hundred thousand attendees continued elements that were farseeing in purpose and vision: "For my hope is that your magnificent march from the shadow of the Washington Monument to the foot of the statue of Taras Shevchenko will here enkindle a new world movement in the hearts, minds, words and actions of men—a never-ending movement dedicated to the independence and freedom of all captive nations of the entire world." (The parade passed the White House led by an African American band expressive of the Aldridge-Shevchenko friendship. President James M. Nabrit Jr. of Howard University had offered a place for the Shevchenko statue on the university campus when opposition to the statue arose in Congress.)

Eisenhower also pointed out, "His statue, standing here in the heart of the nation's capital, near the embassies where representatives of nearly all the countries of the world can see it, is a shining symbol of his love of liberty. It speaks to those millions of oppressed." (Embassy representatives have continually taken notice.) The president continued, "In the same spirit, it is not merely for today, but for all time to come that we today present to the world this statue of Taras Shevchenko, Bard of Ukraine and freedom fighter, to perpetuate man's faith in the ultimate victory of freedom."[23] Twenty-five-plus years later, victory in Central Europe and the former USSR vindicated all Americans of different heritages who had faith in and fought for the statue.

As with all monumental events, consequences ensued, both empirically important and anecdotally interesting. Khrushchev won the race in unveiling a Shevchenko statue in Moscow on June 10, with considerable nationwide and international propaganda. Washington's unveiling was scheduled for May, but delayed mainly because of the controversy and its effects on other operations. Although it can be said that Khrushchev won in the short run, he lost in the long run, including his chairmanship. In the meantime, on June 15, at a Party-to-People GOP Forum in Philadelphia, a panel that included Eisenhower recommended a captive nations plank for the upcoming 1964 Republican Party Convention's platform, which was realized and set a course of action into the Reagan period. Then and later, unfortunately, and despite broad Democratic congressional support of the captive nations movement, the position of the Democratic National Convention was less intense.

President George H. W. Bush, upon his arrival in Kyiv on August 1, 1991, pointed to the Shevchenko statue in Washington, paraphrasing the famous passage, "When will we have a Washington with a new and righteous law? One day we shall have him!" Speaking at Shevchenko University in Kyiv on May 12, 1995, President Clinton declared, "It is fitting that we are meeting at this institution, named for Taras Shevchenko. More than thirty years ago, America recognized his passion for freedom by erecting a statue of Shevchenko in the heart of our nation's capital. Now, at last, America also honors this great champion of liberty in the heart of Ukraine's capital."[24] At a monument to victims of communism in Lviv, First Lady Hillary Rodham Clinton also made the point on November 17, 1997: "Just eighteen blocks from the White House in Washington there is a monument to your great poet and national leader, Shevchenko, built at a time when Ukraine was still a captive nation."

Depending on future developments, it is not unreasonable to anticipate that our future presidents visiting Ukraine would express similar tribute. Nor is it an overstatement to posit the thought that President George W. Bush's interjection in an address in neighboring Warsaw, Poland, preceding the forty-third observance of Captive Nations Week in 2001—"The Europe we are building must include Ukraine"—is highly in tune with the Shevchenko vision.

The story is ongoing. A statue guide to foreign heroes featured a photo of the Shevchenko statue in September 1997.[25] And in this century, a dribble of the old controversy appeared in the *Washington Post*, "Park Places" (November 12, 2000), proposing the removal of the photographed Shevchenko statue and others. But a week later, again featuring the statue, the *Post* published a more than adequate rebuttal under "Don't Knock Them Off Their Pedestals" (November 19). Indeed, the Shevchenko statue chapter remains open ended, and not just an episode or interlude.

CHAPTER 11

# Countering Russian Propaganda

*A Crucial American Public Diplomacy Mission*

Our thinking throughout the entire Cold War was heavily tainted by myths, half-truths, and skewed policy proposals. But several times we did the right thing, even if it took a while. Here we examine some of these events, including those that continued right through to the end of the Soviet Union. First, we will examine how the United States tried to counter Russian propaganda through the Voice of America and other information efforts, including the many missteps along the way, particularly in regard to Ukraine and other captive nations. Next is an insider's look at the 1952 Republican National Convention, where battling opinions on liberation vs. containment were on display. Rounding out this section is a look at the speech delivered by President George H. W. Bush in Kyiv in August 1991, nicknamed "Chicken Kiev" by its detractors.

The Voice of America (VOA), launched in 1942 under President Roosevelt in the effort for a World War II victory, operated largely in the German language. Under President Truman and his "Campaign of Truth," the course, pursued later by Reagan, was unmistakable: the Psychological Strategic Board stationed in the White House, its coordination of all governmental broadcasting activities, and the setup of Radio Free Europe and Radio Liberation under the US International Information Administration. Eisenhower established in 1953 the US Information Service, shifting control from the White House, but openly advancing the liberation theme until the disputed conversion of Radio Liberation into Radio Liberty. In the Nixon administration, United States Information Agency (USIA) director Frank Shakespeare attempted to infuse truthful public policy, but to no avail. However, he succeeded in a directive sanitizing radio scripts with misleading concepts such as "the Soviet nation," "Soviet people," and so on.

Following the Truman course of action, though more intensely and comprehensively to the pitch of the "evil empire" concept, Reagan returned the control of words to the White House. This control, with no interference in news reports but with a heavy emphasis on values and support of US foreign policy in features and editorials, was placed under the National Security Council. The White House speechwriter's office also played an important role. Reagan's Westminster speech to the members of the British Parliament in June 1982 underscored the values of freedom and predicted that Marxism-Leninism would wind up on "the ash heap of history." Thus, it wasn't just military arms to Afghan freedom fighters alone, but also what I call "words-arms." (Parenthetically, Radio Free Europe's détente-minded management hesitated at first to report Solidarity's strikes for workers' freedom.)

Commendable as it was to establish in December 1949 the Ukrainian section during the embryonic stage of the Voice of America (and this in part the result of citizen political pressure), the content of the Ukrainian language broadcasts was, without exaggeration, incredible. Literally a translation into Ukrainian of the Russian language broadcasts, the message to listeners in Ukraine highlighted the glorification of Russian heroes and conquerors, such as Alexander Nevsky, Ivan the Terrible, and Peter the Great. Ukraine's poet laureate Taras Shevchenko was portrayed as a shining product of, first, Russian and, then, Ukrainian peasantry. And a Russian bishop (as though no Ukrainian American bishop existed) was selected to extend Christmas greetings to the people of Ukraine.

My talks with Foy Kohler, who served as chief of the International Broadcasting Division in New York and later as our ambassador to Moscow, were a source of astonishment to him. It was evident that scores of individual protests hadn't reached his ears. He graciously acknowledged the mistakes, and soon the quality of the Ukrainian broadcasts improved substantially. In addition, the influence of so-called democratic Russian émigrés, who manned the operations with their incorrigible appetite for the "one and indivisible" Russian Empire, à la Kerensky and others, was eliminated—but State's policy restriction remained. (During those years, one of State's public affairs publications depicted the USSR in terms of Russia West and Russia East.)

The renowned columnist and editor of *US News and World Report*, David Lawrence, wrote in his column of October 4, 1950: "Apparently the broadcasts must not do anything to induce the people of the Soviet Union to change their governmental or social structure. Yet nine out of ten members of Congress have believed all along that this is what they were appropriating money for." Questioning the politeness of the State Department in these broadcasts, he added, "Why can't it tell the peoples who make up the Soviet Union that their governmental structure is a menace to world peace today and that, unless it is changed, the world will drift someday into large-scale war?"[1]

In his critical column, Lawrence pointed to the many observers who regarded Ukraine "as constituting the Achilles heel of the Soviet Union." He urged that instead of the Department of State, "some other agency should undertake such broadcasts." The former point was decisively demonstrated in 1991 when Ukraine's declared independence spelled the collapse of the Soviet Union; the latter point was realized by 1958 with the creation of the US Information Agency. However, in the 1990s, while a number of communist dictatorships and captive nations have remained and the need for democratic reinforcement in the former communist states has been urgently pressing, once again shortsighted arguments and efforts emerged to revert Voice of America to the State Department. The omnipresent phenomenon of generational gaps in thinking and perspective continues to haunt us.

Now for another mini-path in the 1950s, leading to the central trail. Broadcast media wallows in information, its very lifeblood. In our policies toward the Russian Communist empire, our message had to be purified and sharpened. Occasioning this purification process was the set of hearings on the newly established United States Information Agency before a House Foreign Affairs subcommittee.[2]

How all this came about is a fascinating story in itself. In early January 1958, I was parking my car outside the National War College building at Fort Lesley J. McNair when I heard someone cry out, "Hey, Doby (my college nickname), have you a minute or two to hear this?" I turned, and it was one of my favorite students, Spencer King, who was a State Department student at the college, very well informed on policy matters, who eventually rose to the ambassadorial level. I greeted him, saying, "Spencer, you'd better make it good."

"Don't keel over now," King said. "USIA Director Allen has launched a plan to eventually eliminate the non-Russian language broadcasts to the Soviet Union."

"You're pulling my leg in this New Year," I shot back. He strongly assured me of the plan's existence and urged that I look into it.

On my own time, the first order of business was to obtain an appointment with Ambassador George Allen. The second step was to inform friends on Capitol Hill of the plan. The appointment was arranged by Congressman Michael Feighan of Ohio, who had been consistently a stalwart exponent of the non-Russian nations concept. I then reached out to Democratic representatives Edna Kelly of New York and Alvin Bentley of Michigan and Republican Rep. Walter Judd of Minnesota, as well as senators H. Alexander Smith of New Jersey (Republican) and Paul Douglas of Illinois (Democrat), all of whom had an intellectual and legislative stake in the subject.

The meeting with George Allen took place a few weeks after King's notice, followed by reports about the plan in the press. The director received me graciously in his office, but our discussion was almost entirely philosophical. He admitted that the plan was under study, and I vigorously recited the reasons for opposition to it. He avoided countering the points of objection; instead, he steered into a seemingly "broader issues" discussion of world trends, larger political entities versus smaller, national states (citing his Yugoslavia and India ambassadorial experiences), the simple objective of the VOA, and peace with the USSR via cultural exchanges and the avoidance of "splinterizing" it. Nothing was said about the supposed transmitter problem or lack of funds. For my part, though disputing him on all of these issues, I said nothing about contesting the plan in Congress.

In a nutshell, the congenial ambassador, who was supposed to lead an agency designated as our truth propaganda apparatus in the Cold War, represented the views, concepts, and thinking traits characteristic of narrow, staid diplomacy. He displayed little knowledge or understanding of the foremost problems in the USSR; no grasp at all of the non-Russian nations concept, viewing (as did most others) the "minorities" and "ethnic groups" in the Soviet Union as resembling ours in the United States; no appreciation of the force of nationalism in the primary empire; and a barren notion of the VOA as simply informing the peoples of the world how Americans and others live and intersect.

Clearly, decisive action had to be taken on the course pursued by the USIA and its director. Centered on the subject of a summit with Moscow's leaders, a memorandum was signed in April by senators Smith and Douglas and representatives Judd and Feighan emphasizing the need for more non-Russian language broadcasts to the Soviet Union. It was addressed to Secretary Dulles and led to a meeting with him by the four. Dulles expressed total agreement on the issue.

The next step was the preparation for an open hearing before an appropriate subcommittee of the House Foreign Affairs Committee, which was the one concerned with State Department organization and foreign operations. The logical person to initiate this was Rep. Edna Kelly of New York, an astute committee member who had previously contacted me on other matters and showed a deep interest in the non-Russian nations concept. In our many discussions, I found her to be open-minded and willing to act upon what she deemed important and vital to our national security.

Anecdotally, I recall an early discussion in which Kelly raised the question, "Doctor, why don't you include Algeria, for example, as a captive nation?" Over the years, she wasn't the only one to pose a similar question. My friend Alfred M. Lilienthal, a widely respected supporter and advocate of Palestinian independence, revealed to me in the 1990s that he had participated in an annual New Hampshire Captive Nations Week commemoration, feeling that Palestinians constituted a captive nation. The adjective "captive" has multiple uses, but its use in relation to communist-dominated nations is an exclusive and technical one. Even some of the annual Captive Nations Week proclamations, presidential and others, have been needlessly confusing on this score.

Covering a broad area was the submitted document signed by Major Petro Fedun, aka Poltava, chief of the Bureau of Information of the Supreme Ukrainian Council in Ukraine (formed in 1944 to resist both Bolshevik and Nazi occupation)—which the State Department had received eight years before. This most revealing document contained an extensive analysis and appeal for a more realistic Voice of America. Among its numerous theses is this sage advice: "The American Radio should talk to the non-Russian peoples of the USSR in their own, patriotic, national spirit."[3] Much, much later, this orientation was skillfully fitted into VOA policy and operations.

Two other items appended to my testimony expanded on Poltava's thesis. First was a report in the *New York Herald Tribune* on Moscow's deep concern with the so-called "remnants of Ukrainian nationalism."[4] Second was a random analysis of VOA's Ukrainian-language broadcast programs in early 1958, most with no relevant references to Ukraine and others with a line or two.[5] The latter demonstrated conclusively at the time the lack of competence and imagination of the agency in interrelating news and events in the free world with the national interests of Ukraine and its people, not to mention the other non-Russian nations in the Soviet Union.

Moscow consistently jammed English and Russian-language broadcasts to the Soviet Union. As reported by Adlai Stevenson, the Russian leader categorically declared to him that communist-dominated territory was off limits to any involvement by the United States or the West, while free world areas are open fields for him by virtue of ideology. The bounds of self-delusion may have no limits, but Khrushchev was making an intimidating propaganda point, which goes a long way to explain in part why Moscow jammed the English and Russian-language broadcasts far less than the non-Russian-language ones. Those policymakers pressing for only the former in VOA knowingly or inadvertently were supporting Moscow's alternating Russification campaign among the non-Russian nations.

Before concluding this chapter, the need for a sound, overall perspective on this vital subject demands several notes of projection down to our period. Yes, I was greatly elated over the checkmate to the Allen plan, not only because of the incalculable harm it could have inflicted on our nation's freedom fight in the Cold War, but also the very stain of crass ineptitude it would have left on our record in this titanic struggle. Thus, after necessary changes were made, I, along with other interested parties, supported the USIA well into the 1990s. The very next year (significantly, two months before Congress passed the Captive Nations Week resolution) my testimony before the House Committee on Appropriations called for substantial funding increases to expand and bolster the non-Russian-language broadcasts to the Soviet Union. Sponsoring the text in the Congressional Record, the highly knowledgeable Representative Bentley of Michigan stated, "The general observations made in this testimony might well be pondered by every American interested in a realistic policy toward the USSR, one with maximum economy and productive results."[6]

Fortunately, the secular trend in the development of the USIA was an upward one, mainly because its relative detachment from the State Department allowed for greater independence in lead personnel and programming. Based on direct, personal experience, I can say that in the Cold War period as concerns the non-Russian concept, the agency h162                                                                        Chapter 11

reached its peak years during the Nixon, Reagan, and George H. W. Bush administrations. I cannot deny the contributions made to the trend by the Democratic administrations, in particular the exceptional Carter one with its human rights advocacy. In relative terms of challenging specificity, imaginative intersecting of free world events and non-Russian nations' interests, skillful editorials, and basic themes, none, with again the exception of the still developing Carter one, could match the peaks represented, for example, in the Olympics phenomenon in 1972 and Reagan's "evil empire" and his annual Captive Nations Week observances—indeed, the highest peak of all.

USIA director Shakespeare's policy directive in 1972 regarding VOA's coverage of the Olympic games in Munich had far-reaching consequences. It was my privilege to serve as a consultant to him for several years during the Nixon administration. Intellectually sharp, prudent, and innovative, Shakespeare, who later became an ambassador, quickly grasped the non-Russian concept and strengthened the non-Russian-language broadcasts to the Soviet Union. His outstanding contribution was the directive ordering explicitly national identification of USSR participants in the Munich games.

Unforgettable in my memory was a meeting in his office on Pennsylvania Avenue that led to this action. Having returned from a White House meeting involving the president and his advisors, Shakespeare informed me of his attempt to initiate a discussion of the non-Russian issue and the parameters for its implementation in the agency. Engrossed at the time with Vietnam, Moscow negotiations, domestic disturbances, etc., "the club," as he depicted it, evinced no interest in the subject, leaving him with the impression of fending for himself in this area. With circumspection and responsible judgment, Shakespeare acted accordingly.

Thus, in VOA's coverage of the 1972 Olympics, when a Georgian, Lithuanian, Ukrainian, or other non-Russian athlete was announced or won a medal, he or she was to be identified as such, and not as a "Soviet" or "Russian," which typified private media coverage.

Consequentially far-reaching? Extending to the 1996 Olympics in Atlanta, the consequences have evolved into (1) mounting pressures in the USSR for separate republic and national designations (e.g., Kazakhstan, KSSR, own flag and insignia); (2) adopted differentiation by private media in the 1976 Olympics in Montreal; (3) an overflow of this demand in petitions to the world Olympic authority; and (4) with the breakup of the USSR its full fruition in the 1996 Olympics. Comments then by broadcasters about the former "united team" may be forgiven for their superficiality. The final results in Atlanta demonstrated how spurious the former propaganda vaunting by Moscow of "Homo sovieticus" had become.

The 1990s have been marked by further revisionist efforts and their conspicuous lack of perspective with regard to our international broadcast apparatus—USIA, Radio Free Europe, Radio Liberty, and Radio Martí. It's the old story of new people without sufficient background or different levels of competence in Congress, the administration, and the respective agencies—familiar cases of revision without the vision. For ostensible reasons of economy, budget-cutting, and sheer reform, the drive from 1993 on to revert the USIA to State Department control (where it was back in the 1950s) evidenced the revising sponsors' lack of vision. As a flexible instrument of public diplomacy projecting in all their institutional details democracy and politico-economic freedom— in sharp contrast to State's characteristic, staid diplomacy bent on negotiations, compromise, at times misdirected "stability," and secret deals—the USIA and its VOA have a tremendous mission to undertake, along with the other international broadcast instruments, in the period ahead. The foci of their typical messages to Central and Eastern Europe, Central Asia, the Far East, the remaining captive nations in Asia, and Cuba should not be minimized.

To believe, as one senator did, that the crucial mission of public diplomacy can be performed by private media indicates a sub-zero appreciation of the propaganda machines heavily subsidized by totalitarian, political states, whether communist or theocratic. In the

1990s, and into the next century, the urgency of perpetuating the ongoing liberation process by singularly advancing democracy and politico-economic freedom among the once-again independent nations and in Russia and the Russian Federation has remained undiminished. Back in World War II, it was plausible to suppress the known truth of the Katyn Forest massacres of over ten thousand Polish officers by the Russian Communists. But after the war it was clearly unjustified for our government to continue such suppression for VOA broadcasts of the facts—which took a congressional investigation to reveal and over thirty years later for an enfeebled Moscow to confirm.

As to what could have been, Radio Free Europe was allowed to establish belatedly its Southern Slavic Service. Had it been earlier, in the late 1980s for instance, it could have strongly counter-balanced state-subsidized Serb and Croat media spreading poisonous ethnic hatred propaganda. With other policy adjustments, it could have played a determining role in staving off the ghastly wars in the former Yugoslavia.

In concluding, let's recall from the USIA hearing Representative Kelly's question about President Eisenhower and Secretary Dulles in UN speeches referring to the "captive nations." My answer in part: "I hope we will come to the point sometime in the near future when we can more realistically apply the 'captive nations' concept to include all the subjugated non-Russian nations under Moscow's imperial rule. I would say that concept even includes the Russian people. In a sense they are captive, captive to a totalitarian regime and government carrying on precedents which go far back into their history."[7] That wish came to reality the following year, a wish based on the fundamental truth of Russian Communist imperio-colonialism and embodied in Congress's passage of the Captive Nations Week resolution. With the congressional act, our central paper trail was cemented.

The situation of our international broadcasts in the early 1980s was best epitomized by the oft-used taunt, "Badly out-talked, out-funded, out-transmitted, and out-gamed by Moscow and its Communist Party proxies." The need for modernization was uppermost, and the content of broadcasts, as well as access to facilities, constituted a seemingly intractable problem. Apart from Solzhenitsyn's later erraticism, to deny him early entrée to the Voice of America, yet to allow Georgi Arbatov, a roving principal propagandist for the Kremlin, indicated the scope of the managerial problem.

Beyond question, the Voice of America, Radio Free Europe, and Radio Liberty were grossly underfunded to compete in words with the Soviet Union. Voice of America's budget, largest of the three, had increased from under $50 million in 1966, a level it maintained as late as 1980, to $167.8 million by 1985. Contemporaneously, the Soviet Union was spending approximately $700 million per annum for its foreign radio broadcasts, well over double the total amount of all US governmental radio operations. Worse still, the Soviet Union's total expenditures for worldwide propaganda were estimated at $3.3 billion, engendering press sections in Soviet Union embassies, foreign communist parties, national liberation fronts, and so forth in a whole array of propaganda conduits.

Adding to the burden of playing catch-up for the administration was the pressing need for modernization of our transmitters and the jamming problem. Reagan proposed $1.3 billion to modernize our words arsenal, even seeking to establish an up-to-date complex of transmitters in Israel's Negev Desert that would be capable of deep penetration into Eastern Europe and Central Asia and of solving the jamming problem. Some of our transmitters were of World War II vintage. We lagged behind not only the Soviet Union but also France, West Germany, and Great Britain. The Voice of America operated at 990 hours per week in forty-two languages, Moscow at 2,175 hours per week in eighty-one languages. We even lagged behind the People's Republic of China. Concerning the jamming of our allied broadcasts, the Soviet Union spent about $300 million—again, more than we were spending on all of our broadcasts in the early 1980s. However, the problem was an intermittent one since the Soviet Union, as a concession to détente in the 1970s, reduced its operations and later in the

1980s found it increasingly difficult to sustain because of limited territorial coverage as our reconstruction progressed, particularly in rural areas. Jamming was terminated in 1988 during the Gorbachev regime.

Enormous credit is due to Charles Wick for the transformation of our words arsenal in both imperative investment and upgraded operations. Since his assignment as director of USIA in 1981, the catch-up process was relentless and adequate for a Cold War victory. His introduction of Worldnet, the first international satellite television network, drew vehement opposition from Moscow, fearing transborder penetration. The idea wasn't new—Shakespeare couldn't realize it under Nixon because of détente. In the framework of the Reagan challenge, Wick succeeded, though he did run into trouble with Moscow's Aleksandr Yokovlev over a deal made for exchanging Soviet Union radio broadcasts and reduced jamming of Voice of America broadcasts. The issue was turned over to the State Department, and it evaporated after appropriate steps had been taken via the World Administrative Radio Conference and the International Frequency Review Board, which found the Soviet Union, Czechoslovakia, and Poland in violation of article 35 of the International Telecommunications Union Convention.

Lessons for now and the future? Briefly, in the unfolding of US global strategy the continuance of research scholarships in this area is indispensable. The prudent balancing of resources and demands will be ever-present for the USIA and the Broadcasting Board of Governors, especially in regard to priorities in foreign policy directions flowing from the White House. Works by Peter Kuznick and James Gilbert (editors of *Rethinking Cold War Culture*) and Arch Puddington (*Broadcasting Freedom: The Cold War Triumph of Radio Free Europe and Radio Liberty*) provide a course of scholarly action deserving of emulation.[8] Both recognize that more could have been done by Voice of America, Radio Free Europe, and Radio Liberty, yet each has more than passing grades. The crucial relationship between the Voice of America and Radio Liberty was especially relevant to the captive nations category in the Reagan Doctrine and the PL 86-90 observances at the White House. In 1982, to strongly argue for nationalism as the core concept in our broadcasts, as had Constantine Jurgela, a lawyer, historian, and guiding light in the Voice of America, was supremely meritorious.[9]

Another lesson is the coordination of Voice of America broadcasts with allies in the world democratization process. The Voice of America, having reached over eighty million listeners in over fifty languages, should operate twenty-four hours a day to further humanitarian and business links of ecoglobalism. Hardly requiring emphasis is the necessary coordination of current broadcasting facilities in the war on terror. There is also the lesson of preparedness, notably as concerns Turkestan or Central Asia, one of the "near abroad" targets of the aggressive Putin policy. Over fifty years ago, when the Uzbek language program in Voice of America was abolished, later restored, and liquidated again, C. L. Sulzberger of the *New York Times* wrote in partial truth, "This is the most delicate and weak region of the entire Soviet Empire" (May 23, 1952).

Then, too, there is the lesson of consistent truth-telling. In the spirit of Wickean innovation, his Worldnet and transborder TV penetration, another consideration would be the utilization of Hollywood's worldwide influence and facilities in portraying the crimes of "Soviet Communism," including genocide. The actor and game show host Benjamin Stein poignantly raised this point in March 2000: "What is the attraction of this evil system for Hollywood and for 'intellectuals' generally that keeps them from facing the truth about how vicious Communism was and is?"[10]

# CHAPTER 12

# Beyond Containment

Containment versus liberation was the topic of endless political debate during the Cold War. To its proponents, containment meant a practical, long-term, patient policy of countering the Soviet Union's expansionist tendencies. To its critics, it meant abandoning the people who had been enslaved by the USSR. The liberation faction preferred a proactive stance aimed at rolling back Soviet power and liberating Eastern Europe.

"Beyond Containment" was the crowning moment attached to the ostensibly pragmatic foreign policy of the George H. W. Bush administration. Similarly, "Enlargement" was the label placed on the policy of the Clinton administration. "Beyond Containment" was the theme song of the Republican National Convention in 1952, used to describe the liberation policy then and long after. "Beyond Containment" meant to blunt Moscow's oppressive and political warfare devices within its three-layered empire and leapfrog over the Maginot-like walls of containment in Asia, Africa, Latin America, and elsewhere. "Enlargement" meant to penetrate Moscow's tenuous hold on the original captive nations in the Soviet Union itself.

The liberation policy of the 1950s finally found its realization thirty years later in the Reagan Doctrine. Motivation, means, opportunity, and goals were identical. President Reagan singularly made full use of the Captive Nations Week Resolution (PL 86-90). With an eye to the tremendous Cold War costs we sustained in human life and economic sacrifices, it can be confidently argued that the contextual circumstances of the 1950s were far more favorable than those of the 1980s.

Regarding "Beyond Containment" and "Enlargement," this is no play on words, nor is it just a verbal coincidence. Nor should it be wrongly interpreted as some historical repeat. Its meaningfulness in our day rests on the fact that the motivation and the explicit freedom goals that constituted the liberation policy materialized in such broad scope and with volcanic impact, leaving most analysts and commentators spellbound at the end of the 1980s and well into the 1990s.

The political story surrounding its acceptance in 1952 will confirm this observation. Discounting the omnipresent fringe groups—the dupes, the self-interested, pro-Soviet elements, professional peaceniks, etc.—far too many of our policymakers and opinion makers failed to comprehend the liberation/containment issue. In addition to other reasons (e.g., limited captive nations knowledge and the distractions of the Korean War), the most basic was the lack of knowledge of systematic Soviet Russian political warfare, which was taught at different times to early Communist Party members. Also, too many Americans weren't even aware of the existence of the Cold War, believing that the challenges posed by our World War II military ally were just problems characteristic of the normal play in international relations.

At the time, the liberation policy was attacked as "a dangerous crusade," "apocalyptic," "a risky policy," "warlike," and other variants of essentially the same idea. Moscow and its satraps bellowed against it. Some myths were perpetuated in commentaries decades later by our better foreign policy minds.

The policy of liberation and its "beyond containment" and "enlargement" features, in contrast to mere containment, were riveted in an open politico-economic commitment to the eventual liberation of all the captive nations. The liberation policy, facing the realities of Moscow's global political warfare, promoted the empire concept aimed at the Soviet Union itself, from the Carpathian Mountains to the shores of the Soviet Far East. It projected a vision and determination not only to fight and defeat communism but also to pave the reconstructive way for real, expansive politico-economic freedom, the rightful independence of subjugated nations and peoples in Moscow's vast empire, and federative and other configurational alternatives conducive to emergent politico-economic necessities. Then, as now, visions of a United States of Europe, an economic European Union, a Siberian federation or confederation of states, yes, a genuine federation, under an appropriate title and based on self-determination in the Russian Federation, were theoretically accommodated by the liberation rationale.

America's geopolitical position in the world during the early years of the Cold War was one of unique world leadership. Although drawn into the Cold War facet of the Korean War, we singularly possessed all of the fundamental assets for the exercise of such world leadership: supreme military power, unparalleled economic strength, and the pride and glory of victory in World War II. Contrary to the groundless criticisms of the liberation policy, its skillful implementation in that propitious and facilitative setting would certainly have disrupted Moscow's global Cold War plans, forthrightly challenged its oft-repeated ploy of peaceful coexistence on firmer grounds of civilized values, and severely impeded its consolidation efforts both within the Soviet Union and in Central Europe.

Despite all its typical bluff and bluster, the Kremlin was in no position—even with stolen nuclear secrets—to engage in another hot war. Both its domestic and imperial situations were punctuated by political instability, deep economic weakness, widespread active and passive resistance, the presence of underground systems, and an urgent need for "peaceful coexistence." For Moscow, that meant time to recover and also time for waging the Cold War.

In terms of objective reality, the opportunity for implementing the liberation policy couldn't have been more ideal. However, the subjective factors that determine will and reason—little recognition of the Cold War in its totality, scarce comprehension of Moscow's political warfare theory and operations, the blatant myths entertained with reference to the Soviet Union and the captive nations as a whole, and recurring isolationism—contributed to a lost opportunity.

The internal logic of the liberation policy persisted in its conclusion that the best way to prevent a hot war was to win the Cold War, without any illusions of an apocalypse or risk-free ventures, but with knowledgeable and informed initiatives placing the enemy and its spurious pretensions of "democracy," "freedom," "national liberation," "economic progress," etc. on a perpetual defensive. In the liberating process and with judiciously seized opportunities, victory might have been possible in a short time and at considerably less cost.

A few episodes illustrate the problems that were encountered in promoting the liberation policy. During the 1940s, I participated in fairly regular luncheon meetings in the Washington Square College cafeteria of New York University, where I was teaching and enjoyed the privilege of becoming a friend of fellow faculty members James Burnham, Sidney Hook, and Anton Friedrich. Much of the give-and-take centered on the Soviet Union, Moscow's global conspiracy, and its political warfare methods. Burnham had already made his mark as an eminent politico-economic philosopher with his acclaimed *Managerial Revolution*.[1] Hook was an outstanding scholar on Marxism; and Friedrich was known for his popular teaching and critiques in the areas of economic thought and systems. Both Burnham and Hook, former Trotsky supporters, had broad backgrounds in communism, and I profited greatly from them, rendering in return my knowledge of the captive nations in the Soviet Union.

The warm relationships and intellectual intermix didn't end with my departure in 1948 for Georgetown University. Hook had already honored a personal request to join a committee aiding refugee and other scholars, and in 1958, on my recommendation, was a guest lecturer at the National War College and appeared on the Georgetown University TV-Radio Forum. During my several visits to New York University, Friedrich continued to offer his critical observations, and Burnham also displayed his continuing interest by addressing an overflowing audience in New York's Carnegie Hall on October 1, 1950, celebrating the tenth anniversary of the Ukrainian Congress Committee of America.[2] He, too, lectured at the National War College in 1958.

But it was in the interim years that our friendship deepened, both professionally and socially. Burnham left New York University to become engaged in a variety of governmental and private projects in the nation's capital. Our exchanges were frequent since he lived with his family in the stately MacArthur house only a few blocks from Georgetown University. Burnham's towering contribution to the liberation policy was his analytically penetrating work published in 1953, *Containment or Liberation?*[3] On Capitol Hill and in the new Eisenhower administration, it moved minds and hearts, but not enough wills.

In the political arena the term "liberation" had been in circulation years and even decades before the 1950s, depending on which captive nations one's attention was focused on. Refugees and émigrés from countries whose independence was destroyed by Soviet Russian imperialism under the cover of communism were familiar with the concept. What was wanting was a unifying foreign policy.

My experience with the Genocide Convention ratification effort convinced me of the need for some alternative political means to advance the liberation policy—in effect a search for a conglomerate constituency. The opportunity appeared in the next two years as a succession of events contributed to a Republican policy of liberation. This began with the role the Republican National Committee played toward the close of 1950 and culminated with Eisenhower's victory in 1952.

Several months after the Genocide Convention hearings in 1950, I struck up a relationship with Albert Hermann. He had been an aide to Sen. H. Alexander Smith of New Jersey and became the executive director of the Republican National Committee. The relationship developed into a friendship that lasted for nearly three decades. "Al," as he liked to be called, was an institution within the institution, a political pro who, except for a short time following Ike's nomination, provided indispensable continuity and memory, rare expertise, wisdom, and warm congeniality in the RNC and the party at large.

In that first phase of our incipient friendship, Al was strongly attracted to three interrelated ideas: the formation of an ethnic division in the RNC, the appeal of a dynamic foreign policy, and the persuasion of RNC chairman Guy Gabrielson, Senator Smith, and others to support programmatic steps aimed at the party's adoption of the policy in the 1952 Chicago convention. The realization of these ideas was not without anticipated difficulties and problems, but on the whole the sailing was remarkably smooth.

Concerning the first idea, with the assistance of Stephen Skubik, a former counterintelligence officer fully conversant with ethnic compositions, a division was eventually established for the dual purpose of gaining popular support of the policy and also breaking the traditional hold of the Democratic Party on the ethnic vote. It was named the "nationalities division" to serve as an oppositional counterpart to the one in the Democratic National Committee. After the convention, it was renamed the ethnic division and eventually the heritage division.

The appeal of the liberation policy to the "ethnics" related to communist-dominated countries proved to be overwhelming, especially with the generally better-educated immigrants following World War II. The RNC chairman's support and inputs by other party authorities followed along. For the first time, with Eisenhower's election, the so-called ethnic vote shifted to the Republican party and expanded until the 1992 presidential election, when a reversal set in because of dissatisfaction with the policies of the George H. W. Bush administration. According to an NBC poll in 1964, even the Goldwater debacle didn't deter its growth.

Of course the policy's appeal extended also to labor groups, veterans' organizations, various civic bodies, and so on. In most cases, it was related to the captive nations thesis, viewing them as our natural allies in the Cold War. Therefore, it shouldn't be surprising that well into the 1990s the essence of the liberation policy has resonated in the advocacies of many of these organizations for principled and yet pragmatic policies toward mainland China, Vietnam, North Korea, Cuba, and areas of the former Soviet Union and Central Europe.

Heading toward the 1952 convention, the enthusiastic cooperation of Guy Gabrielson and others allowed a program of action that included the dissemination of information on the policy's essentials, the family scope of the captive nations, recruitment of spokespeople in the field, the scheduling of Republican speakers at conventions and meetings, and preparations for organizational endorsements of the presidential nominee. For example, in my capacity as president of the Ukrainian Congress Convention of America, I obtained its endorsement of Eisenhower's candidacy for its "courageous advocacy of a realistic foreign policy of liberation toward the enslaved nations in the Soviet Empire."[4]

My association and then friendship with Rep. Charlie Kersten (R-WI) included a number of memorable experiences. At the beginning of 1952 he permitted me to conduct two polls out of his office in the Longworth House Office Building in preparation for the Republican National Convention that summer. Manned by excited Georgetown students tracking down Republican members, the operation sought their support of a liberation policy and the genocide treaty. The results were sizably positive for the policy but less so for the treaty.

The aforementioned poll conducted out of Kersten's House office early in 1952 was part of the program, and John Foster Dulles's article on liberation that May, which was reproduced and circulated widely, gave a considerable boost to the pre-convention campaign.[5] Finally, in Chicago, wedged in between labor leader Walter Reuther and Senator Nixon (R-CA), I had the pleasure of testifying on the issue before the convention's foreign affairs committee. But, more importantly, several thousand copies of the pamphlet *Republican Policy of Liberation or Democratic Policy of Containment* were distributed to all delegates and participants in the convention.

Sad as it is with most campaigns, the winners come in sweepingly, the losers are indiscriminately eliminated. Much to the credit of his sense of honor and integrity, Goldwater in the 1964 post-convention turnover curbed the liquidation by retaining the invaluable services of Al Hermann, whose neck was on the line again. Al was not so lucky in 1952. He, as well as Skubik and others in the nationalities division, were eliminated because of their personal support of Senator Taft. I alone remained as a consultant, still admiring and loving Taft for his superlative human qualities, keen intellect, and party leadership, but feeling that the country was politically ripe for a distinguished war hero. However, the changes in the renamed ethnic division led to a new and warm association with Arthur Bliss Lane, who had served as our ambassador to Poland.

As the presidential campaign got under way, General Eisenhower delivered a resounding speech to the American Legion convention espousing the liberation policy. Some Democrats and opponents in the media and other sectors railed against it as "a warlike policy" and variations galore. Early in September, I received a call from Arthur Summerfield, who was in command of Eisenhower's campaign and later became our postmaster general, warning that pressure was mounting in several quarters of the party to scrap the term "liberation." I naturally resisted, and with the support of Bliss argued for its retention, qualifying it as "eventual." "Liberation" remained in use— sometimes qualified, often not. Four years later, in his reelection campaign, President Eisenhower spoke of "peaceful liberation."

Another revealing incident in the 1952 campaign was a brief conversation with Sen. Alexander Smith at a liberation dinner in September. Before the dinner, the senator, who had been serving as a liaison between Eisenhower at Columbia University and Taft in Canada, took me aside and said in these approximate words, "Doc, the general and some people about him aren't too clear as to what the liberation policy entails and what can be done. They feel that its aggressive overtones may be detrimental to the campaign." In the moments available, I informed him of the decision made at headquarters earlier that month; emphasized that a detailed blueprint of the policy was unnecessary in the campaign; and offered to brief Ike and his close associates on the practicalities of the policy. I never heard from the senator.

Evidently the reason for Smith not pursuing my offer was the tactical change in the Democratic presidential rhetoric. Not that the war scare was eliminated, but rather that "containment" was being disowned. A striking example was the TV debate on August 21, 1952, between Averell Harriman and John Foster Dulles. Harriman kept challenging Dulles or any Republican to show where or when Truman or Acheson ever used the term "containment." This, to be sure, was a valid point about which Dulles showed immediate concern. Frantic word went out to research the subject. Considering the difficulties facing an already overburdened research unit in the RNC and the time factor, the research, to my knowledge, was never completed. I often wondered whether Harriman's challenge was founded on meticulous research. In any case, the seeming crisis soon evaporated.

My position on the challenge was that although any additional bit of knowledge is beneficial, it was relatively minor and could hardly sway the campaign. For a backstop, if that was necessary, we could have easily maintained that whether or not Truman or Acheson used the term, their policies were not adequately liberational, and this was the difference. Theoretically and practically, the liberation policy was necessarily based on containment. Moreover, countless Democrats in Congress, the executive branch, and our society at large, individually if not organizationally, were strongly in favor of it.

How was the policy implemented and what could have been done? My article published in the international journal, *The Ukrainian Quarterly*, in some measure answers the question.[6] It apparently made a favorable impression on Rep. Alvin Bentley of Michigan, who not only introduced it into the Congressional Record but also was inspired by its message to vigorously support certain measures of liberationist meaning.[7] The Captive Nations Week resolution was one. The other, in a sensational race with Khrushchev, was his sponsored resolution on the Shevchenko monument in the nation's capital. Both hit Moscow's bull's-eye.

It has frequently been stated that the Eisenhower administration paid only lip service to the liberation policy. This is not entirely correct. A real first step was taken (with the complete backing of Secretary of State Dulles) with the formation of the Kersten committee to establish the indispensable public opinion groundwork for the policy's implementation. But the next equally indispensable step was never realized. This would have been the creation of a planning and operational mechanism, solely responsible to the president, mandated exclusively to deal with Moscow's worldwide political warfare. To expertly manage political warfare, Moscow's government had its Communist Party mechanism; we had nothing comparable to it.

Confronted by all of this, proponents of the liberation policy could only resolve to continue with their advocacy of the chief premises of the policy—in particular the empire concept pertaining to the Soviet Union itself—and, equally important, their vigorous opposition to policies containing serious errors of thought and action.

# CHAPTER 13

# Cold War Victory and the Collapse of the Soviet Union

Entering now into the post-Reagan years, we ask: Who won the Cold War (not entirely cold, yet in reality World War III)? What primarily caused the Soviet Union's downfall? We begin with the infamous "Chicken Kiev" episode, the policy direction under President George H. W. Bush, and the liberated captive nations following Reagan's incumbency.

The speech delivered by President George H. W. Bush in Kyiv in 1991 received worldwide publicity, and it has since been referred to as "Chicken Kiev." Some analysts interpreted it to the tune of "one huge policy gaffe in our history"; others viewed it as a pragmatic address in the prevailing circumstances. Still others accused Bush of playing politics, citing the gap between his principled captive nations renditions at home and his actions abroad. To evaluate it firmly in its broadest scope, consideration must be given to the president's captive nations record, his policy toward Ukraine, the Gorbachev-Bush relationship, the delayed recognition of independent Ukraine, and his 2004 revisit to "Chicken Kiev" in Kyiv.

Bush's statements on the captive nations well preceded his presidency. During the Reagan tenure, they fully supported the president's Captive Nations Week proclamations and addresses. When Reagan proclaimed Afghanistan Day in 1982, asserting that the Soviet Union "must understand that the world will not forget—as it has not forgotten the peoples of the other captive nations from Eastern Europe to Southwest Asia—who have suffered from Soviet aggression," his vice president elaborated on the conceptual linkup (Afghanistan, Poland, and all of the captive nations). He emphasized, "Let's not forget the other nations that have suffered the same fate, both within and without the Soviet Union . . . countries from the Baltic States to the Ukraine to Uzbekistan."[1]

Among other examples, Bush addressed the Captive Nations Conference Banquet during the 1983 Captive Nations Week in Washington's Hyatt Regency, elaborating further on the linkup in Central America and elsewhere. He began his address with, "This year, during Captive Nations Week, we mark a grim anniversary—the fiftieth anniversary of the forced famine in the Ukraine, in which five to seven million people lost their lives."

As to Bush's proclamations of Captive Nations Week, a review would show the same tenacity of devotion to the liberation of all captive nations, with some variations in coverage and settings as compared to Reagan's. One variation concerned the consistent White House and assembly addresses for signing. Another was the fluctuation in content and a drift toward generalization, particularly in 1991 when the Bush-Gorbachev relationship became amiably intense. All of the proclamations enunciated the principles of freedom and independence for all captive nations but varied in references to the United Nations Charter, the Helsinki Final Act, and the like.

The 1991 proclamation, for instance, was a relatively short one and clearly overgeneralized. In sharp contrast, in 1992, a presidential year and the Soviet Union nonexistent, the proclamation and Bush's strong address at the Three Saints Russian Orthodox Church in New Jersey were in full Reagan form. While mentioning Vietnam, North Korea, and China, Bush said, "At long last, the captive nations of the old Soviet empire are free"; celebrated "the free world's triumph in the Cold War"; and expressed gratitude to President Yeltsin for the realized American contribution to Russian democracy. Overall, it can be said that the Bush record on Captive Nations Week was positive and highly spirited.

Now for President Bush's explosive address, dubbed "Chicken Kiev." In that fiery year of 1991, and almost three weeks before the famous coup against Gorbachev, the president arrived on August 1 at Kyiv's airport and addressed a welcoming assembly. He spoke of the Shevchenko statue in Washington, quoting the poet's call for a Washington in Ukraine, and cited America's help in the aftermath of the Chernobyl nuclear tragedy. He extolled Ukrainians for being the first to establish Christianity in that part of Europe and for the return to Kyiv of the patriarchs of both the Ukrainian Orthodox and Catholic churches for the first time in forty years. Also, he held out the promise of more US economic and cultural ties with Ukraine and other republics while retaining official relationships with Gorbachev's government.

With this prelude, the shock of "Chicken Kiev" came when the president later appeared before the country's Supreme Soviet to declare: "Yet freedom is not the same as independence. Americans will not support those who seek independence in order to replace a far-off tyranny with a local despotism. They will not aid those who promote a suicidal nationalism based upon ethnic hatred." To invidiously transform the spirit of a nation responding to a call for freedom and independence into "suicidal nationalism" hardly stands for friendship, to say the least. The attempt to rationalize this we'll see below.

An informed reflection on this ill-conceived statement would instantly show the contradiction with Bush's Captive Nations Week proclamations and addresses and his administration's misreading of the dynamic events both in Russia and in the non-Russian nations. The reactions to the gaffe were widespread and sharp. The republic of Georgia, for example, responded, "The heir of Washington, Jefferson, Lincoln and others arrives and carries on propaganda in favor of the union treaty."

In Congress, both Republicans and Democrats denounced the gaffe. Democratic Sen. Dennis DeConcini of Arizona delivered a speech the very next day, declaring, "The president's veiled attempts to equate the relationship between the center and republics with American federalism ignores both the brutal history and the involuntary nature of this nation" (Congressional Record, August 2, 1991). Prematurely, but with long-run political effect, resolutions by DeConcini and Republican Sen. Alfonse D'Amato of New York and representatives Donald Ritter (R-PA) and Dennis Hertel (D-MI) sought full sovereignty for Ukraine with diplomatic recognition. Much has been written on the subject, such as the 1993 Naval Postgraduate School publication, *From "Chicken Kiev" to Ukrainian Recognition*, and in numerous accounts with observations similar to that of AFL-CIO President Lane Kirkland, who criticized Bush in 1992 for "scolding democratic Ukrainian separatists." What remains here, however, was the nature of the Bush policy regarding strategic Ukraine.

For the critical period of 1989–91, several background notes are in order to determine the policy direction of the Bush administration. What may arguably be construed as the roots of Western Gorby-mania, British prime minister Margaret Thatcher emphatically expressed to Ukrainians in June 1991 that she did not wish to witness any disintegration of the Soviet Union. This remark, after her meeting with Gorbachev in London, revealed her belief that the leader was one the West could do business with. In that same time, Bush welcomed Gorbachev at the White House, raising his theme "beyond containment."

The theme had been sounded and developed a year before in addresses at Texas A&M and Boston University, projecting a vision beyond containment "toward a new era, an era of enduring cooperation." Diplomatic injections of issues on Lithuania, Nicaragua, and others were not excluded. By the fall of 1990, Bush pleaded with Gorbachev for his support of the UN resolution to end Iraq's occupation of Kuwait in return for proposed US political and economic aid as the Russian leader struggled to save the Soviet Union. Obviously, a significant shift from the "evil empire" direction—and certainly that of PL 86-90—to one of heightened conventional diplomacy and realpolitik was under way, with status quo, reactive negotiations, and hopes for serendipitous breaks that had characterized our period of failed détente.

While genuine revolutions of submerged nations were in process within the Soviet Union, Yugoslavia, and Czechoslovakia, the Bush administration played the role of stabilizer, preserving the "territorial integrity" of the respective imperial states. Marlin Fitzwater, the chief White House spokesman, reinforced this: "The Yugoslavia people would be best served by a country that's unified." And Secretary of State James Baker, following his meetings with Yugoslav leaders in Belgrade on June 27, 1991, unambiguously asserted, "We came to Yugoslavia because of our concern about the dangers of a disintegration of this country."

The book coauthored in 1998 by President Bush and his national security advisor, Brent Scowcroft, A World Transformed, reveals with considerable candor the administration's stance on "the nationalities," "Chicken Kiev," and the prospect of the Soviet Union's collapse. Concerning the limited view of the nationalities seeking merely to challenge the extent of Gorbachev's reforms, the authors admitted, "In some ways, the United States may have made the same kind of mistake in reading the situation. For years we have tended to assume the Soviets had had more success in stamping out parochial nationalism than proved to be the case."[2]

Regarding "Chicken Kiev," they engaged in a bit of rationalization (if not another admitted miscalculation). On saying "suicidal nationalism" in the context of occurrences in Yugoslavia, Moldovia, and other Soviet republics, "The reference to local despotism was not directed specifically at Ukraine. It was aimed at a number of areas where an upsurge of intolerant nationalism threatened the outbreak of major violence."[3] Georgia or Armenia could have been chosen for the stated purpose with moderated wordage.

The authors' accounts of White House concerns over the issue of nuclear arms and the disintegration of the Soviet Union were revealing. Bush's general view on the Soviet Union was "to help the nation cope with its immediate problems." In the National Security Council meetings, the issue of nuclear arms diffusion was necessarily considered in the event of the Soviet Union collapsing. In a candid admission, Scowcroft reflected, "we never really drafted a tight administration policy on the potential breakup of the Union" due to different perspectives.[4] Ukraine, which had been a center of nuclear arms production, announced its non-nuclear pledge in 1990. The illuminating work by Kostyantyn Morozov, *Above and Beyond: From Soviet General to Ukrainian State Builder*, explores this development.[5]

The orientation of Secretary of Defense Richard Cheney was significant and prescient (later, too, on the recognition of Ukraine). As depicted, in a search for a proactive design and avoidance of missed opportunities, Cheney argued, "We are reacting. . . . The voluntary breakup of the Soviet Union is in our interest. If it's a voluntary association, it will happen. If democracy failed, we would be better off if they're small," meaning the fifteen independent countries.[6] Scowcroft publicly acknowledged his postscript about the Soviet Union's fall: "An event I had never imagined I would see in my lifetime had actually taken place."

Ukraine had already declared its independence at the time of the Madrid peace conference in October 1991, where pressure was exerted on Bush to preserve the Soviet Union for the sake of stability and for certain rules of the game. In reality, the rules of the game as set by Gorbachev had ironically been endorsed since the "Chicken Kiev" speech ("Freedom is not the same as independence"). After that speech, Bush wrote a letter to Gorbachev, stating, "The visit to Kiev was a good one, and I hope I did not inadvertently cause any problems. . . . Perhaps some Ukrainians were disappointed, because they wanted to hear a clarion call for 'independence now.'"[7] This disclosure in his 1999 memoir, *All the Best, George Bush: My Life in Letters and Other Writings*, amply shows his miscalculation of the response to his unforgettable address, not only by "some Ukrainians" but by people worldwide, including members of Congress.

Basking in the West's Gorby-mania, the ousted Russian leader was quick to take full advantage of an outrageous invitation to speak in

1992 in Fulton, Missouri, the site of Churchill's Iron Curtain speech in 1946. He emphasized our misunderstanding about the Cold War and our sharing with Stalin our responsibility for it. Yet, upon his ouster from leadership of the dying Soviet Union the previous December, he did creditably offer one wise piece of advice to Bush—"Watch out for Russia. They will zig and zag. It won't be all straightforward."[8] Gorbachev should know—in view of his zigzags on perestroika and the non-Russian problem that provided scarce ground for belief in his rules of the game.

Concerning US diplomatic recognition of Ukraine, here again, in contrast to White House and State Department opinions, Cheney urged an early recognition after Ukraine's referendum on December 1 overwhelmingly affirmed its August 24 declaration of independence. Formalistically, the recognition didn't come to pass until December 26, after the Soviet Union's formal dissolution and Gorbachev's resignation on December 25. Poland was the first to recognize Ukraine, Canada the second, Iraq the thirty-sixth, and we—the heirs of independence from empire—ranked thirty-seventh. This was hardly the way to win hearts and minds in a former captive nation. Our awakening on this score finally occurred in 2005.

Thirteen years later, President Bush revisited Kyiv, and in part, "Chicken Kiev," this time to students and faculty at the Taras Shevchenko National University. His address was thoroughly inspirational, constructive, and emblematic of his lifelong convictions as shown in his Captive Nations Week proclamations and speeches. But his attempt to erase the ill-worded stains of "suicidal nationalism" and "freedom is not the same as independence" by saying, "Had your leaders acted irresponsibly or precipitously . . . that could have prompted a crackdown from the Soviet Army" was feeble.

Just twenty-three days after the gaffe, Ukraine's leaders declared the nation's independence. Shrewdly planning for that moment of historic opportunity, Ukraine's leaders acted most responsibly as the Soviet economy decayed and the "Soviet Army," composed of over 40 percent non-Russians, was already in open disarray.

Again: Who won the Cold War? What was the prime cause of the Soviet Union's fall? Gorbachev, Yeltsin, and George H. W. Bush were on the same wavelength regarding the unity of the Soviet Union. The Russian leaders were completely cognizant of the geo-politico-strategic nature of Ukraine, as indeed were most of the Russian elite, while Bush was not. He even invoked "no interference in the internal affairs" of the Soviet Union, a charge the Kremlin unrelentingly made against Carter and Reagan.

This issue of Ukraine's strategic value goes as far back as the 1950s. For another anecdote, I'll never forget President Eisenhower's expression when in 1956 I had the privilege to present him with a "Memorandum on the Strategic Importance of Ukraine to the National Interest of the United States," which was subsequently published in the Congressional Record.[9] It was one of quizzical skepticism. Bush demonstrated the same blind spot when, preparing for the 1992 presidential election, he overlooked in his acceptance speech at the Republican National Convention in August the essential role toward Cold War victory played by the captive nations behind the Iron Curtain.

Meg Greenfield of the *Washington Post* singled this out in her column, "Who Gets Credit?" She noted "a 58-minute acceptance speech . . . without once even briefly mentioning the anguish and suffering and bravery of these people whose handiwork it truly was."[10] To be sure, the handiwork toward Cold War victory was broader in scope.

Other observers, aware of the president's stirring Captive Nations Week proclamation and address the previous month, seized upon the gap. This exposed George H. W. Bush to the criticism of "politicking." Whatever the judgment made of Bush's policy in the critical 1990–91 years, embracing a weak direction, poor preparation and advice, and insensitive language, a fair balancing of all factors certainly cannot obscure his long-term dedication to the liberation of all captive nations. Fortunately, the sweeping impact of the Reagan Doctrine under the banner of "evil empire" and the indomitable independence forces within the Soviet Union prevailed.

Looking east, the pattern of assessment on the Cold War was set by Gorbachev, who in January 1992 declared, "I do not regard the end of the Cold War as a victory for one side. The end of the Cold War is our common victory." This view—with its contradictory variations—was widely held despite the collapse of the Soviet Union. As for nebulous variations, the former longtime Soviet ambassador to the United States, Anatoly Dobrynin, wrote in his 1995 memoirs, "Nobody won the Cold War."[11]

Now looking to the West for examples, George Kennan and many others, regardless of their varying promises, concluded in the vein of his words, "No one won the Cold War."[12] Not surprisingly, the answer to the question was overwhelmingly the opposite—we and our allies won it. More specifically, Reagan (who confided to and surprised Richard Allen, later his first national security advisor) clearly expressed before assuming the presidency his premise on the Cold War: "We win and they lose."[13] Having pursued successfully this objective, Reagan would have been the first to refute the oft-repeated view that "Reagan won the Cold War without firing a shot."

As demonstrated by decisive vote margins in two presidential elections, the great communicator was fully aware of the bases of his support. Through his constant, direct appeals, he tapped one important base in congressional supporters of PL 86-90 and its centerpiece of empire, nationwide Captive Nations Week organizations, anti-communist groups, informed media columnists, and labor, as best represented by President George Meany of the AFL-CIO—all galvanized by his courageous and confident leadership. When thought through, the shot was not to be out of a gun, but rather out of the progression of a leading concept, the "evil empire." Reagan provided the vision, courage, leadership, and the will to win. The United States, with its democratic allies and others, unmistakably won the Cold War in the terms of global political warfare.

Yet, bearing in mind the essential distinctions, this Cold War victory is not the same as the Soviet Union's collapse. As in the cases of Nazi Germany and Imperial Japan at the end of World War II, which remained intact as national entities (in the case of Germany despite efforts by secretary of the Treasury Henry Morgenthau and others to dismember it), the Soviet Union, if it were a national organism, would also have remained intact at the end of Cold World War II. Also, just as ideological Nazism had been defeated, communism as such was defeated. Logically, our Cold War victory of course contributed immensely to a cosmic historical condition, but by itself cannot account for the fall of the Soviet Union. In 2005, the Russian Federation's authoritarian President Putin, pursuing his imperialist "near abroad" policy, viewed the fall not as a historic opportunity for independence and freedom, but rather "a major geopolitical disaster of the century."[14] A year later, Gorbachev agreed with him, saying, "Things certainly needed to change, but we did not need to destroy that which had been built by previous generations."[15]

Our victory has yet to be celebrated in the form of an International Victims of Communism project that would complete—along with the Korea and Vietnam war memorials—the Cold World War III story. Meanwhile, some individual memoirs, revisionist histories, and journalistic accounts will doubtlessly elide the basic distinctions. The cited Dobrynin example will continue in different forms. To publicize his book *In Confidence*, the former long-term Soviet ambassador to the United States appeared in October 1995 on CBS's *60 Minutes*. In answer to the above question, he answered, "No, we defeated ourselves."[16] This is comparable to saying that in the 2004 World Series, the Boston Red Sox didn't win, the St. Louis Cardinals defeated themselves.

The favored ambassador, who had enjoyed privileged access to secretaries of state Dean Rusk and Henry Kissinger, actually produced a book fraught with misinformation and skewed observations, such as Khrushchev venting simply "his emotions" against PL 86-90, the myth of Cuba as a Soviet proxy, the image of the "evil empire" being "straight from Hollywood," and so on.[17] Many of these notions have continued to circulate in the new century.

What really caused the Soviet Union's downfall? To answer "the independence of Ukraine" would undoubtedly precipitate in the minds of both the informed and the uninformed readers a profound skepticism. Yet with the "evil empire" challenge from the outside, a reasonable explanation resides in the cause of national independence and freedom, focused on Ukraine. Possessed with basic economic resources, with a long history of opposition to foreign Russian rule and colonialism, Ukraine in its status of geopolitical, strategic significance proved to be the prime agent in the Soviet Union's breakup after it declared its independence in 1991.

Similar to the pre–World War II period, the Soviet Union would have been intact without the independent Baltic nations; and with Ukraine in the Soviet Union, the other non-Russian nations would have been deprived of leverage to preserve their independence. But far more significantly from the viewpoint of political power, both Gorbachev and Yeltsin strove to the very end to preserve the unity represented by the Soviet Union. Later, the imperial drive for "unity" didn't subside, as typified by Yeltsin's Commonwealth of Independent States and his drawing the line on independence by Tatarstan and the Caucasian nations, in effect preserving the first layer of the evil empire (the Russian Soviet Federative Socialist Republic, or RSFSR), which Yeltsin emphasized to Gorbachev. Putin's "near abroad" policy and Single Economic Space, with Moscow the center, represented the same imperial impulse.

CHAPTER 14

# The Third Plateau
## *Remaining Captive Nations*

In light of current developments in both the liberated and defeated areas, the uppermost question is, "Will there be further progress toward a complete vindication of the law or a recession marked by lost gains?"

A significant chapter in this vein that escaped the attention of the majority analysts occurred in Congress in 1993. It involved President Yeltsin, the Russian embassy, both the House and Senate, President Clinton, the National Captive Nations Committee and its affiliated organizations, and a few empire-inclined Russian émigrés.

The chapter began with the Yeltsin-Clinton summit in Vancouver at the beginning of April. With the theme of seeking better US-Russian Federation relations, a deal referred to as a "partnership package" resulted from the ostensibly successful meeting. Clinton summarized it as such: "I agreed to a comprehensive review of all the Cold War statutes and other limitations on our relationships with Russia."[1] Cunningly, Yeltsin sought this package in meetings with Secretary of State Warren Christopher and others in the administration. Moreover, while the summit was in process, he was engaged in preparations for an armed assault against Chechnya, which commenced on April 6 and in open combat lasted for two years. Also, clinging to his Eurasian view, he directed his policy toward the PRC in a friendship alliance designed to counter America's superpower status.

A few days after the summit, a delegation from the Russian embassy hustled to Capitol Hill for a meeting with Rep. Lee Hamilton (D-IN), who chaired the Foreign Affairs Committee. It presented to him a list of Cold War statutes for elimination. As reported in some media and indicated by the chairman's reaction, PL 86-90 was on the list. Anticipating items such as the Jackson-Vanik trade restrictions, espionage, technology transfers, and so forth, the chairman was "puzzled" by all of this.[2] He may have been puzzled momentarily, but, as demonstrated by his forceful leadership on the issue later, he was keenly aware of the stratagem involved. Countering this maneuver, Clinton issued a Captive Nations Week proclamation that year.

By May 31, 1997, contrary to his original plan and personal assumptions, Yeltsin signed in Kyiv the Treaty of Friendship, Cooperation and Partnership between the Russian Federation and Ukraine.

Viewing this, we can reflect back on the defeated attempts by Kennan, Rusk, and others to eradicate the law—for different reasons, to be sure. On the positive side, recall that Ambassador Pamela Harriman, in her article in 1992 titled "Our Moscow Blinders," stressed that "we can understand the reactions of countries pillaged by Moscow for 75 years. We can create a foreign policy that sees issues whole, not from one point of view."[3] On the negative side, two years earlier, a half-truth article in the *Wall Street Journal* claimed, "Republicans repeatedly got Congress to pass resolutions establishing 'Captive Nations Week' commemorations set aside for Americans to pray for the liberation of people behind the Iron Curtain."[4]

The Russian delegation, receiving no support on the House side, then concentrated on the Senate, working well into the summer on the elimination of the law. Amid consultations and protests from the law's supporters, this effort failed to achieve its prime objective. However, an amendment submitted in July by Senator Claiborne Pell (D-RI), chairman of the Foreign Relations Committee, stopped short of repealing the law, but, in the interests of "bettering US-Russian relations" and obliterating "irritants to the Russian government," proposed "updating" the law.[5]

Pell's move on updating the law precipitated an avalanche of technical objections, consultations, and further protests. Minority views in the report warned, "The revision of Public Law 86-90 . . . should not be construed as an attempt to minimize the intense suffering of millions whose nations were invaded by communist Russia between 1920–1922 and later by the Soviet Union. . . . The minority would like to note that since its adoption in 1959 the Captive Nations law has been an effective vehicle in the struggle against Communism."[6]

Those pursuing the crafted emasculation route aimed to preserve the spirit but "update" the law by eliminating specifics, construed as "irritants" to the Russian government. A press release by the National Captive Nations Committee, titled "Rewriting History to Please Moscow," apparently struck home when, at the conclusion of this phenomenal chapter in November, Senator Pell commented on the accommodating Senate bill that its purpose "is not to rewrite history." Among other items, the release emphasized, "As to 'irritants,' any reference to Russian Communist imperialism, which led to the inauthentic Russian Soviet Federative Socialist Republic (RSFSR, predecessor of the present Russian Federation) and the USSR facades, is taboo. Briefly, this rewriting of history is like having sought better US-German relations by expunging any mention of the Holocaust and Nazi German imperialism." Also, by logical implication, the Soviet Union was no longer to be viewed as an "evil empire"—all in the torrent of extreme exuberance to form improved relations with the Russian Federation, a desirable end in itself, but necessarily based on realism.

Before Congress recessed till after Labor Day, two events occurred to transform the course of the process. First, soon after President Clinton had issued his Captive Nations Week proclamation on July 15, the executive branch soundly called for the full retention of PL 86-90—no repeal, no amendments. The proposal, classified as S. 1296 on the Senate side, pragmatically stipulated in its Finding and Affirmation that his action "should not be construed as being directed against Russia,

Ukraine, or the other independent states of the former Soviet Union, connoting an adversarial relationship between the United States or signifying or implying in any nuances unfriendliness toward such states."[7]

In the House in early August, the White House proposal was designated as H.R. 3000. By fall, the process moved rapidly on both sides, in part to meet the Clinton-Yeltsin Moscow summit deadline. The second important event was the farsighted, determined position expressed by Hamilton: "I believe that the US must move quickly to reshape a policy toward Ukraine that is better able to protect and promote US and Ukrainian 'interests.'"[8] His position was later decisive in the final outcome of this chapter and also well buttressed by analysts and commentators concerned with Yeltsin's "near abroad" policy. A year before, columnists Rowland Evans and Robert Novak had raised the question "A New Russian Empire?" citing Moscow's actions in Tajikistan, Azerbaijan, and the Baltic states, and advising "pressure should show whose side Washington is on in the need to speed troops withdrawals, and coercion against other republics, and create true democracy."[9]

During this period of Congress's treatment of PL 86-90, the scholar John Lenczowski wrote a piece titled, "Prospects for a New Russian Imperialism and Implications for the United States," about Russia's "challenge of conducting relations with 14 new countries on its borders whose independence many Russians view as illegitimate."[10] In the media, analysts spotlighted Russian military operations in Azerbaijan to replace democratically elected President Abulfaz Elcibey and warned that similar events could occur elsewhere in the former Soviet Union.

The prominent politico-military analyst William Odom described Yeltsin's increasing dependence on the military, the doctrine of "peacekeeping" in the "near abroad," and expanding military expenditures, including high pay for over 150,000 "contract" soldiers to serve in "dangerous places," adding, "In a word, a new Russian empire is in the making."[11] Another penetrating op-ed, "The Russian Empire Strikes Back," written by John Hannah (*New York Times*, October 27, 1993) cogently summarized the situation: "Mr. Yeltsin has sought to safeguard Russia's relations with the West by more subtle muscle-flexing. Economic blackmail and rogue army units have been his weapons to coerce the former republics into the Moscow-dominated Commonwealth of Independent States." He concluded, "With Ukraine's re-subjugation, Russia—Yeltsin's democratic Russia—will have gone far toward reconstituting its old empire."

When Congress resumed sessions after Labor Day, the process was accelerated, both to resolve the PL 86-90 issue and to equip the president for his Moscow summit. This finalized the first surprise, but also gave birth to the second one, namely a memorial to the Victims of Communism.

In the House, the Foreign Affairs Committee reported favorably in October on H.R. 3000, following a lively debate led by Representative Rohrabacher of California. Defending PL 86-90, the congressman pinpointed the issue in this vein: "We will support the long-term hope for democracy in the former Soviet Union by maintaining our policies against tyranny and aggression and standing firm in our defense of freedom and self-determination."[12] In addition, he raised the memorial bill, Joint Resolution 237, arguing for its inclusion in H.R. 3000. By mid-November, Chairman Hamilton presented the latter for a vote in the House, citing the support of its leaders, Rep. Richard Gephardt (D-MO) and Robert Michael (R-IL), to which could be added such longtime supporters of PL 86-90 as representatives Gerald Solomon, John Dingell (D-MI), and numerous others. In his remarks, Hamilton assured Rohrabacher of his support of the law and significantly underscored his additional support of JR 237, the memorial bill. As he put it, "I also will support this provision should it come back as an amendment to this bill from the other body."[13]

Finally, a week later, this extraordinary, post–Cold War chapter ended with the Senate passing, in essence, H.R. 3000. Chairman Pell introduced its parallel measure, S. 1672, commenting, "The purpose of this bill is not to rewrite history, but to amend or repeal laws that impede our relations with Russia, Ukraine, and the other countries of the former Soviet Union."[14] He added, "When the president travels to

Moscow in January, he will be able to tell President Yeltsin that our
laws are up to date."

Apparently encouraged by the initiatives taken in the House, Senate leaders George Mitchell (D-ME) and Robert Dole (R-KS), who
were long-term PL 86-90 supporters, played a fundamental role in
guiding the administration proposal (no repeal, no amendments).
They also proceeded to incorporate in the final Friendship Act an
amendment authorizing the National Captive Nations Committee to
take steps toward the foundation of an international memorial honoring the victims of communism, as provided in H.J.R. 237—the second positive surprise.[15] Sen. Jesse Helms (R-NC), who was primarily
responsible for the memorial amendment, accurately commented, "I
am pleased to note that the administration is not opposed to the memorial and that Congressman Hamilton has stated for the record
that he expects the other body to accept this addition."

Thus we see the net results of this unique chapter in the early post–
Cold War period: PL 86-90 kept in its entirety; Yeltsin's policy exposed, suggesting his fear of the law; and the authorization for the
international memorial, which President Clinton approved on December 17, 1993, and enacted into Public Law 103-99.[16] The president's
early stand on PL 86-90 was obviously quintessential in determining
the proper course for Congress on the Yeltsin stratagem. On the
whole, his Captive Nations Week proclamations, both gubernatorial
and presidential, conformed well with the law—not comparable to
the Reagan proclamations, but definitely above those before.

Clinton's July 15, 1993, proclamation enunciated the point: "As
America declared its independence, our country provided inspiration
for all those who did not enjoy the rights that we hold to be self-
evident, we cannot abandon those we have encouraged." Clearly, it
would have been a manifest contradiction to have satisfied Yeltsin's
scheme. Indeed, Clinton's July 10, 1992, proclamation as governor of
Arkansas included the captive nations in "North Caucasia," "Idel-
Ural," "Mainland China," etc., revealing at least his basic instincts on
the scope of the issue.[17] Contrary to criticism of Clinton's limitations

on foreign policy, a further read of his 1992 article on "A New Covenant for American Security," published in the *Harvard International Review* and reproduced elsewhere, would show his grasp of the promotion of global democracy as "vital to our national interests"; the need to "work closely with the newly independent Ukraine, as well as the former Soviet Union republics who pursue democratic reforms"; and his advocacies for the creation of Radio Free Asia and leadership in politico-economic globalization.[18]

All of this, however, is not to imply that Clinton was beyond serious flaws in policies and impromptu political observations. For example, at the Group of Eight summit in Moscow in April 1996, he falsely compared the drive for independence by Chechen freedom fighters to our Civil War, painting it as an internal Russian matter and Yeltsin as a Lincoln. This wasn't the first time the fantastic comparison arose. State Department spokesman Mike McCurry in 1995 made the same comparison in his briefing to reporters on US-Russian Federation relations, explaining, "We have to, you know, look at the full scope of issues that define [the relationship]."[19]

• • •

In the current climb to the third plateau, the vision of freedom and democracy presents the prospect of another historic opportunity for global democratization in a world driven by irresistible economics, connections, and technology. That the United States possesses the necessary assets of moral, politico-economic, and military power to achieve much of this process goes without saying. The predeterminants for the maximum capitalization of these assets are strong, prudent leadership and societal understanding and will in a real evolving context of its Manifest Destiny.

On the scale of comparative power, the greatest danger to our national security resides in the PRC and the Russian Federation, the remaining empires containing numerous captive nations that have to cope with both communist party authoritarian rule and foreign domination.

A thriving awareness of the two-ring composition of the former Soviet Union must be maintained. The first ring—the RSFSR—comprised
what is now the Russian Federation; the second ring included the
now independent non-Russian republics. Moscow's leaders from
Lenin on saw the necessity for maintaining the two rings if the inner
empire were to undertake its world mission, not to mention the indis-
pensability of strategic Ukraine. Within the existing first ring, both
Yeltsin and Putin have demonstrated their policy in Chechnya and
other Caucasian nations, as well as controlling from "the center" nationalist deviations in Tatarstan and others in the Idel-Ural region;
Sakha-Yakutia in Siberia; and in the far east the former Far Eastern
Republic. Both have stridently pursued through several instruments
their "near abroad" policy, a neo-imperialist attempt to undermine
the independence of the non-Russian republics and expand the power
of the center.

Catapulted into power by Yeltsin on December 31, 1999, Putin as
acting president lost no time to travel to Chechnya. In his address to
Russian troops there, he emphasized, "This is not simply about restoring home and dignity to the country. This is about how to bring
about the end of the breakup of Russia. That is your fundamental
goal."[20] This longstanding policy statement raised the pertinent question: Was the independence of the non-Russian republics an act of
"the breakup of Russia"?

Five years later, soon after his humiliating political defeat in
Ukraine's Orange Revolution, Putin, who already had opined that
the fall of the Soviet Union was a national tragedy, had also restored
a number of Soviet Russian symbols in the Russian Federation's
political and social fabric and had exploited the old Soviet nonsense
of "noninterference in internal affairs." Extending this medley of
thoughts and actions to impress his audience, he asserted in a staged
session with invited foreigners: "We are not going back to a Russian
empire. Only an idiot could imagine we are striving toward that. It is
not possible, and Russia has no interest in having the whole world
against us." As the acclaimed manager of what he has dubbed a

"managed democracy" under a coterie of former KGB operative colleagues and Unity party loyalists, he has employed authoritarian
methods to solve the Russian Federation's mammoth socioeconomic
problems. To many careful analysts, his oft-quoted favorable poll rat-
ing of 70 percent, ominous in itself, is in part a measure of the citizens' impotence in a controlled society.

Putin's rhetorical and tactical zigzags have consistently reflected one
of the most basic trends in the period. Except for stubborn Chechnya
and adjoining Caucasian nations, Putin has sought to control the now
independent former republics of the Soviet Union—not by imperial
conquest but with a "sphere of influence," with Moscow at the center.
With abundant resources in the Russian Federation, the Russian president has earned the title Energy Tsar because of the state's increasing
control of energy enterprises. Oil and natural gas have served as an
essential means of leverage as concerns the non-Russian republics.

As for the other remaining empire, the large Chinese nation on the
mainland is bordered by millions in non-Han nations, such as East
Turkestan, Tibet, and Inner Mongolia, with a long history of resisting
Sinicization, a process similar to Moscow's Russification programs.
The Chinese Communist Party has intensified the eradication of all
nationalist opposition, which often runs afoul of Chinese Muslims
with different preferences.

In the 2007 Eurasian landscape, the peoples' war for independence
had been won by the Baltic nations, Ukraine, Georgia, Armenia,
and others, but imperialist pressures by Moscow have persisted.
Democratic unrest in Azerbaijan punctuated the adoption of orange
as the color of the democratic opposition to authoritarian rule. In
Russia proper, fear of a street revolution, a genuine democratic Red
Revolution—unlike the coup d'etat in October 1917—found some
expression.

Problems facing the "Stans" in Central Asia expanded further as
the Shanghai Cooperation Organization revealed its true nature. The
Shanghai Cooperation Organization, made up of the PRC, Russian
Federation, Kazakhstan, Uzbekistan, Tajikistan, and Kyrgyzstan, was

originally established to fight Islamist terrorism. By July 2005, a new objective, engineered by the two empires, called for the withdrawal of foreign forces (US bases) from the Stans in view of the decline of active fighting in Afghanistan, adding pointedly that the presence of such forces destabilizes Central Asia. Clearly, the two empires are fearful of the spread of universal values in the region. A few months later, Moscow and Beijing engaged in a formidable military exercise dubbed as a peace mission. The question that emerged at the time was whether circumstances and attitudes would overcome the deeply rooted cultural attitudes of the 1960s, when Russia was viewed as the "northern barbarian" and China as the "yellow peril."

In the climb to the third plateau, these points serve as a working outline of the captive nations orientation. As for current blinders that obscure realities, the habit of equating the Russian Federation with Russia and the PRC with China is similar to the long past one of Soviet Union = Russia. Perhaps most intriguing in Moscow's imperial effort to maintain the first ring and create its sphere of influence while regaining a creditable world power status is its relationship with Beijing. It could portend a long-run threat to the democratic world, but under present conditions it demands no more than close attention.

Back in the mid-sixties, a well-informed Turkestani activist met me in my Georgetown University office to seek American assistance in the heated rivalry between Beijing's campaign for the independence of western Turkestan and Moscow's drive for the independence of eastern Turkestan. Recalling former OSS leader Donovan's visitations in his Sutton Place apartment by Chinese Muslims dealing with the area in the early 1950s, I explained the impracticality of my visitor's message under political conditions then. But I advised him, somewhat to his satisfaction, that he convey to his sponsor their need for worldwide media preparedness once the conditions emerge, as indeed they did with the Soviet Union's downfall. Beijing won in the rivalry, while Moscow lost.

The importance of revamping the relationship between the Russian and Chinese empires was recognized by Gorbachev when he appeared in Beijing in 1989 and witnessed the turmoil that eventually led to Beijing's deadly crushing of student protest in Tiananmen Square. It was President Yeltsin who, after the Soviet Union's collapse, forged a friendship to counter the unipolar status of the United States by stressing the desirability of world multipolarity. Following suit, Putin, Yeltsin's protégé, furthered this trend by signing the Sino-Russian friendship and cooperation treaty in 2001. This then led to the formation of the Shanghai Five, later renamed the Shanghai Cooperation Organization, of the empires and four independent Central Asian states. Under the guise of antiterrorism, control of Islamic fundamentalism, antiseparatism, Central Asian stability, and anti-US missile defense systems generally and in Asia, the SCO has led to mutual deals between Beijing and Moscow, such as Chinese support of Moscow's operation in Chechnya and Russian support of Beijing's stand on Taiwan.

By 2005, the Shanghai Cooperation Organization openly expressed its dominant interest in excluding the United States and its democratizing influence in Central Asia. On July 6, it demanded a withdrawal timetable from the United States of its military bases in the region in view of the decline in active fighting in Afghanistan. To expedite the process, the Russian Federation in October finessed an offer to Afghanistan involving the sale of helicopters and equipment for $30 million. Two months earlier, August 18–25, in what was deemed by many in the West as an extended charade, the two imperial powers staged Peace Mission 2005, a military exercise which displayed formidable Russian weapons for China's military modernization and also for Russian income. Aside from the long-term thought of a combined nuclear threat resulting from the actual modernization of both powers, there exists—considering the huge internal politico-economic problems confronting each power—the lingering thought of whether the two will slip back into the respective attitudes exchanged in the 1960s and 1970s about "the yellow peril" and "the northern barbarian."

As for mainland China, the connection with PL 86-90 has on record been quite extensive since the early 1960s. The law has specifically included the captive nations of mainland China, Tibet, East

Turkestan, and others; and the independent Republic of China on
Taiwan had for decades annually commemorated Captive Nations
Week through broadcasts to the mainland. In many respects the story
of the PRC is unlike that of the Soviet Union and the Russian Federation. Apart from its immense population and internal political, economic, and social problems, it has in subtle and judicious ways made
rapid international strides, including attracting US and foreign investments and joining the World Trade Organization. Following the course
of development set by Deng Xiaoping, the PRC has overshadowed the
Russian Federation under Putin. In both domains, the human rights
record has remained dismal, although totalitarian restraints in the PRC
are a far cry from the Maoist years that had accounted for the most
victims of communism. In the Putin period, authoritarian curbs are
also far removed from the days of Lenin and Stalin. However, the cen-
tralization of power in Moscow is in the Chinese direction.

Moscow's near-abroad tactics have not ceased. Some of them were
discussed in May 2005 on the occasion of the sixtieth anniversary
of the end of World War II, held in Moscow and attended by President George W. Bush, Latvian President Vaira Vike-Feiborga, and over
fifty additional world leaders. The issues covered the Soviet Union's
occupation of the Baltic states; the Russian Army crimes of rapes, loot-
ing, and killings, and later the additional massive deportation of Balts
to the Soviet Union; and the current near-abroad tactic of demanding
special rights for Russians in the independent non-Russian states.

President Putin, who had viewed the collapse of the Soviet Union
as the greatest geopolitical catastrophe of the century, refused to re-
nounce the secret 1939 Molotov-Ribbentrop pact that sealed the
Baltic occupation. He cited the already done 1989 Soviet Union parliament renunciation (incidentally that of another state, not the
Russian Federation), thereby indicating the Russian myth of having
been invited to occupy the Baltic republics. Instead of highlighting
the occasion with honest reconciliation and admission of the crimes
committed by the former Soviet Union as Germany had for its crimes,
the wily Putin displayed his KGB bent in his determination to keep

the near-abroad policy intact. In a more proactive mode, President George W. Bush, whose faith in the Russian soul was apparently already on the wane, visited Latvia and Georgia, where a democratic color revolution had occurred, carrying the spirit of his message given at the anniversary: "Yet this attempt to sacrifice freedom for the sake of stability left a continent divided and unstable. The captivity of millions in Central and Eastern Europe will be remembered as one of the greatest wrongs of history."

Continuing this second segment of the former captive nations story, the picture is complicated by the numerous forces and factors at work in the independent non-Russian states. Most important for an overview of this second segment is that the entire area is in the throes of a non-Russian Revolution III. The preceding struggles in 1917 and 1991 were for independence and national sovereignty; the one since has been for democracy and freedom to develop internally without external neo-imperialist pressures and a new brand of captivity. The crux of the matter lies primarily in the near-abroad policy waged as a fundamental part of the Putin doctrine. Its first goal has been the full realization of the Commonwealth of Independent States (CIS), with Moscow as its perennial center. Its goal is to institutionally counter the European Union and NATO. The process would include the strengthening of Putin's authoritarian political position in the Russian Federation, the further reduction of any serious liberal, democratic opposition, the presentation of the restored Russian power in the world, and—most essentially—maintenance of the first ring, namely the Russian Federation with its captives and the near abroad (the former second ring) serving as a convenient buffer for any number of operational purposes.

Turning to Ukraine, the outbreak of the Orange Revolution in November 2004 furnished more than ample evidence of this march. Publicized worldwide, the spectacular event in Kyiv's Independence Square, the *Maidan Nezalezhnosti*, crystallized the moral and material support the determined and chiefly young protesters were raising from the populace at large. So impressive were the effects that adoption of the color orange by democratic reformers ranged from Azerbaijan and Egypt to Taiwan.

Following are some of the background events and persons that played important roles in recent history, particularly involving Ukraine and Russia. The Russian Duma in 1996 annulled the Commonwealth of Independent States agreements that had dissolved the Soviet Union. In 1997 Yeltsin and Ukraine's President Kuchma signed in Kyiv the Treaty of Friendship, Cooperation and Partnership respecting territorial integrity and sovereign equality. Ukraine was one of the first to join NATO's Partnership for Peace program, to shed ahead of schedule its nuclear arsenal, and to sign the Nuclear Non-Proliferation Treaty. In response to the International Monetary Fund, Ukraine embarked on delayed economic reforms to warrant Western aid. In Russia, despite widespread poverty, declines in social services, a breed of business oligarchs, corrupt government, and so on, Putin pushed his campaign for a Common Economic Space agreement (Russian Federation, Belarus, Ukraine, and Kazakhstan) leading to a customs union and a bloc countering the EU. By January 29, 2003, Putin designated the weak Kuchma as head of the Commonwealth of Independent States. Kuchma had been implicated in the murder of the journalist Georgiy Gongadze, while his proconsul and former Russian Federation prime minister, Ambassador Viktor Chernomyrdin, publicly propagandizes the CIS as against the EU for Ukraine and cynically quipped to the citizen demand for the Russian Federation's apology for Stalin's crime of genocide by famine: "Ask Georgia, since Stalin was Georgian."

Putin intervened personally in Ukraine's 2004 presidential election. He became heavily involved, meeting with Kuchma monthly, spending energy money estimated in excess of the $300 million spent in the Belarus president-for-life referendum, and openly backing Viktor Yanukovych, who campaigned, among other things, for the inclusion of Russian as the second official language. The falsification of election results was widespread, Ukraine's Supreme Court intervened, and the liberal democrat Viktor Yushchenko won.

An ardent advocate for a free market economy, the rule of law, societal reforms, and integration with Western Europe and sound relations with the Russian Federation, the young president, who was poisoned during the political scrimmage, quickly reformed his cabinet of participants in the revolution harboring conflicting views on privatization and the role of government in the economy. Just as quickly in a program for expanded trade and investments in Ukraine, he staked out his goals of obtaining a release from outdated obstacles in the Jackson-Vanik amendment to ensure normal trade relations with the United States, admission to the World Trade Organization, and the attraction of secure foreign investments in Ukraine, as typified under his tenure by the $4.8 billion investment by Mittal Steel, the world's largest steel producer. Fiscal problems were weighty, but an economy that entered the new century with a GDP over $200 billion and a growth rate averaging 8.4 percent by mid-decade (in 2004 alone at 12 percent) showed promise.

American policy, which is of pivotal importance in the arena, deserves comment. During the 1990s, President Clinton was the first to visit independent Ukraine (the stopover by President Nixon was to a captive nation). The Clinton administration responded warmly to the strategic importance of Ukraine, both diplomatically and economically, but as disclosures of corruption and governmental misgovernance mounted under the Kuchma regime, including a poor human rights record, the drive for productive partnership in the administration and in Congress deflated. With the George W. Bush administration in the first term and also with Congress, the condition of US-Ukraine relations didn't improve. In his second term, Bush praised Kuchma for sending troops to Iraq, but the issue of freedom and democracy in Ukraine was not openly mentioned. The Orange Revolution, however, changed the situation by 180 degrees as the president and Congress welcomed President Yushchenko on the level of "strategic partnership."

Moving on to the Caucasian region and southwest Asia (which PL 86-90 pointed to long before the area became of general analytic interest), it is important to bear in mind the Russian arsenal of levers and tactics and also the independent non-Russian resistance to their employment. You can add to Moscow's arsenal of oil and natural gas dependency its promotion of internal division, military bases, ambassadorial proconsuls, support for fraudulent electors, pretentious peacekeeping operations, and border and visa restrictions in this drive for a neo-imperialist sphere of influence. The bottom line of non-Russian resistance has been the preservation of independence and the freedom to develop internally despite clouds of corrupt governance, party strife, and superficial democratic institutions. Crucial to the evaporation of these clouds is the broadening and intensification of international relations on the part of these non-Russian nations, entailing nongovernmental organizations and the Organization for Security and Cooperation in Europe. No democratic tradition characterizes any of these nations. The sobering thought of how long it took Western nations to solidify democratic institutions deserves consideration.

The "Stans" in Central Asia represent a substantial Eurasian area of what the renowned geopolitical analyst Halford Mackinder somewhat prematurely defined as the World's Heartland over a century ago. From many viewpoints it has become so today. In our Captive Nations List, Turkestan, the "land of Turks," is used because of its centuries-long designation, depicting the eastern part under Chinese domination in the eighteenth century and the western part with the Russian conquest in the nineteenth century. The Soviet Union proceeded quickly in 1924 to bring an end to Turkestan, though not in its military maps, by dividing the area into the five "Stans" embracing Kazakhstan, Kyrgyzstan, Uzbekistan, Tajikistan, and Turkmenistan, which later Khrushchev narrowly exploited as "the virgin lands" for cotton production.

In our time, the dream of a grand Turkestan as a Central Asian state hasn't evaporated entirely. All of the republics, geographically the largest in size of the independent non-Russian ones, are seeking politico-economic links with the West, India, Pakistan, Iran, and others. Generally, varying degrees of authoritarian rule, rampant corruption, retention of power, extensive poverty, KGB-style repression of opposition during elections, and other blights of the past persist behind appearances of democracy. Yet these require necessary qualifications in terms of the perspective in security, stability, democracy, and energy where democratic institutions had been unknown for centuries.

The situation in the strategic area of Central Asia is not fundamentally oil and gas—the actual means and weapons—but rather one of political warfare between former captive nations striving to preserve their independence and varying freedoms and the two encroaching remaining empires: the Russian Federation and the PRC.

As to the remaining captive nations under communist party rule—those in North Korea, the PRC, Laos, Vietnam, and Cuba—US policies must adjust to them. Trends in Vietnam, Laos, and the PRC justify in varying degrees liberal adjustments. The North Korean ones, centered on the nuclear threat, also lend themselves to policy change in the event of nuclear disarmament. As for Cuba, the longstanding dictator, Fidel Castro, facing death might still have sparks of spiritual depth as revealed in his letters while imprisoned back in 1953. In any case, different conditions from those of the Cold War, the adjustments made toward other captive nations, and a careful monitoring of ours with Cuba should be enough to convince one of allowing at this time free travel to the country. The adjustment benefits would be a concourse of people, exchange of ideas, including democratization, humanitarian advantages to deprived Cuban families, and a guaranteed encouragement to the economy's entrepreneurial areas, all with transparency and accountability.

• • •

It should be obvious now why the president and Congress avoided being hoodwinked by Yeltsin's scheme for getting rid of PL 86-90. For this post–Cold War period, and well into the future, the law will stand firm and accommodating in its solid framework for our understanding and forming rational, timely policies in the huge complex of globalized issues and tragedies.

# Epilogue

*David B. Rivkin*

Lev Dobriansky died in 2008 at the age of 89, leaving behind this manuscript, written out in longhand on legal size paper. His daughter, Paula Dobriansky, and her colleague, Pratik Chougule, set out to turn this first, incomplete draft into a finished book.

Lev Dobriansky was born in New York City in 1918 and thus his life was contemporaneous with that of the Soviet Union. Son of Ukrainian immigrants, he was a staunch anticommunist who believed that the Soviet Communist Party–controlled state was inherently both internally repressive and internationally expansionist. He was also always deeply skeptical that the Soviet Communist Party would ever moderate its behavior through diplomatic, security, and trade dialogue, rejecting the ever-popular theory of Soviet convergence with the West.

However, while fully acknowledging the malign influence of Soviet-style communist ideology, Dobriansky argued throughout his entire career that there were other, more long-standing policy drivers of Moscow's repressive and aggressive behavior. With this in mind, Dobriansky's most important academic and public policy contribution was his thesis that the key enduring theme of Russian history, religion, and political culture was its overarching imperial drive—the perennial desire to absorb neighboring countries and build the largest land empire in the world. Russia's oft-proclaimed specious assertions that it was the Third Rome and that Russian Orthodoxy was the only true version of the Christian faith added an additional messianic component to its empire building. This imperial drive remained unaltered during the Soviet period.

Dobriansky has also consistently maintained that, for a variety of geopolitical, economic, and cultural reasons, Ukraine loomed particularly large within the context of Russia's empire building. His thesis concerning the importance of the peculiarly nationalistic nature of Russian imperialism was criticized by some Western scholars who preferred alternative explanations for Soviet domestic and international conduct. Dobriansky's view of the importance of Ukraine was well captured in his favorite saying: "Russia minus Ukraine equals zero."

Accordingly, Dobriansky became a tireless public champion for what he called the "captive nations"—Ukraine and other countries and ethnic groups that had fallen prey to the pre-1917 tsarist empire and, following the Russian Revolution and a brief period of independence, experienced the same fate in the new version of Moscow's empire. Living and teaching in Washington, DC, he was a witness and key participant in many of the most important events in twentieth-century American political history.

Aside from his scholarly writings on the subject, Lev Dobriansky was the indispensable drafter and the intellectual and political force—from his perch as the head of the largest Ukrainian organization in the United States, the Ukrainian Congress Committee of America—behind Public Law 86-90, the Captive Nations Week resolution. Every president, Republican and Democrat, from Dwight D. Eisenhower on, has issued a proclamation during the third week of July.

The resolution reaffirmed the captive status of numerous ethnic groups and nationalities that were forcibly incorporated into the Soviet Union, acknowledged their desire for independence, and robustly rearticulated US support for such independence. Appreciating the resolution's analytical vigor and symbolic importance, Moscow has regularly attacked it as the worst example of American Cold War diplomacy.

We are grateful that Dobriansky lived to see the collapse of the Soviet Union in 1991, an event he had worked toward relentlessly for most of his adult life. Indeed, it is rare for anyone who was both an academic and policy practitioner to see firsthand such a complete vindication of his work. Even then, he kept writing down his impressions of the drastic changes that occurred in that part of the world until he died in 2008. He knew that, despite the end of the old USSR, there would still be "captive nations" around the globe, places where citizens lacked freedom and opportunities for democratic self-governance.

Indeed, the author's experiences in the twentieth century provide valuable background to current conflicts. Viewing the events from 1991 until his death, he paid particular attention to the eagerness of the non-Russian republics to gain their independence and the surprise and anger that elicited in Moscow; the Yeltsin-Gorbachev contest; widespread demonstrations in the non-Russian republics; frantic efforts in Moscow to hold the empire together; equally frantic efforts among Western governments and intelligence agencies to adjust to the rapid changes; the debate over "who won the Cold War"; Vladimir Putin's authoritarian role in the government of the Russian Federation; Boris Yeltsin's decision to invade Chechnya; debate in Congress over whether to maintain, update, or repeal PL 86-90; Russia's relations with China; and political developments in several formerly "captive" nations.

This book would have been primarily a memoir except for a tragic and historic twist that fully validated Dobriansky's thesis about the indispensable role of Ukraine within the context of Moscow's imperial drive: Russia's annexation of Crimea in 2014, its support of separatist militias in Ukraine's Donbas region, and finally Russia's full-scale invasion of Ukraine on February 24, 2022. These actions have been buttressed by Putin's robust articulation of the Russian imperial drive, allegedly driven by the imperative to regather all of the former constituent parts of the Russian and Soviet empires.

With that in mind, Dobriansky's insights into the Russian attitude toward Ukraine and other nations that were previously part of the USSR have become particularly prescient and have gained additional significance for American decision makers. This book has become a valuable guide for American citizens and policymakers who are facing Putin's efforts to rebuild Russia's imperial edifice through blatant aggression.

Lev Dobriansky has passed on, but PL 86-90, his signature accomplishment in a life spent fighting totalitarianism, lives on. This book serves as a monument to his foresight, perseverance, and desire for democracy and freedom for all people.

# Postscript

*Pratik Chougule*

Lev Dobriansky passed away in January 2008 before he was able
to complete this book. As seen in the concluding chapter, he was
researching how the captive nations had developed since the collapse
of the Soviet Union. He was also formulating insights on how US
policy could help the people of these countries realize their aspirations for national self-determination, democracy, and human rights.

Captive Nations Week observances continue across the country
every third week of July. Since the law's enactment, every president
since Eisenhower has commemorated Captive Nations Week by issuing a proclamation. Members of Congress have routinely submitted
statements for the Congressional Record. Governors, state legisla-
tures, and mayors across the country have issued proclamations. And
references to the captive nations have appeared during various presidential election cycles in the party platforms of both major political
parties.

Lev Dobriansky's central recommendation to policymakers was to
preserve PL 86-90. Far from being a Cold War–era relic, or simply an
occasion for annual remembrance, he viewed the law as a framework
for how the United States could advance its own interests by supporting the captive nations' pursuit of national sovereignty and liberal
democracy. As evidence, he pointed to the zeal with which activists at

the front lines of Russian and Chinese aggression have persisted in marking Captive Nations Week well after the Cold War's end. Taiwan's leadership, as an example, continues to mark the occasion every year.

Numerous institutions continue to advance Lev Dobriansky's legacy. Papers related to his work on the captive nations can be found in the archives of the Hoover Institution at Stanford University, Georgetown University, the National Captive Nations Committee Collection at Syracuse University, and the Ronald Reagan Presidential Library. The full, unedited version of this manuscript is available in the Hoover Institution's Ukraine Collections. The Victims of Communism Memorial Foundation, which Lev Dobriansky cofounded and chaired, deserves special mention for its leadership every year in hosting a Captive Nations Week summit and issuing a State of the Captive Nations report. The Ukrainian Congress Committee of America continues to publish *The Ukrainian Quarterly*, where he served as an editor. The UCCA is a founding member of the Ukrainian World Congress, which helps the global Ukrainian diaspora mark Captive Nations Week. The Fund for American Studies, which hosts an annual lecture on political economy in Lev Dobriansky's honor, plans to convene events related to this book.

# Captive Nations Week

## Public Law 86-90; 73 STAT. 212
## [S. J. Res. 111]

Joint Resolution providing for the designation of the third week of July as "Captive Nations Week."

Whereas the greatness of the United States is in large part attributable to its having been able, through the democratic process, to achieve a harmonious national unity of its people, even though they stem from the most diverse of racial, religious, and ethnic backgrounds; and

Whereas this harmonious unification of the diverse elements of our free society has led the people of the United States to possess a warm understanding and sympathy for the aspirations of peoples everywhere and to recognize the natural interdependency of the peoples and nations of the world; and

Whereas the enslavement of a substantial part of the world's population by Communist imperialism makes a mockery of the idea of peaceful coexistence between nations and constitutes a detriment to the natural bonds of understanding between the people of the United States and other peoples; and

Whereas since 1918 the imperialistic and aggressive policies of Russian communism have resulted in the creation of a vast

empire which poses a dire threat to the security of the United
States and of all the free peoples of the world; and

**Whereas the imperialistic policies of Communist Russia have led,
through direct and indirect aggression, to the subjugation of the
national independence of Poland, Hungary, Lithuania, Ukraine,
Czechoslovakia, Latvia, Estonia, White Ruthenia, Rumania,
East Germany, Bulgaria, Mainland China, Armenia, Azerbaijan,
Georgia, North Korea, Albania, Idel-Ural, Tibet, Cossackia,
Turkestan, North Vietnam, and others** [emphasis added]; and

Whereas these submerged nations look to the United States as the
citadel of human freedom for leadership in bringing about their
liberation and independence and in restoring to them the enjoy-
ment of their Christian, Jewish, Moslem, Buddhist, or other
religious freedoms, and of their individual liberties; and

Whereas it is vital to the national security of the United States that
the desire for liberty and independence on the part of the peoples
of these conquered nations should be steadfastly kept alive; and

Whereas the desire for liberty and independence by the overwhelming majority of the people of these submerged nations constitutes
a powerful deterrent to war and one of the best hopes for a just
and lasting peace; and

Whereas it is fitting that we clearly manifest to such peoples
through an appropriate and official means the historic fact that
the people of the United States share with them their aspirations
for the recovery of their freedom and independence: Now,
therefore, be it

*Resolved by the Senate and House of Representatives of the United
States of America in Congress assembled, That*

The President of the United States is authorized and requested to
issue a proclamation designating the third week of July 1959 as

"Captive Nations Week" and inviting the people of the United States to observe such week with appropriate ceremonies and activities. The President is further authorized and requested to issue a similar proclamation each year until such time as freedom and independence shall have been achieved for all the captive nations of the world.

Approved July 17, 1959, by President Dwight D. Eisenhower.

# Captive Nations List 1980

The original list of captive nations can be found in PL 86-90, which is included in Appendix A.

The last time the Captive Nations List was updated was in 1980. The table below includes all the captive nations recognized by the National Captive Nations Committee and the year when they became captive.

**Captive Nations List (CNL)**

| Year of Communist domination | Country (people) |
| --- | --- |
| 1920 | Armenia* |
| | Azerbaijan* |
| | Byelorussia* |
| | Cossackia* |
| | Georgia* |
| | Idel-Ural (Tatarstan et al.)* |
| | North Caucasia (Chechnya et al.) |
| | Ukraine |
| 1922 | Far Eastern Republic |
| | Turkestan (not East T.) |
| 1924 | Mongolia (not Inner) |

Note: An asterisk (*) denotes captive non-Russian nations in USSR.

(*continued*)

**Captive Nations List (CNL)** *(continued)*

| Year of Communist domination | Country (people) |
|---|---|
| 1940 | Estonia*<br>Latvia*<br>Lithuania |
| 1946 | Albania<br>Bulgaria<br>"Yugoslavia" (Serbs, Croats, Slovenians, etc.) |
| 1947 | Poland<br>Romania |
| 1948 | Czechoslovakia (Czechs, Slovaks)<br>North Korea |
| 1949 | East Germany<br>Hungary<br>Mainland China |
| 1951 | Tibet |
| 1954 | North Vietnam |
| 1960 | Cuba |
| 1964 | South Yemen |
| 1975 | Angola<br>Cambodia<br>Laos<br>Mozambique<br>South Vietnam |
| 1977 | Ethiopia |
| 1978 | Afghanistan |
| 1979 | Nicaragua |

Note: An asterisk (*) denotes captive non-Russian nations in USSR.

# Notes

### Introduction

1. Lev E. Dobriansky, *U.S.A. and the Soviet Myth* (Old Greenwich, CT: Devin-Adair Company, 1971), 14.

### Chapter 1: Captive Nations, Then and Now

1. Nikita Krushchev, "On Peaceful Coexistence," *Foreign Affairs* 38, no. 1 (October 1959): 1–18.

2. Mikhail Gorbachev, *Perestroika: New Thinking for Our Country and the World* (New York: HarperCollins, 1987).

### Chapter 2: The First Plateau: Public Law 86-90—Stemming the Tide

1. Cong. Rec., July 2, 1958, 11791–92: also, 104 Cong. Rec., part 10, 12,989.

2. "Captive Nations Week," Cong. Rec., June 22, 1959, 11,398.

3. For Lippmann's attack, see "Nixon in Russia," *New York Herald Tribune*, July 28, 1959. See also "The Declaration on the Captive Peoples," *New York Herald Tribune*, February 24, 1953.

4. "Captive Nations Week," Cong. Rec., July 9, 1959, 13,116.

5. See "Socializing Virginia Rusk: Our Super Diplomatic Asset," Associated Press, March 17, 1956.

6. "Khrushchev-Rusk Meeting," TASS, August 9, 1963, reprinted from "Daily Report, Foreign Radio Broadcasts, Friday, August 9, 1963," Washington, DC, Foreign Broadcast Information Service no. 155, 1963: BB 9–10.

7. Harrison Salisbury, "A 'Free' Sinkiang Held Soviet Aim," *New York Times*, March 2, 1970.

8. James Rupert, "Soviet Central Asian Republics Seen on Road to Independence," *Washington Post*, December 14, 1991.

9. Mikhail Sholokhov wrote several books, most notably *And Quiet Flows the Don*, which was published in installments in the magazine *Oktyabr* from 1928 to 1932. He was awarded the 1965 Nobel Prize in Literature.

10. Dean Rusk, *As I Saw It* (New York: W.W. Norton & Co, 1990), 544.

11. Rusk, *As I Saw It*, 544.

12. Laszlo Ladany, *The Communist Party of China and Marxism, 1921–1985* (London: Hurst, 1988), 10–19.

13. For example, John B. Dunlop, *The Faces of Contemporary Russian Nationalism* (Princeton, NJ: Princeton University Press, 1983), 286–87.

14. *Forward-Looking Addresses in the House of Representatives Together with Documents on the Captive Nations Week Movement*, House Document No. 91-184, Ninety-First Congress (Washington, DC: US Government Printing Office, 1969), 3.

15. Republican Committee on Program and Progress, *Decisions for a Better America* (New York: Doubleday & Co., 1960), 151–53.

16. "Text of the Governors' Report on Soviet Visit," *New York Times*, August 1, 1959.

17. Mikhail Gorbachev, *Memoirs* (New York: Doubleday, 1996), 688.

18. Boris Yeltsin, *The Struggle for Russia* (New York: Random House, 1994), 68, 113, 310, respectively.

19. Yeltsin, *Struggle*, 35.

20. Yeltsin, *Struggle*, 215.

21. Yeltsin, *Struggle*, 285.

22. "Diplomat Says New Far East Republic 'Likely,'" *Nihon Keizai Shimbun* (Tokyo), February 27, 1990.

23. See, for example, John P. Dunlop, *The Rise of Russia and the Fall of the Soviet Empire* (Princeton, NJ: Princeton University Press, 1993), 276. Galina Starovoitova was assassinated on the evening of November 20, 1998, shot to death outside her St. Petersburg apartment. At the time of her death, she had declared her intention to run for governor of Leningrad Oblast.

24. Respectively: In *Sovetskaya Estoniya*, April 27, 1990, quoted in Dunlop, *Rise of Russia*, 114; Yuri Afanasiev, "The Coming Dictatorship," *New York Review of Books* 38, no. 3 (January 31, 1991): 38.

25. John M. Goshko, "Ethnic Strife Replaces Cold War Rivalries," *Washington Post*, July 14, 1991.

26. "U.S. on Secession: Maybe," *New York Times*, June 28, 1991.

27. Thomas Friedman, "Baker Urges End to Yugoslav Rift," *New York Times*, June 22, 1991.

## Chapter 3: Puncturing Moscow's Central Nerve

1. *NATO's Fifteen Nations* (August–September 1963): 94.

2. *Hearings before the Subcommittee on Europe of the Comm. on Foreign Affairs, House of Representatives*, 87th Cong. (1962), 195.

3. A. M. Rosenthal, "Nixon Aim Vague, Khrushchev Says," *New York Times*, July 22, 1959.

4. *Evening Star* (Washington, DC), July 23, 1959.

5. Henry Shapiro, "Khrushchev Says U.S. 'Interferes,'" *Washington Post*, July 24, 1959.

6. United Press International, Moscow, July 23, 1959.

7. Richard M. Nixon, *Six Crises* (New York: Doubleday, 1962), 250, 252, respectively.

8. Ernest Barcella, "Text of Notes at Nixon-Khrushchev Talks," United Press International, July 26, 1959.

9. "The Two Worlds: A Day-Long Debate," *New York Times*, July 25, 1959.

10. "Nixon Greeted by Applause at Soviet Fair," *Evening Star* (Washington, DC), July 25, 1959.

11. Nikita Krushchev, "On Peaceful Coexistence," *Foreign Affairs* 38, no. 1 (October 1959): 7.

12. *Ukrainian Bulletin* (New York) 2, nos. 19–20 (October 1–15, 1959): 6.

13. "U.S. Better Than Exhibit, Visitors Say," *Washington Post*, August 17, 1959.

14. Khrushchev, "Peaceful Coexistence," 6–7.

15. "The International Situation and Soviet Foreign Policy," report given at the third session of the USSR Supreme Soviet, October 31, 1959.

16. Nikolai Podgorny, "Address to the UN General Assembly," New York, October 4, 1960.

17. *The Fifteen Soviet Republics, Today and Tomorrow* (London: Soviet Booklets, 1959–60).

18. I. P. Tsamerian and S. L. Ronin, *Equality of Rights Between Races and Nationalities in the USSR* (Paris: UNESCO, 1962).

19. Stewart Alsop, "The Berlin Crisis: Khrushchev's Weakness," *Saturday Evening Post*, December 16, 1961:18.

20. Reuters report datelined Banska Byotrica, Czechoslovakia, August 29, 1964.

21. Edward Crankshaw, *Khrushchev Remembers*, trans. Strobe Talbott (Boston: Little, Brown, 1970), 106.

22. "Moscow's Reaction to Captive Nations Week," Georgetown University Forum, Cong. Rec., August 25, 1960, 17,675–77.

23. Associated Press report datelined Prague, July 24, 1959.

24. Fred Theroux, "That 'Captive Nations Week' Has Many Diplomats Puzzled," *Sunday Star* (Washington, DC), July 26, 1959.

25. Report in *Scinteia* (Bucharest, Romania, newspaper), July 23, 1960.

26. Report in *Romania Libera* (Bucharest, Romania, newspaper), July 23, 1960.

27. Report in Soviet North American news service in English, Moscow, July 22, 1960.

28. *For the Return to the Homeland*, East Germany, No. 57/444 (August 1960), cited in Lev E. Dobriansky, *The Vulnerable Russians* (New York: Pageant Press, 1967), 75.

29. "Eisenhower Appeal a Diversion Tactic," Prague Radio, July 22, 1960.

30. *Daily Report: Foreign Radio Broadcasts, Issues 146–150* (Washington, DC: Foreign Broadcast Information Service, 1960), 5.

31. United Press International, July 29, 1959.

32. Nixon, *Six Crises*, 247.

33. Richard Nixon, *The Memoirs of Richard Nixon* (New York: Grosset & Dunlap, 1978), 205.

34. *Memorandum to the Vice President*, October 30, 1959, available at: Nixon, Richard., 10/11/1959–11/11/1959. Lev E. Dobriansky papers, GAMMS447.1.32. Georgetown University Manuscripts.

35. Available at: Nixon, Richard., 10/11/1959-11/11/1959. Lev E. Dobriansky papers, GAMMS447.1.32. Georgetown University Manuscripts.

36. "Fulbright Cites Nixon Regrets," *Evening Star* (Washington, DC), October 19, 1960.

37. "Faked Photos in Golden State," *Washington Post*, November 2, 1962.

38. Drew Pearson and Jack Anderson, "Nixon's Positions," *Washington Post*, August 4, 1968; Drew Pearson, "Why the Russians Don't Relish Nixon," *Washington Post*, April 20, 1968.

39. "Captive Nations Week—1960 Results," in CIA—RDP80B01676 R003600060033-3, memo approved for release on August 21, 2002, 5, https://www.cia.gov/readingroom/docs/CIA-RDP80B01676R003600060033-3.pdf.

40. Cong. Rec., August 25, 1960, 17,691.

41. Cong. Rec., March 8, 1961, 3,292.

42. Cong. Rec., 83rd Congress, First Session, US Senate, August 3, 1953.

43. Rusk, *As I Saw It*, 544.

44. George Kennan, *Memoirs 1950–1963* (vol. 2) (Boston: Little, Brown, 1972), 293.

45. George F. Kennan, *On Dealing with the Communist World* (New York: Harper and Row, 1964), 19.

46. Kennan, *Communist World*, 13.

47. Kennan, *Memoirs*, vol. 2, 97.

48. Kennan, *Memoirs*, vol. 2, 98.

49. Kennan, *Memoirs*, vol. 2, 292.

50. "Communism's Captives," 1964 Platform of Republican National Convention, San Francisco, July 14, 1964, Cong. Rec. July 22, 1964, 16,027.

51. *Freedom Commission and Freedom Academy, Hearings Before the Subcommittee to Investigate the Administration of the Internal Security Act and Other Internal Security Laws of the Comm. on the Judiciary*, Eighty-Sixth Congress, on S. 1689, to create the Freedom Commission for the development of the science of counteraction to the world communist conspiracy, June 17–19, 1959.

52. *Providing for Creation of a Freedom Commission and Freedom Academy, Hearings Before the Comm. on Un-American Activities*, House of Representatives, 1964–65.

53. *Study of Population and Immigration Problems, Hearings Before the Committee on Judiciary*, House of Representatives, 196.

54. "Fulbright Asks Details of Goldwater's Views," *Evening Star* (Washington, DC), July 25, 1961.

55. Radik Batyshin, "Conference as a Means Against Chaos; National Movements of Urals-Volga Region for Unification of Their Republics," *Nezavisimaya Gazeta* (Moscow), December 12, 1992.

56. See John Boardman Whitton and Arthur Larson, *Propaganda: Towards Disarmament in the War of Words* (Dobbs Ferry, NY: Oceana, 1963).

57. Associated Press, report datelined Tbilisi, Georgia SSR, June 9, 1962.

58. Walter Millis, "The Political Control of an International Police Force," Peace Research Institute, April 1963. Published under US Arms Control and Disarmament Agency Grant ACDA/IR-8, vol. 2, A-14.

## Chapter 4: A Second Plateau: The Reagan Revolution—US Strikes Back

1. Erik von Kuehnelt-Leddihn, "Restless Baltic Republics," *National Review*, March 20, 1981, 292–93.

2. "Soviet Nationalities Survey," Department of State, Bureau of Intelligence and Research, December 1984.

3. Susan D. Fink, "From Chicken Kiev to Ukrainian Recognition" (master's thesis, US Naval Postgraduate School, 1993), 15.

4. See, for example, Edward Derwinski, "Captive Nations Week," Cong. Rec., July 19, 1982.

5. Ambassador Jeane Kirkpatrick, address to the Captive Nations Conference, July 18, 1983, Cong. Rec., August 3, 1983, 17,6462–64.

6. Cong. Rec., July 24, 1984, E3254–55.

7. See, for example, Briefing Book, "Selected National Security Issues" December 1985, Folder: Selected National Security Issues December 1985 [Copy 1], RAC Box 9, NSC Executive Secretariat: Trip File, Ronald Reagan Library.

8. "Lethal Terrorist Actions Against Americans 1973–1985," Department of State, 1986; "Terrorist Attacks on U.S. Business Abroad," Department of State, 1986.

9. Jiri Valenta and Herbert J. Ellison, "Soviet/Cuban Strategy in the Third World After Grenada," report from 1984 conference at Naval Postgraduate School, Monterey, CA; "The Soviet-Cuban Connection in Central America and the Caribbean," Department of State and Department of Defense, Washington, DC, 1985.

10. "Soviet Political Treaties and Violations, Staff Study for the Subcommittee to Investigate the Administration of the Internal Security Act and Other Internal Security Laws, of the Committee on the Judiciary, United States Senate, Eighty-fourth Congress, First Session" (Washington, DC: US Government Printing Office, 1955); *History of Major Soviet Treaty Violations*, Cong. Rec., September 30, 1983, S19,937–38; "Foreign Presidential Report on Soviet SALT Violations Brings Total to 50," Cong. Rec., March 4, 1986, S1958–60.

11. See Harvey Klehr, John Earl Haynes, and Kyrill M. Anderson, *The Soviet World of American Communism* (New Haven, CT: Yale University Press, 1995).

12. Thomas P. O'Neill and William Novak, *Man of the House* (New York: Random House, 1987), 295.

13. See Father Joseph Denischuk, *Two Hundred Thousand Miles across America* (Regina, SK: Peerless Printers, 2000), 175–76.

14. Ignatz Synystsyn, "A Scandalous, Scandalous World," Kiev, July 21, 1982.

15. Radio Kiev, July 20, 1982.

16. Warsaw Radio, July 22–23, 1982.

17. Cited in Lev Dobriansky, "The Captive Nations in U.S. Global Strategy," *Ukrainian Quarterly* 38 (Autumn 1982): 242; and "Arbatov Sneers at Captive Nations," *Chicago Sun-Times*, July 19, 1982.

18. Gary Lee, "Kremlin Official Blasts Reagan," *Washington Post*, November 22, 1986.

19. *Komsomolskaya Pravda*, April 4, 1984.

20. *Kommunist Azerbaidzana*, June 1984.

21. Whoever wrote the editorial should have researched the paper's previous analyses and reports on the real forces in that region of the world, equating the non-Russian ones to those that resulted in the Declaration of Independence.

22. These were sources of misinformation for journalists, analysts of all sorts, and doctoral candidates in Russian history. Several textbooks copied the imperial Russian schemes of Nikolay Karamzin, Sergey Solovyov, Vasily Klyuchevsky, and other Russian historians. Significantly, despite its faulty Marxist scheme, M. N. Pokrovsky's *Brief History of Russia* (London: Martin Lawrence, 1933) displayed far more sense by the early distinctions between Muscovites, then later Russians and Ukrainians. Flawed but worthwhile sources include George Vernadsky's *A History of Russia*, 3rd edition (New Haven, CT: Yale University Press, 1951); Bernard Pares's *A History of Russia*, 5th edition (New York: Alfred A. Knopf, 1947); the more accurate *Russia, A History and an Interpretation* by Michael Florinsky 2 vol. (London: Pearson College Division, 1953); and John Lawrence's *A History of Russia* (New York: Farrar, Straus and Cudahy, 1960). Better yet is Paul Dukes's *A History of Russia: Medieval, Modern, Contemporary* (New York: Macmillan, 1974). Many ill-formed conceptions by academics persisted until the 1980s, when the combination of the Reagan challenge and events in the Soviet Union galvanized the necessity for more balanced scholarship. Quite understandably, reversing academic trends on the Soviet Union was a slow process. For instance, a political science professor wrote in the November 1987 issue of the *Foreign Service Journal*, "It is clear . . . that within the Russian terms lies the potential renaissance of a powerful nation-state." The "terms" referred to were Gorbachev's perestroika and glasnost, and for the professor, "the powerful nation-state" with its people "the Soviets" was the Soviet Union. The apologetic work by Dimitri Simes, an author who traveled with and interpreted for Richard Nixon when the former president visited the Soviet Union, should be of curious interest. With a title somewhat contradicted by much of its content and an admixture of sound ideas (e.g., "Soviet/Russian empire") and fictitious ones (e.g., "Kievan Russia"), *After the Collapse: Russia Seeks Its Place as a Great Power* (New York: Simon & Schuster, 1999) is an attempt to link Nixon's supposedly Wilsonian-bred policy and the Soviet Union breakup. Simes offers two specious arguments: first, that it is a "gross exaggeration to claim that President Reagan's foreign policy was the sole, or even the principal, reason for the Soviet collapse"; and second, "When it came, no Russian or foreign analyst had anticipated the Soviet implosion."

### Chapter 5: Support for Freedom Fighters in the Soviet Empire

1. The Russian invasion of Ukraine took place after Lev E. Dobriansky's death. This paragraph has been added by the volume editors to reflect what its significance would have been to the original author.

2. *Hearings on S. Res. 8 Before the Committee on Foreign Relations and the Committee on Armed Services*, February 1–28, 1951, Cong. Rec., 251–60.

3. "The Anti-Soviet Underground: National Independence and Self-Government at Stake," *Vital Speeches of the Day*, January 15, 1952: 222.

4. "Will Aid to the Underground Crack the Kremlin Wall?" Georgetown University Radio Forum, Washington, DC, January 20, 1952.

5. Michael Hoffmann, "West Bitter Haven for Red Refugees," *New York Times*, September 19, 1951; Statement to the President's Commission on Immigration and Naturalization by Edward M. O'Connor, "Escapees from Communism," October 27, 1952, Psychological Strategy Board Files, Class 300-Administration, 1951–1953 383.7, Educational Programs for Iron Curtain Escapees, Project ENGROSS, Box 29, HSTL.

6. "Letter to Secretary of State John Foster Dulles," introduced by Senator William Purtell (R-CT), Cong. Rec., January 17, 1957, 721–22.

7. Zbigniew Brzezinski, "Toward a Modern, Non-Imperial State," *Washington Post*, August 23, 1991.

8. Felix Morley, "Three Envoys to Russia," *Barron's*, April 13, 1953, 7.

9. *Hearings Before the Comm. on Foreign Affairs, Special Subcommittee on H. Con. Res. 58*, Cong. Rec., July 15, 1953, 22–88.

10. Cong. Rec., Senate, October 17, 1951, 13,322.

11. Address delivered at the United Ukrainian American Relief Committee Convention, Metropolitan Opera House, Philadelphia, October 13, 1931, transcript available in *Ukrainian Weekly* 44 (October 29, 1951): 2.

12. Cong. Rec., Appendix, July 5, 1952, A4542.

13. "Encouragement for Slaves," *New York Journal-American*, April 27, 1953.

14. "Their Cause Is Ours," *Democrat and Chronicle* (Rochester, NY), March 30, 1953.

15. "Three of a Kind: On House Concurrent Resolution 58," introduced by Rep. Lawrence H. Smith, Cong. Rec., March 29, 1954, A2384–86.

16. "The Dilemma of the State Department—On Diplomatic Relations," introduced by Rep. Lawrence H. Smith, Cong. Rec., June 11, 1954, A4315–17.

17. *Review of the United Nations Charter, Hearings Before the Subcommittee of the Comm. on Foreign Relations*, Cong. Rec., March 17, 1955, 1829–51; also, "Fact and Fantasy on Ukraine and Byelorussia in the U.N.," introduced by Rep. Lawrence H. Smith, Cong. Rec., May 11, 1955, A3208–11.

18. *Review of the United Nations Charter, Hearings Before the Subcommittee of the Committee on Foreign Relations*, Cong. Rec., March 17, 1955, 1829–51, 1849–51.

19. *Review of the United Nations Charter, Hearings Before the Subcommittee of the Committee on Foreign Relations*, Cong. Rec., March 17, 1955,

1829–51; Romand Olesnicki, "Memorandum on Membership of the Ukrainian S.S.R. in the United Nations and the Forthcoming U.N. Charter Amendment," 1844–49.

## Chapter 6: Non-Russian Revolutions

1. Susan Eisenhower, "Why Bait the Bear?" op-ed, *Washington Post*, July 18, 1995.

2. *Hearing Before the House Foreign Affairs Comm.*, "The Partnership for Freedom: A Statement in Support of the Proposed Mutual Security Program," Secretary of State Dean Acheson, June 26, 1951.

3. Ambassador Madeleine Albright, address, *International News Broadcast*, Moscow, September 6, 1994.

4. See *A Short Outline of the History of the Far Eastern Republic* (Washington, DC: The Special Delegation of the Far Eastern Republic to the United States of America, 1922), 56–59.

5. Lev E. Dobriansky, "The Soviet Centrifuge," *Human Events* 10, no. 29 (July 22, 1953): 1–4.

6. Lev E. Dobriansky, "The Roots of Russia," *United States Naval Institute Proceedings* 89, no. 4 (April 1963): 40–57.

7. Dobriansky, "Roots of Russia," 41.

## Chapter 7: The Semantics of Liberation

1. Richard Gid Powers, *Not Without Honor: The History of American Anticommunism* (New York: Free Press, 1996), 262.

2. Statement introduced by Rep. Timothy P. Sheehan, Cong. Rec., July 9, 1953, A4213–15.

3. James Burnham, *Containment or Liberation?* (New York: John Day, 1953), 236.

4. The Three Secrets of Fátima were a series of holy apparitions reportedly given to three young Portuguese shepherds in 1917. The secrets, as publicly revealed decades later, have been interpreted as pertaining to hell, the two world wars, and modern-day persecution of Christians.

## Chapter 8: Human Rights and the Faith Community

1. William Korey, *NGOs and the Universal Declaration of Human Rights: "A Curious Grapevine"* (New York: St. Martin's Press, 1998), 223.

2. "President's Message Urging Ratification of Genocide Treaty," Cong. Rec., February 19, 1970, S2039.

3. *Genocide Convention, Hearings Before the Comm. on Foreign Relations*, 1977, Cong. Rec., 114–16.

4. "Ratification of Genocide Convention," unclassified telegram September 24, 1984; "Senate Failure to Ratify the Genocide Convention Only Helps the Soviet's Anti-American Propaganda Campaign, According to the Reagan Administration," Sen. William Proxmire, Cong. Rec., October 1, 1984, S12,506.

5. Article in *United Evangelical Action* magazine introduced in Cong. Rec. by Rep. Samuel S. Stratton, March 20, 1962.

6. Donald Miller memorandum to author, July 16, 1995.

## Chapter 9: Captive Nations—Who's Next?

1. Richard Pipes, "The Fall of the Soviet Union," in *The Collapse of Communism*, ed. Lee Edwards (Stanford, CA: Hoover Institution Press, 1999), 46.

2. Correspondence with author, August 10, 2000.

3. For additional details, see Stefan T. Possony and L. Francis Bouchey, *International Terrorism: The Communist Connection* (Washington, DC: American Council for World Freedom, 1978), 1–2.

4. Speech in Moscow, 1920.

5. Department of State, "Background Notes, USSR," Publication 7842 (Washington, DC: US Government Printing Office, 1968), 1, 3.

6. Department of Defense, National War College, "Critical Evaluation of NWC Curriculum," August 6, 1969, 4.

7. Telegram sent to President Eisenhower by author, July 30, 1959, from Waterford, CT.

8. Freedom House, "The Map of Freedom," *Miami Herald*, January 2, 1978.

9. Paul Goble, "East/West: Analysis from Washington—A List Without an End," Radio Free Europe / Radio Liberty, July 9, 1998.

## Chapter 10: The Novelist and the Poet

1. Aleksandr Solzhenitsyn, "Misconceptions About Russia Are a Threat to America," *Foreign Affairs* 58, no. 4 (Spring 1980): 805–6.

2. Solzhenitsyn, "Misconceptions," 806.

3. Richard Pipes, "Dealing with the Russians: The Wages of Forgetfulness," in *US-Soviet Relations: The Next Phase*, ed. Arnold L. Horelick (Ithaca, NY: Cornell University Press, 1986), 283–84.

4. Aleksandr Solzhenitsyn, *Rebuilding Russia* (New York: Farrar, Straus and Giroux, 1991), 16.

5. Moscow television series, September 25, 1990.

6. "Shevchenko: A Monument to the Liberation, Freedom and Independence of All Captive Nations" (Washington, DC: US Government Printing Office, 1964), 119.

7. For a comprehensive rebuttal to the *Washington Post*'s editorials, see Roman Smal-Stocki's rendition in "Shevchenko: A Monument," 73–85.

8. M. Parkhomenko, "Taras Shevchenko and Champions of the 'Cold War,'" *Sovietskaia Kultura*, Moscow, December 24, 1960.

9. L. Novichenko, "Our Contemporary," *Kommunist*, no. 4 (March 1961).

10. I. Diachenko, "Get to Your Senses, Madmen," *Robitnycha Hazeta*, April 8, 1961.

11. "Russian Tsar and Poet Taras Shevchenko," *Văn Nghệ* (Hanoi) no. 99 (March 19, 1965).

12. "Europe's Freedom Fighter, Taras Shevchenko 1814–1861," document no. 445 (Washington, DC: US Government Printing Office, 1960).

13. John McKelway, "Free Man or Slave? Cold War Warming Up over Obscure Poet," *Evening Star* (Washington, DC), September 28, 1960.

14. Charles E. Wingenbach, "A New Twist in the Cold War," *New York Herald Tribune*, October 15, 1960.

15. Robert Young, "Dead Poet Now a Live Issue," *Chicago Sunday Tribune*, November 6, 1960.

16. Stephen S. Rosenfeld, "A Ukrainian Poet Gets Statue Billing," *Washington Post*, September 29, 1963.

17. "New Jersey Town Kills Proposal for Shevchenko Street," *Washington Post*, December 5, 1963.

18. "Communists Love Shevchenko," *Washington Post*, December 29, 1963.

19. "Communists Love Shevchenko." See also Robert J. Lewis, "The Status of a Statue," *Sunday Star* (Washington, DC), November 10, 1963; "Association Again," editorial, *Evening Star* (Washington, DC), December 4, 1963.

20. "Shevchenko: A Monument," 14. See also Frederick Brown Harris, "Spires of the Spirit—Another Washington," *Sunday Star* (Washington, DC), October 13, 1963.

21. "Shevchenko: A Monument," 40–43.

22. *Nomination of James Russell Wiggins, Hearing Before the Comm. on Foreign Relations*, Cong. Rec., September 30, 1965, 35–58.

23. Address by Gen. Dwight D. Eisenhower at the Unveiling of the Monument to Taras Shevchenko, Washington, DC, June 27, 1964, Cong. Rec., House, 88th Congress, July 2, 1964, 15924–25.

24. Bill Clinton, "Remarks by the President to the People of Ukraine," White House, Office of the Press Secretary, May 13, 1995, 1.

25. "D.C. Statue Guide to Foreign Heroes," *Embassy Flash*, September 1997, 19.

**Chapter 11: Countering Russian Propaganda: A Crucial American Public Diplomacy Mission**

1. David Lawrence, "Curb on Appeal by 'Voice' to Soviet People Assailed," *U.S. News and World Report*, October 4, 1950, 8.

2. *Hearings by the House Committee on Foreign Affairs, Subcommittee on State Department Organization and Foreign Operations*, 85th Congress, October 6, 1958, 102–61.

3. Petro Fedun, "Appeal of the Ukrainian Underground to the Voice of America," August 1950, cited in *Hearings by the House Committee on Foreign Affairs, Subcommittee on State Department Organization and Foreign Operations*, 85th Congress, October 6, 1958, 110.

4. Barrett McGurn, "Ukrainians Are Told to Like the Russians," *New York Herald Tribune*, March 14, 1958, cited in *Hearings by the House Committee on Foreign Affairs, Subcommittee on State Department Organization and Foreign Operations*, 85th Congress, October 6, 1958, 116.

5. Lev E. Dobriansky, "Summary Analysis of Ukrainian-Language Broadcasts of Voice of America," January 19–29, cited in *Hearings by the House Committee on Foreign Affairs, Subcommittee on State Department Organization and Foreign Operations*, 85th Congress, October 6, 1958, 118.

6. "The USIA and the Non-Russian Nations in the U.S.S.R.," introduced by Rep. Alvin M. Bentley, May 27, 1959, Cong. Rec., A4464-65.

7. *Hearings Before the House Committee on Foreign Affairs, Subcommittee on State Department Organization and Foreign Operations*, 85th Congress, October 6, 1958, 159.

8. Peter J. Kuznick and James Gilbert, eds., *Rethinking Cold War Culture* (Washington, DC: Smithsonian Books, 2001), 232; Arch Puddington, *Broadcasting Freedom: The Cold War Triumph of Radio Free Europe and Radio Liberty* (Lexington, KY: University Press of Kentucky, 2000), 382.

9. Constantine Jurgela, letter to national security advisor William Clark, June 5, 1982; response from Richard Morris, special assistant, June 11, 1982; "Radio Liberty," editorial, *Washington Post*, November 24, 2004.

10. Ben Stein and Phil DeMuth, *How to Ruin the United States of America*, (Carlsbad, CA: New Beginnings Press, 2008), 51.

**Chapter 12: Beyond Containment**

1. James Burnham, *The Managerial Revolution: What Is Happening in the World* (New York: John Day, 1941).

2. *Ukrainian Bulletin*, November 1, 1950, 2–3.

3. James Burnham, *Containment or Liberation? An Inquiry into the Aims of United States Foreign Policy* (New York: John Day, 1953).

4. "Truman Will Widen Campaign Activity," *New York Times*, September 6, 1952.

5. John Foster Dulles, "A Policy of Boldness," *Life* 32, no. 20 (May 19, 1952), 146–57.

6. Lev E. Dobriansky, "The Inescapable Liberation Policy," *Ukrainian Quarterly* 14, no. 2 (June 1958): 124–36.

7. Dobriansky, "Inescapable Liberation Policy," introduced by Rep. Alvin M. Bentley, Cong. Rec., July 31, 1958, A6889–92.

## Chapter 13: Cold War Victory and the Collapse of the Soviet Union

1. White House Release, March 21, 1982.

2. George Bush and Brent Scowcroft, *A World Transformed* (New York: Knopf, 1998), 499.

3. Bush and Scowcroft, *World Transformed*, 516.

4. Bush and Scowcroft, *World Transformed*, 544.

5. Kostyantyn Morozov, *Above and Beyond: From Soviet General to Ukrainian State Builder* (Cambridge, MA: Harvard Ukrainian Research Institute, 2001).

6. Bush and Scowcroft, *World Transformed*, 541.

7. George H. W. Bush, *All the Best, George Bush: My Life in Letters and Other Writings* (New York: Scribner, 1999), 531.

8. David Remnick, "Gorbachev Tells Bush, 'Watch Out for Russia,'" *Washington Post*, December 27, 1991.

9. "Memorandum on the Strategic Importance of Ukraine to the National Interest of the United States," Cong. Rec., January 17, 1957, 668–69.

10. Meg Greenfield, "Who Gets Credit?" *Washington Post*, August 24, 1992.

11. Anatoly Dobrynin, *In Confidence: Moscow's Ambassador to America's Six Cold War Presidents (1962–1986)* (New York: Crown, 1995), 612.

12. Leslie Derfler, ed., *An Age of Conflict: Readings in Twentieth-century European History*, 2nd ed. (New York: Harcourt Brace, 1997), 352.

13. Richard Allen, "The Man Who Won the Cold War," Hoover Digest 2000, no. 1 (January).

14. Katie Sanders, "Did Vladimir Putin Call the Breakup of the USSR 'The Greatest Geopolitical Tragedy of the 20th Century?'" *Politifact*, March 6, 2014, quoting translation from Kremlin archive: "Above all, we should acknowledge that the collapse of the Soviet Union was a major geopolitical disaster of the century. As for the Russian nation, it became a genuine drama. Tens of millions of our co-citizens and co-patriots found themselves outside Russian territory. Moreover, the epidemic of disintegration infected Russia itself."

15. "Russia: Gorbachev Reflects on the Legacy of the Coup," Radio Free Europe / Radio Liberty, August 18, 2006.

16. Anatoly Dobrynin, *60 Minutes*, CBS, October 1, 1995.

17. Dobrynin, *In Confidence*, 197, 527, respectively.

## Chapter 14: The Third Plateau: Remaining Captive Nations

1. Bill Clinton, "The President's News Conference with Boris Yeltsin of Russia in Vancouver," April 4, 1993, American Presidency Project.

2. Associated Press, "Repeal of Cold War Laws, Language Sought," *Washington Times*, April 6, 1993.

3. Pamela Harriman, "Our Moscow Blinders," *Washington Post*, June 26, 1992.

4. David Shribman, "GOP Constituency from Soviet 'Captive Nations' Reacts to Bush's Stance with Anger and Sadness," *Wall Street Journal*, April 6, 1990.

5. Foreign Relations Authorization Act, Fiscal Years 1994 and 1995, Report No. 159, Senate, July 23, 1993, 58.

6. Foreign Relations Authorization Act, Fiscal Years 1994 and 1995, 73.

7. Cong. Rec., July 27, 1993, S9554.

8. Lee Hamilton, "United States Policy Toward Ukraine," Cong. Rec., August 2, 1993, E1934.

9. Rowland Evans and Robert Novak, "A New Russian Empire?," *Washington Post*, July 8, 1992.

10. Cong. Rec., September 28, 1993, E2255.

11. William Odom, "Yeltsin's Deal with the Devil," *Washington Post*, October 24, 1993.

12. "The Friendship Act," Dissenting Views of Honorable Dana Rohrabacher on the Report of H.R. 3000, Cong. Rec., October 15, 1993, 2.

13. "Friendship With Russia, Ukraine and Other New Independent States Act," Cong. Rec., November 15, 1993, H. 9636.

14. "Friendship Act," Cong. Rec., November 22, 1993, S16,996.

15. "To revise obsolete laws related to the Cold War," Committee on Foreign Relations, S. 1672, Cong. Rec., November 18, 1993, 35–36.

16. "Friendship Act," Cong. Rec., November 23, 1993, S17,051.

17. Proclamation, State of Arkansas, Executive Department, July 10, 1992.

18. Bill Clinton, "A New Covenant for American Security" (speech), Georgetown University, Washington, DC, December 12, 1991.

19. "US Compares Chechnya Revolt with American Civil War Period," *Washington Post*, January 4, 1995.

20. Daniel Williams, "Russian Stresses Victory in Chechnya," *Washington Post*, January 2, 2000.

# About the Author and Contributors

## Lev E. Dobriansky

Upon Dr. Lev E. Dobriansky's death, the *Washington Times* wrote, "It is rare that a man dreams big, dedicates his life to a project and sees it to fruition before his death. Yet, this is precisely what happened with Lev E. Dobriansky, a scholar, educator, American patriot . . . and a relentless anti-communist."

Dobriansky taught economics for over thirty-five years at Georgetown University, New York University, and the National War College, and published more than five hundred articles and books, including *The Vulnerable Russians* (Pageant Press, 1967) and *U.S.A and the Soviet Myth* (Devin-Adair, 1971). At Georgetown, he founded and served as director of the Institute on Comparative Political and Economic Systems.

Dobriansky penned the Captive Nations Week Resolution, which was passed by Congress in 1959 as Public Law 86-91. Under this resolution, every US president since Eisenhower has issued a proclamation of Captive Nations Week annually. He also testified before the House Un-American Activities Committee regarding Nikita Khrushchev's role in Stalin's crimes against the Ukrainian people. Dobriansky additionally wrote Public Law 86-749, the Shevchenko

Monument Resolution, and was one of the founders, later chairman emeritus, of the Victims of Communism Memorial Foundation.

Nominated by President Ronald Reagan in October 1982, Lev E. Dobriansky served as US ambassador to the Bahamas from 1983 to 1986. In 1986 he was awarded the Ellis Island Medal of Honor, and in 2005 he received the Truman-Reagan Medal of Freedom for his leadership and activism in support of those oppressed worldwide.

**Ambassador Paula J. Dobriansky**, a national security expert and diplomat, has held high-level US government positions including under secretary of state for global affairs (2001–9), the president's envoy to Northern Ireland (2007–9), and director of European and Soviet affairs in President Reagan's National Security Council. She has over thirty years of government and international experience across senior levels of diplomacy, business, and defense. She is vice chair of the Atlantic Council Scowcroft Center, a senior fellow at Harvard University Belfer Center, and on the Victims of Communism Board of Trustees. She is the daughter of Dr. Lev E. Dobriansky.

**Pratik Chougule** is a visiting fellow at the Fund for American Studies. As a researcher at Boston College's Center for International Higher Education, Chougule authored the book *American Universities in the Middle East and U.S. Foreign Policy: Intersections with American Interests* (Brill, 2022). He was previously an editor on the Trilateral Commission's task force on Russia. During the George W. Bush administration, Chougule served at the State Department in the Office of the Under Secretary for Arms Control and International Security. Chougule graduated Phi Beta Kappa from Brown University and holds a JD from Yale Law School.

**David B. Rivkin Jr.** is a partner in the Washington office of Baker Hostetler LLP and cochairs the firm's appellate and major motions practice. He served in a variety of legal and policy positions in the

Reagan and George H. W. Bush administrations, including stints in the White House Office of the General Counsel, the Office of the Vice President, and the Departments of Justice and Energy. Before starting a legal career, Rivkin served as a defense and foreign policy analyst, focusing on Soviet affairs, arms control, naval strategy, and NATO-related issues. Rivkin holds a JD degree from Columbia University Law School, a master's degree in Soviet affairs from Georgetown University, and a bachelor of science degree from Georgetown University's School of Foreign Service. He is a member of the District of Columbia Bar and the Council on Foreign Relations.

# Index

Voice of America *(continued)*
   Radio Liberty and, 166–67
   Ukrainian section, 156–57
   Uzbek language program, 167
   weekly operations hours, 165
Volpe, John, 35

*Washington Post*, 63, 147–51,
   154, 186
*Washington Star*, 151
Weintal, Edward, 96
Wherry, Kenneth S., 84
Wherry Resolution (S.R. 8), 84
White Russians, 29
White Ruthenia, 29
Wick, Charles, 166
Wiggins, James Russell, 148, 152
Wiley, Alexander, 85, 103
Wilkinson, John, 72
Wojtyla, Karol, 128–29
World Administrative Radio Confer-
   ence, 166
*World Transformed, A*
   (Scowcroft), 183
Worldnet, 166

Yanukovych, Viktor, 204
Yeltsin, Boris, 39, 93
   appearance on *Nightline*, 37
   attempt to cast an anti-empire
    image, 38
   "cold peace," 17
   Commonwealth of Independent
    States, 189
   "near abroad" policy, 194, 198
   ousting of Gorbachev, 16
   revamping relationship between
    Russian and Chinese
    empires, 201
   Treaty of Friendship, Cooperation
    and Partnership, 192
   Yeltsin-Clinton Vancouver summit,
    191–92
Yokovlev, Aleksandr, 166
Young, Robert, 148
Yugoslavia, 40–41, 59, 86–87,
   139, 183
Yushchenko, Kateryna, 68
Yushchenko, Viktor, 204–5

Zelaya, Henry, 78